th hillel

BETH HILLEL
W... Illinois 60091

sented by

honor of

Conversation With...

Books by Rabbi William Berkowitz

CONVERSATION WITH
LET US REASON TOGETHER
HERITAGE AND HOPE
TEN VITAL JEWISH ISSUES
STUDY GUIDE AND SYLLABUS FOR
  TEN VITAL JEWISH ISSUES
I BELIEVE: THE FAITH OF A JEW

Conversation With...

edited by
Rabbi William Berkowitz

Bloch Publishing Company
New York

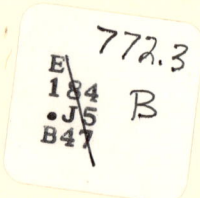

BETH HILLEL LIBRARY
WILMETTE, ILLINOIS

Copyright, 1975 by
William Berkowitz
Library of Congress Catalogue Card Number: 75:5487
I.S.B.N. 0-8197-0391-5

All rights reserved. No part of this book may be
reproduced in any form without written permission from
the publisher, except for brief passages included in
a review appearing in a newspaper or magazine.

Printed in the United States of America.

Dedicated to the unforgettable memory and influence of my parents, who raised me in a home that was singular for the diversity and richness of its conversation and where dialogue was an on-going challenge.

CONTENTS

Ralph David Abernathy	1
Theodore Bikel	19
Rose N. Franzblau	37
Alan King	59
Arthur Morse	83
Alan F. Guttmacher	111
Benjamin H. Kahn	137
Margaret Mead	163
Ida Kaminska	191
Ramsey Clark	207
Marie Syrkin	231
Saul Alinsky	253
Erich Segal	279
Jacques Lipchitz	303

FOREWORD

The Institute of Adult Jewish Studies brings forth the best minds of our times to reason together in an atmosphere of heritage and hope—expressing the things they believe concerning today's vital issues.

Each time I attend, there is a sense of having witnessed something of a miracle involving many hands and hearts. The very fact of its continued existence as a viable seminar for more than two decades does enormous credit to its inspired and gifted founder and moderator.

The seed of knowledge which Rabbi William Berkowitz planted as a service to our community has flourished and spread to attract young and old from every part of our great metropolis. It has been replicated by congregations throughout the country and is, undoubtably, the precursor of the concept of a free Jewish University.

Hundreds of thousands have attended—and every student is on a 'scholarship'. It is a deep, rich and rewarding reservoir of culture from which all may drink freely; a unique phenomenon in today's economy.

The caliber of speakers and their message is matched in few centers of learning. They are drawn from the highest levels of today's life and learning, from every area of human involvement. The world is our stage, and the actors at each Institute session are drawn from the loftiest echelons of literature and art, the top ranks of industry and the professions, the world of scholarship, the political arena, and many areas of government and diplomacy.

Like the conductor of some complex and soaring symphony of intellect, Rabbi William Berkowitz astutely and brilliantly leads his guests along glowing corridors of enlightenment—lined with the wisdom of our ancient Torah—but leading through the echoing truth of yesterday to the most vital application in the world of today. The weekly dialogues—Socratic in character, scintillating in quality—are in themselves hours of magnificence and lasting effect. Their impact should be felt by even wider audiences; their influence should exceed the walls of our Sanctuary.

This book, the fifth compendium of its kind, edited by Dr. Berkowitz, conquers the transient status and space limitations of these widely lauded convocations. Its pages preserve a distillation of current topics and opinion, fused at many points with the perspective of our people and our faith, and treasured up for a life beyond life.

This volume merits a place of honor in our homes—and in our hearts.

CHARLES H. SILVER
President
Congregation B'nai Jeshrun

Conversation With...

RALPH DAVID ABERNATHY

RABBI BERKOWITZ: Ralph Abernathy was born in Alabama, grandson of a former slave. He embodies the struggle of the Black and poor people for a share of the freedom and affluence in America, the struggle which has become the hallmark of the seventies. Dr. Abernathy, who succeeded the late and unforgettable Martin Luther King, Jr., as president of the Southern Christian Leadership Conference, is the nation's foremost advocate of the non-violent struggle for human rights. He led the movement in the streets of Birmingham, in the march to Resurrection City in Washington, D.C., from the pulpits of numerous churches, in the fields of the South. He has also been honored by a broad variety of civic agencies and has been called on for lectures in this country and around the world.

Dr. Abernathy, tell us in brief a little about the history of the Southern Christian Leadership Conference. How many members do you have, and who makes up this membership?

DR. ABERNATHY: The Southern Christian Leadership Conference had its beginning in Montgomery, Alabama, in December, 1955. At that time there was a Negro woman who said, "I work as a seamstress in a department store downtown in Montgomery and for twenty years I have been forced to stand up over empty seats in city buses." On December 1, 1955, Mrs. Rosa Parks, for some strange reason which she could not explain, decided that she was just too tired to get up that evening when ordered by the bus driver to give her seat to a white passenger. She was seated in the rear section of the bus, the section which was commonly left for Black individuals. In Montgomery there was a law that the bus driver always determined where the Blacks' seats and the whites' seats were separated. Unlike Birmingham and nearly every other Southern city, we did not have big signs that clearly indicated the White section and the Black section. We had an imaginary line, left to the discretion of the bus driver. When Mrs. Parks refused, naturally this was revolutionary and she was taken from the bus in a most brutal fashion and was thrown into jail. I did not get the news until five o'clock the next morning, the second of December, when Mr. E.D. Nixon, a pullman porter, called me and said, "Dr. Abernathy, we have waited long enough to do something about the bus situation here in Montgomery, and I would like to call a meeting of community leaders this evening in order that we may address ourselves to this particular problem."

I informed him of my new friend, Martin Luther King, Jr., the new pastor of the Dexter Avenue Baptist Church, who had come to the city just a few months prior to that, with whom I had spent long nights talking about the social ills of the State of Alabama, the South and of our community in general. I urged that Mr. Nixon contact Dr. King, but he said, "No, I don't think I need further contact. I think that I have spoken to you, and I think the Lord has directed me in speaking to you, so I leave it up to you."

I spoke with Dr. King and Dr. King said to me, "Well, suppose you work on it. Use the basement of my church for the meeting. I am a new pastor and I must give my program to the church for its final adoption very shortly. I need to spend this day working on that program." I immediately mimeographed handbills and got to work. The school kids passed them out, and the many friends among the faculties and students of the school took them home with them. This was the beginning, and later that evening we gave it the name of "The Montgomery Improvement Association," which was expanded into the Southern Christian Leadership Conference.

Strangely enough, our demands in 1955 were very simple. We were trying to have an improved form of segregation, if you *can* have an improved form of segregation. Our demands were three, and I remember them very well. One was that whites would get in at the front of the bus and the Blacks at the back of the bus. Once they had boarded, and wherever they met, this would be the dividing line. Number two, there would be no so-called reserved seats for white passengers over which Black passengers would be forced to stand even though they were not occupied by white persons. Number three, there would be employment of Black bus drivers on predominantly Black bus routes. Of course, we thought that this would be over within, at most, three or four days, but it did not take three or four days. It stretched out over a period of 381 days, for when the city of Montgomery refused to respond favorably to these simple demands, we went into court—the federal court—in which we asked that the city of Montgomery be ordered to do away with segregation of its city buses. The churches all bought station wagons, and we formed car pools during this period of over a year. Finally, we were ordered into court to show reason why our car pools should not be abandoned.

I remember one incident in court that day, coming in to see

Judge Jones, who had been given the nickname in Montgomery of "Injunction Judge Jones" because he gave so many injunctions against what appeared to be right and just for all of the people. We noticed that Judge Jones was terribly upset. It was a Monday, near the noon hour, and the prosecuting attorney went up and talked to the judge quietly. The judge then declared a recess. Mr. Rex Thomas of the Associated Press came over to Dr. King and myself, who were seated at the table as defendants, and said that on this day the Supreme Court had just rendered a decision stating that the segregated system on Montgomery city buses was unconstitutional.

Judge Jones was finally back in his seat and continued with great haste to issue an injunction stating that our car pools were illegal and forbade us to make use of them. But this did not bother us very much because we knew we had about eight or ten days before the order would come from Washington to the District Court in Montgomery, Alabama.

At a mass meeting that night one sister could not remain quiet and she spoke out loudly, "Thanks be to God, today God done spoke from Washington." That was the beginning of the Southern Christian Leadership Conference. We did not issue memberships per se, except for individuals living in communities where there were no SCLC chapters or affiliates. These groups were all affiliated with the Southern Christian Leadership Conference. One became a member of his local organization, and then the local organization sent its membership to the national organization.

It is very difficult, therefore, to say how many constituents we have and what our numbers are, because when we planned our organization we decided that we would not set up a series of strict rules of organization because we were going to have a movement of people and let them come as long as they were dedicated to the philosophy and principles and ideals of our Judeo-Christian heritage. We are a movement rather than an organization.

RABBI BERKOWITZ: Dr. Abernathy, when you spoke about the sister claiming God spoke from Washington, you reminded me of a classic story appropriate to this season of Hanukkah. A little boy wrote to God and said, "I would like to get $100 as a Hanukkah present." He addressed the envelope to "God" in care of the postmaster in New York City. When the Post Office got the letter they did not really know what to do with it, and they felt they did not have the right to open a letter addressed to "God," so they sent the letter to the Postmaster General in Washington, who opened it. The Postmaster General, who was a religious man, felt that if no response came to the boy he would be frustrated and disappointed; he might even become an atheist or an agnostic. So the Postmaster put a ten-dollar bill in an envelope and sent it to the boy. When the boy opened it, he saw that he had received ten dollars from God. That night he prayed to God and said, "Dear God, I addressed a letter to you asking for a hundred dollars for a Hanukkah present, but they routed your letter through Washington where, as usual, they took off ninety percent."

Speaking of Washington, I would like to ask you what your judgment has been of the Nixon Administration on schools, in the North and South, Black Capitalism and the economic government of Blacks.

DR. ABERNATHY: I am a former school teacher and taught school for a brief period. If you had asked me this question a couple of years ago, I would have given the Nixon administration an "I" for "incomplete" because I think it needed more time. A little later on, I possibly would have given it a "C," but at this stage, at this late hour in the game, I have to give the Nixon administration an "F" because in my estimation the Nixon Administration is totally insensitive to the needs and the problems which face us as a nation.

As far as Black capitalism is concerned, I think that is just a catch-word, and I will never be fooled by any type of rhetoric.

I am as much against Black capitalism as I am against White capitalism. I am against any system that would rob and deny the individual his constitutional and God-given rights and say to people that they must lift themselves up by their own bootstraps when they don't even have a strap, much less a boot. To me, it is really phony for the Nixon Administration to talk about Black capitalism.

As far as the educational system is concerned, I do not think that the Nixon Administration has done anything other than further confuse the issue. Mr. Nixon now says he is against busing. Anyone in his right mind knows we will never have quality integrated schools in this country with the housing situation as it is unless there is busing. In all seriousness, the issues are even more confused today than ever before, because the Nixon Administration deals in myths, and myth is much worse than a lie. When you hear a lie, you know exactly how to deal with it. A myth is a half-truth, which people believe easily.

The Nixon Administration has failed to give us the one Black member in the Cabinet, which we achieved under Lyndon Johnson. We really are not getting anywhere on the question of school issues. In the South, as we make steps forward, those who are opposed to making those steps have the highest executive offices in the United States of America. Since 1954 we have had the Supreme Court's ruling on school desegregation. The question is very, very clear—the problem is the problem of implementation. And there have been lawyers in the Justice Department who have risen up in rebellion against the Nixon Administration because the Justice Department has not taken the stand that it should take on these particular issues.

RABBI BERKOWITZ: Dr. Abernathy, to use your example of report cards, that "I" for incomplete, the "C," the "F" and the "A," how would you, or how would the Black community grade John F. Kennedy and Lyndon B. Johnson?

DR. ABERNATHY: I think that the John F. Kennedy Administration would certainly receive what it deserves; that is an "A." Mr. Kennedy came forth and brought new life and vitality and gave new hope to the youth of the nation and encouragement to the old in our country. He said the right things and he sought to do them, not always because he wanted to do them, but simply because of the pressure that was applied. It is unfortunate for the Johnson Administration; had it not been for the war in Vietnam, I feel in all sincerity that Lyndon Baines Johnson would have gone down in history as possibly one of the greatest, if not the greatest, of all Presidents. But because he was caught up in this whole Vietnam business, a Godless, senseless war that took place in Vietnam, because he did not have the courage to take a stand, because he did not have the courage to be unpopular, and because he was more concerned about the Gallup poll than he was about the sensible humanity polls, Mr. Johnson will not go down as such. Had it not been for the anti-war Moratorium, he might have run for the presidency again, but it was the youth of America, the young people, who spoke with great clarity against that war in Vietnam. You have to give Lyndon Johnson credit—he was a Texan and he was a Southerner; but he was one of the most astute politicians of all time, and he saw the handwriting on the wall and decided that he would not attempt to be a part of what might have been a failure. In that light, I would have given Mr. Johnson a "C plus" because he did what he thought was right, and that was to remove himself from the candidacy and not run for the presidency again.

RABBI BERKOWITZ: Dr. Abernathy, together with Dr. King, your contribution in terms of coming to grips with the problems of the Black community is basically rooted in the philosophy of the non-violent movement. This is not always a popular concept. For example, since the Nazi period, a great deal of criticism has been expressed by some people who said that the Jews, because of their non-violence, were slaughtered like sheep. Yet you have said, and Dr. King said, that non-violence is not a method for cowards. It does resist, it is active non-violent resistance to evil. It does not seek to defeat or humiliate the opponent, but to win his friendship and understanding. Using this as a spring-board, would you spell out the philosophy of the non-violent movement?

DR. ABERNATHY: The philosophy of the non-violent movement is that an individual who is seeking to gain his constitutional and God-given rights must not only win those rights for himself, but he must win his brother in the process and preserve and save, if at all possible, the society of which he and his brother are a part. I firmly believe that non-violence has been misunderstood and misinterpreted. Many individuals have felt that it is the weapon of the weak. But it is the weapon of the strong. So often the question is raised with me about the militants in this country and, of course, I feel that there is no group in this country that is more militant than the SCLC and those of us who have sought to practice non-violence in our struggle. The non-violent movement believes firmly in changing the system and bringing about change within the system. It maintains faith in humanity and faith in one's brother and in all mankind. We feel that we are all the children of God and every individual is capable of being convinced.

RABBI BERKOWITZ: How do you get this message across to someone who, for example, is faced with a billy club, or a gun, or with actions which arouse the normal angers and passions of individuals? You understand the philosophy, Dr. King understood it. You are a leader, an exponent, a teacher and a preacher, but how do you communicate to the average man this understanding of what you are trying to get across—which is, without question, one of the noblest ways of achieving results without the expense of human life.

DR. ABERNATHY: Well, thank you, Rabbi, this gives me a little broader scope with which to deal. Non-violence is not only a philosophy but a strategy, a technique that we use in our struggle. For me, of course, violence is immoral, it is wrong, but even if it were not morally wrong, strategically it is wrong for Black people and for poor people in this country. Blacks make up some 11 percent of the population of the United States; as poor people we make up one-fifth of the population. From the point of view of strategy, it would be pure folly for us to turn to violence. The people who control—the police who have the tear gas, the Mace, the billy clubs and the guns—the people who are waiting for us in the street—ready to beat us up, to shoot us down, and to kill us in cold blood—are representatives of the power structure. From the point of view of strategy, any individual seeking to stand up for his constitutional and God-given rights imitates the worst in that society when he uses violence. He is not exercising to the fullest extent his intelligence or his brain power. I have seen this in action. I have even said from a platform that if anyone can show me a living violent movement that works, I will be very happy to study it and maybe I might even become a part of it. All I hear is a lot of rhetoric about it. I do not see any violent movement that has been effective in this country. Have you ever been tear-gassed? Have you ever been Maced? Have you ever seen a brutal policeman come at you with a .45 on his hip and a blackjack in his hand? They are trained in violence and they know how to deal with violence, and that is their particular field. Take them out of their field altogether and practice non-violence against them, and they are totally at a loss. I saw it in Birmingham, Alabama.

You have heard a great deal about "Bull" Connor. He was an awful bull down there. He was a rough fellow, terrible and awful, but we changed him from a bull to a steer, and we did it through non-violence. I never will forget how he came out of the 16th Street Baptist Church in Birmingham one day, and when he saw us coming he ordered that the fire hoses be turned on. The pressure from those hoses was so great that one minister was pressed against the wall of the 16th Street Baptist Church and had three ribs broken. Others of us had our feet literally swept out from under us. We got up and we kept on marching to freedom towards our destination, downtown Birmingham. Then Mr. Connor decided that he would call out his dogs, and he turned the dogs loose on us. And the Black people who confronted the dogs would pat them on the head. After all, we had been treated like dogs all our lives and I should think we could get along together. They made friends with the dogs and kept on marching to downtown Birmingham. Then Mr. Connor said, "What can I do with these Negroes; I just can't stop them." So he went for a tank, which he painted white to represent white supremacy. Some of us had been in the armed forces, and we had discovered that a tank can only be used to do harm at some distance, because if you get up close, the barrels of the guns just cannot be directed so low. So we just climbed on top of the tank, and it kept going around in circles with Negroes on top of it saying, "I am on my way to freedom land, and I am not going to let nobody turn me around."

Finally we filled up the Birmingham jails, we filled up the Bessemer jail, we filled up the Fairfield jail, we filled up other jails. We filled up the fair grounds in Birmingham. They had me in Birmingham jail and I heard Bull Connor on the telephone; he called and said, "For God's sake, don't send no more niggers over here. I have nowhere to put them." I don't know what the person on the other end said, but he said, "All the jails are full, don't send any more over here. I don't have anywhere to put them. I can't keep them." I don't know what the other party said, but he went on, "I don't care what they want. If they want to sit at the lunch counter, go ahead and let them sit at the lunch counter, but don't arrest another damned nigger, I got too many on my hands now."

All I am saying is that what we must realize in this struggle is that if we turn to violence we are playing the game that the enemy wants us to play. He is trained in it, he knows exactly how to deal with it. When you use soul power, soul force, something they do not know anything about, the enemy does not know how to deal with it.

For any revolution, a violent revolution, to be successful, one of two things must happen. One, you must have the vast majority of the population in sympathy with your cause, and that is what happened with the war in Vietnam. A couple of years ago I was in Vietnam, and I discovered that the majority of the Vietnamese people did not look upon themselves as South or North Vietnamese. They considered themselves as one people, and they gave refuge and they took those people in and they let them stay overnight. They did not fight the guerrillas. In Cuba the vast majority of the Cuban people were in sympathy with Castro's movement and fed up with Batista; consequently, they gave aid and comfort to the revolutionaries.

The second way a violent movement can be successful is to get control of the army. Nobody in his right mind, and I do not care how Black he is, would believe that Black folks could ever be in control of the Army of the United States. The last time I checked to see how many Black officers we had, although I do not follow Army statistics much, all we had was one general. How are we going to get control of the Army? So when we turn to violence, we are playing right into their hands.

If you can win through violence and if you do not have any other weapon, I might advocate violence. I would use a gun rather than be a coward. If you are not able to defend yourself through non-violence, if you do not have non-violent weapons with which to defend yourself, then you have to turn to other weapons. I would never go along with cowardice. I do not think that God can use a coward in his band. But at the very same time, I feel that if a policeman came in right now to arrest you and you look up to him and say, "Sir, are you a policeman of the City of New York? And you act in such brutal fashion? It is almost unbelievable that New York could have men like you on the force because I am sure you did not intend to twist my arm as you did. I am sure. I accept your apology, young man." You will make a human being out of a beast that way, through your use of non-violence.

I believe very firmly that the philosophy of "an eye for an eye and a tooth for a tooth," if followed to the ultimate conclusion, would result in a blind society and a toothless generation.

In Atlanta, soon after the death of Governor Eugene Talmadge, a Black lady got on the bus and dropped her coin, the only dime she had to ride the bus. The bus driver said, "All right, but you better get up and find that coin and put it in the slot." She said, "That's all right, young man, I'll find it, but I am going to tell God about you." And the white bus driver answered, "Oh, good God, Madam, I'll find it, for I don't want you to pray for me, you all did pray Talmadge to death. I'll get that dime for you."

I think that you have to use other methods in the struggle. If you asked me who is violent today, I would have to tell you that it is the state that is violent, it is the government that is violent. Remember the construction workers in New York with their violence and their beating and brutalizing people? The President of the United States, Richard M. Nixon, or his former Vice-President, Spiro Agnew, arranged for those people to come to the White House, where they were honored and praised for what they did. You and I are living in critical times, and unless we really rise up and face this situation and meet this force with a more powerful force, we are lost. We talk about soul force so much in the Black community. Unless we use it, our civilization and our nation is on the way to its doom. I believe in non-violence, and I am going to continue to lift my voice in favor of non-violence. But do not mistake my non-violence for passivity. I am going to fight evil and sin as vigorously in my day as Amos did in his day.

RABBI BERKOWITZ: In the Negro and Jewish communities there has been a long history of meaningful and cooperative action to remove the barriers of discrimination. This was made possible by continuous and regular communication between these two segments of our society. However, during the last few years this communication for all practical purposes has become somewhat non-existent. How do you account for this? What suggestion would you make to bridge this current communication gap?

DR. ABERNATHY: I would like to say that the Anti-Defamation League made a study which revealed that Black anti-semitism is not as prevalent as we heard—not even as prevalent as anti-Semitism among whites. I think that whenever we find Black individuals with a feeling against Jewish people, it is simply because they feel that their community is being invaded, and they feel that the right to control those communities is being taken away from them. I do not feel that this is Black anti-Semitism at all; it is really a desire to control our own communities and have the say over our beliefs and what happens within our communities.

A normal Black person, during the course of the day, would see only four or five white individuals. Of course, he sees the grocer down on the corner, the policeman, the schoolteacher, and the social worker. In most cases, at least three or four of these individuals are Jewish in Black communities—for instance, in the ghettos here in New York and in many of our large cities. This feeling is really against white people, and it manifests itself not on a religious basis but on the basis of color.

And then, I think, we are being used, both Black people and Jews, by the system. Whenever they see us at each other's throats, they get a great deal of satisfaction in knowing that we are accomplishing what they have not been able to accomplish—that is, the destruction of two great people. We must never play into their hands on this point.

Black people and Jewish people have much in common and I would just like to make this statement: Our position has always been that we support the right of Israel to exist as a nation. I have been to Israel and I look forward to returning there. Our position has always been that the best solution to the problems in the Middle East is the guarantee of Israel's right to exist and a program to end poverty among the Arab people. A continued arms race between Israel and the Arab countries could bring disaster to the Middle East and possibly confrontation—a world war between Russia and the United States.

The Jewish people have been both participants and strong financial supporters of the struggle of Black people, and the involvement of Jewish people is still welcome and is most needed. The Jewish people should be especially sensitive to the aspirations of black people to control their own communities and destinies. Black anti-Semitism is not really widespread in the Black community, and where it does exist, it should be recognized as a reflection of Black people's resentment against outsiders in their community. Blacks and Jews in many American cities face both a challenge and an opportunity. If we unite as substantial minorities, we can lead the way toward creating a new kind of city, providing jobs, decent housing, quality education, safety and a clean environment for all.

Black people and Jewish people have a unique history of oppression, and out of this experience they should teach America how to be a decent society. Just as you, centuries ago in your history, were caught in Egyptian bondage and captivity, Black people are in their Egyptian bondage and captivity now. You wandered for forty years, but you found your way out. Doubtless there were many misgivings, frustrations and anxieties; there were even questions posed to Moses. We wander in our wilderness today. You have a history of oppression not only in the United States but in other parts of the world. We also have a history of oppression. I would hope that somehow we will not be fooled by everything we read in the newspapers and that we will not believe everything that has been lifted out of context. We must realize that this is really the scheme of the power structure: to divide us, to separate us and to keep us apart.

We know about Egypt—we are presently in Egypt; help us out of our Egypt, so that we can deal with you and the forces of good will. It was David, for whom I am named, who said that the earth is the Lord's and the fullness thereof. Now, if David is correct, why is it that less than 10 percent of the population of the United States controls more than 90 percent of the wealth in this country? We are sick and tired of people who are hungry and children who are dying of starvation and malnutrition. This is God's world. There is enough in it for us all, but all that evil men need is for good men to do nothing. I hope that we will not do nothing. Above all, I hope that we will not be guilty of becoming hysterical when we read or hear about some Black anti-Semitism. This is not to say that there are not some Black people who are anti-Semitic. This is not to say that there are not some Jewish people who exploit the communities where their stores and businesses operate. The whole Jewish community must not be penalized because of the actions of a few, and neither must the whole Black community be penalized for the actions of a few Black individuals who are anti-Semitic.

I call on the Jewish community to join the marches and demonstrations and become active supporters of this movement. We have had and still have great support from the Jewish community, and that support must be greater now than ever before so that together we can deal with the power structure. Unless we do that, they are going to do all within their power to destroy your Israel and to keep us out of our kingdom—but they cannot do it if we get together and do our thing.

RABBI BERKOWITZ: Dr. Abernathy, what is your most precious memory of the late Dr. Martin Luther King? Is there one particular moment that you spent with him that you cherish more than any other?

DR. ABERNATHY: That is a very difficult question to answer because we spent so many, many moments together. I would guess that the moment I really cherish the most is that moment I have already alluded to this evening. Martin Luther King left Montgomery and the Dexter Avenue Baptist Church and returned to Atlanta to serve as co-pastor with his father. He tried every trick in the book to get me to go to Atlanta with him as the director of the SCLC, and finally I said no. Well, Dr. King was not a great man for details. I always prided myself on being a detail man. When he went to Atlanta, he did not have his driver's license changed within thirty days as you must once you become a resident of the state. One night, while driving out to see Lillian Smith, the late Southern author, Dr. King was stopped and, of course, he had his Alabama license and, of course, he was known. Now it came to pass that they gave him some kind of warning which placed him on probation.

We were deeply involved in the student movement in the city of Atlanta, and Dr. King, being right there in Atlanta, participated with the students. They were all arrested. Dr. King and the students were to be released after a day. When he was getting ready to come out of jail, the judge told him that he was very sorry but Dr. King could not go because they had orders from the DeKalb County sheriff to hold him and that he had to be transferred to that county.

They came for him and they put him in shackles and carried him out to the DeKalb County jail, and Judge Mitchell gave him six months at hard labor. The next morning about two o'clock, the jailers came and called him by his name and said, "All right, King, get up," and they put shackles and handcuffs and chains on him, and he had to go down and get into a car. He asked, "Where are you going?" They didn't tell him but they cursed him and said, "Don't you ask us anything." Dr. King later told me that he was not prepared to ask any more questions, and he just got ready to die.

They drove him three hundred miles or so to Reidsville State Penitentiary, the main one in Georgia, but at the time he did not know where they were going. The entire day passed, and I was not in communication with Dr. King because I did not know that he had been moved. Finally the news broke. As soon as I was told that he had been transferred, I went to Atlanta and we went into court with our lawyers. Judge Mitchell came out and said, "I want this court to know right now that I run this court, and I don't take orders from anybody. The brother of one of the presidential hopefuls called me last night, but I made up my own mind, they did not make it up for me. I want everybody to understand that. So I have decided that I am going to let Martin Luther King be released and lift his sentence."

I had chartered a little plane to go down with the lawyers and get Dr. King. When we got there, the warden, who was a very fine, elderly white gentleman, muttered something and said that he would go and get Reverend King. When the warden went to get Dr. King, he did not tell him what had happened—he just brought him back to the office. I was standing there in the office and Dr. King looked at me. In a very intimate setting we always called each other by our actual names—strangely enough, my real name is David and his real name is Michael. When he walked into the office of the warden, he said, "Oh, David!" and I said, "Michael!" He asked, "Where have you been so long? It seemed like it took an eternity to get here. Where have you been? I have been waiting for you so long."

Looking back now, I can see that this was one of our closest, perhaps most joyous moments together. The time he had spent in jail, only twenty-four hours, had seemed like an eternity to him. And I realized, and he, too, that our closeness, our support for each other could not be measured in terms of time or in words. We meant more to each other than we could ever express.

RABBI BERKOWITZ: In discussing with Dr. Ralph David Abernathy some of the things which are closest to him, what has come out is not so much a dialogue, I think, as a sermon, a sermon of the highest kind, for it springs from a deep feeling for the dignity and sacredness of humanity, and from personal experience in striving for that idea. It has been a sermon on human relationships, preaching warmth, freedom and love.

We, the Jewish people, have had our Egypt, as Dr. Abernathy has told us. I am not sure that we are completely out of it even yet. But our Jewish tradition of freedom has been a light to the world, and it is a light which is bright only when it illumines all people. To that end, we share Dr. Abernathy's aspirations for the complete liberty of his own people.

THEODORE BIKEL

RABBI BERKOWITZ: In this age of specialization, Theodore Bikel emerges as an amazing and unique personality. He has achieved fame in radio, television, the movies and on Broadway. He is a leading versatile actor and an internationally known artist. Added to this wealth of talent are other aspects of a career that have made him one of the most respected and beloved figures of our difficult times.

Today we discuss a great deal the themes of survival, acculturation, assimilation. Let me ask you this. In what way is your life different from that of your parents and grandchild?

MR. BIKEL: That is a loaded question right from the start. You already know the difference. We are trapped by our times. We would like to think that we shape our time, but this is a lie, we do not. We are fashioned by the mores surrounding us much more than were our fathers and grandfathers. First, they were shut out of the environment around them. They were ghettoized, not only by government control, but by personal choice and by the very rejection they experienced in the diaspora.

Now this is no longer true. The environment around us is quite ready to accept us—well, not accept us, because that would make us equals—but let us say, ready to absorb us. And indeed we are being absorbed by the culture around us. This is quite true and not insignificant. We must remember that we live in a predominantly Christian culture, and we keep falling into the trap of molding ourselves to be like our neighbors.

I do not know the difference between a church bingo and a synagogue bingo game, or between a Christian martini and a Jewish one. To me they are the same kind of living and basically an un-Jewish way of life. It may be called an American way of life; I call it a vastly underrated danger. Those who will tell you that the American way of life means adapting to the melting pot are either lying or hypocritical. To begin with, America is not a melting pot but a kaleidoscope. A melting pot is a no-color color, a no-shape mishmash. In a kaleidoscope, on the other hand, each element has its own distinct personality and beauty, and that is what is meant by man being different from fellow man—his differences not making him less qualified or less entitled to the benefits of the society around us.

Equality means equal access, equal opportunity. It does not mean a sort of general steam-rolling process. That is why the word "acculturation" really is in itself a misnomer. It is a euphemism for assimilation in itself. I think it is to be condemned.

Life now is much different from what it was in the days of my father. I am not saying that much good has not happened, naturally, but I do not count acculturation or assimilation among the blessings. There are good things that have happened to us and I hope we will come to them later, but the acculturation or assimilation part of it is definitely a minus.

RABBI BERKOWITZ: You have said that your upbringing as a

Jew has always been vitally interlinked with your upbringing as a human being and as a person. There was no one time of the day when it was said, "Now we concentrate on being a Jew." Against this background we hear so much today about Jewish heritage, Jewish ideals, questions of survival. What in your opinion are the values in the Jewish heritage that justify Jewish distinctiveness, Jewish survival?

MR. BIKEL: First of all, it is almost a commandment to survive, and I do not mean to survive physically. That is too easy. I mean creative survival, I mean meaningful survival, so that tomorrow's Jew will not merely say, "I am here," but "I am here and I am a Jew."

And what does it mean to be a Jew and what is in this vessel—this vessel filled with Jewish content? Does it only have that nomenclature attached to it as a hollow ringing of the past? That is really the crux of the question. Why should we, indeed, survive? One might ask, Why should any people survive?

RABBI BERKOWITZ: You have expounded magnificently in the written and spoken word the specific values that you see in the Jewish heritage that make for this kind of Jewish survival. Looking back across four thousand years, what has been handed down to you from the past? What is meaningful to you as a human being?

MR. BIKEL: The first of these is the Jewish ethic itself, which is very often misunderstood or misquoted. At times, other people want to claim it for themselves, and then they call it the Judeo-Christian ethic. Yet, the Jewish ethic contains something which I fail to find in others. Obviously, to be a good human being is the basis of any religion or any culture that looks to divide good from evil, right from wrong. Any such culture does that, and we are no different from the others in this, but where we are unique is in our insistence on the openness of the human being.

Religion with Jews is an everyday matter. No other religion really insisted on interlinking everyday living with observance. The washing of hands, the eating of food, the breaking of bread—all of these are tied to our thoughts of ancestry, of group existence and, if you are religious and are not ashamed of it, to God. Other people do not have that. Other people maintain that Sunday morning is for God, the rest of the week is for man. In the Jewish ethic, I believe we are not even entitled to reach for God unless we reach for man. In this respect we are vitally different and for that alone we must seek to survive.

Another day-to-day basic thing that other people also do not have is the concept of *tzedakah,* for which other people have two different words. "Charity" is one of them. But charity is not a thing that a Jew can choose to do or not to do. "Good deeds" are not something that you can elect to do or not to do. These are deeds that you must do. These are what makes a Jew.

RABBI BERKOWITZ: What you are saying is that the Jewish faith is a way of life. The centrality of Jewish theology is rooted in two relationships, the relationship between man and his Maker and between man and his fellow man. I remember as a child two people at Yom Kippur running back and forth and up and down the aisle. I asked my parents and grandparents what they were doing, and I was told that they were running to ask forgiveness from their fellow man, because the principle is that God, on the Day of Atonement, does not grant atonement of sins unless we seek forgiveness from our fellow man.

What steps do you think should be taken to assure the survival of American Jewry?

MR. BIKEL: If you want survival, in one succinct phrase—it is learning. Usually, when people say *Torah,* what they mean is to pay reverence to that Scroll we call the *Torah.* But *Torah* is something altogether different. Also, the rabbi is not a priest, he is not even the equivalent of a priest. His function is instructive, not ritualistic. Rabbi Berkowitz is a rabbi, I am a *Kohen*. My point is that the rabbi is a teacher and the *Torah* is learning.

You are not born a good Jew. You are not born any kind of a Jew. You have to work at being a Jew and that means investing time, investing energy and investing concentration, and there is one place only where you can get it and that is the bookshelf. It is vital and indispensable; there are no shortcuts.

RABBI BERKOWITZ: With regard to the cultural productivity of American Jewry, some literary critics maintain that all creative writers should write frankly and honestly and from their personal experience. Some Jewish leaders feel, however, that Jewish writers when writing for the general community have a prior responsibility to the Jewish community and should not reflect adversely on it. An obvious example was *Portnoy's Compaint.* What is your opinion?

MR. BIKEL: Well, I have always been amused at those of my elders who say *Nisht far Di Goyim,* "Don't talk in front of the Gentile." Any writer worth his salt, any writer who professes to be truthful, must seek the truth, and when he sees it around him, he must write it as he sees it. That is not to say that *Portnoy's Complaint,* to follow up your example, should either be liked or revered or called—and this is what I find ridiculous—a masterpiece. It may be a masterpiece of descriptiveness, but that is another discussion. It is typical to some extent; there must be kids like that around and lots of mothers like that.

Art is not supposed to be photography. If you take twenty types you have known in your life, and you crystallize them into one, this is also valid. It is valid in literature. But the point is that the outside world then tends to take this as fact, the prototype of Jewish literature, Jewish writing and Jewish sensitivity. There is no way we can stop them from doing it. They have always done that to us. They have taken the fact that we eat matzos on Pesach and have called us "matzo fressers" and that was it. They notice little else.

I cannot stop non-Jews from noticing only *Portnoy's Complaint* and his masturbation complex and his mother. All I can do is draw their attention to the fact that there are other books and other images. For example, Chaim Potok's *The Chosen*, or *My Name is Asher Lev*, describes something entirely different, with truth and insight. You draw their attention to the fact that there are other things, that Jews are this and that, man is good and man is evil, man is base and man is noble—both at the same time—and sometimes one at one time and the other at another time. That's what you tell people. But no one has any right to tell a writer, "Don't write that."

RABBI BERKOWITZ: What is Jewish culture? Can Judaism exist in a secularist, nationalist, what we might call a cultural mold, or is religion a necessary component of Jewish civilization and Jewish culture?

MR. BIKEL: I can answer both questions as one, really. Again, it is easier to define what is not Jewish culture than what is. You can consider the various manifestations of Jewish culture and you can tell yourself that the culinary is certainly not Jewish culture, that anybody these days eats and enjoys lox, bagels and kosher-style food. We are told on television that you don't have to be Jewish to drink Manischewitz wine on any occasion, secular or religious. And you don't have to be Jewish to enjoy Jewish humor or to dispense it, and you don't have to be Jewish to adore *Fiddler on the Roof*.

If this is so, then the question inexorably poses itself, "What do you have to do to be Jewish?" Because as America seems to have become more Jewish or Jew-conscious, Jews have become less so. I believe that Jewish culture has several aspects—ethnic and religious, as well as sociological. It is obviously Jewish culture to enjoy and read Yiddish literature in the original rather than in translation. In translation I can read Dutch or Bulgarian; I can read anything in translation. But since Yiddish happens to be one of two of our national languages, its cultivation is in itself Jewish culture.

The second aspect is Hebrew. It is both ancient and modern, with an ancient literature and a modern literature growing by leaps and bounds. This, too, is Jewish. The musical aspects of both of these, the music with Yiddish text, and the music with Hebrew text, liturgical or secular, are Jewish culture.

The way the Talmud has evolved over many, many centuries of our sages talking with each other and with their disciples, is another facet. The *pilpul* is a way of looking at things, a way of arguing, a way of making counterstatements to statements, of doing battle with each other and emerging with several plausible answers, and then, out of several plausible ones, four good ones, out of the four good ones two excellent ones. and out of the two excellent ones, one extraordinary one. This, too, is Jewish culture.

Of course, the religious aspect, the aspect of worship, is also Jewish culture. I am the last to say that one who practices only one of these features, let us say one who only cultivates Yiddish, should be excluded from the definition of Jewishness. As a matter of fact, the greatest rabbis have said that he has as much right to enter the synagogue as anyone, when and if he chooses, and he has as much right to be buried in the Jewish cemetery as anyone else. He has as much right to have *kaddish* said for him, and certainly as much right to form part of a *minyan* as only a Jew can, even if he has never before walked through the doors of a synagogue.

As to the second part of your question, Rabbi, if there is a valid, secular way of Jewish cultural survival without the religious aspect, the answer from where I sit is yes. Of the ethnic, linguistic, religious or political definition of

Jewishness, you can subscribe to any one and still survive as a Jew. But if you have none of these, then you don't have Jewish culture.

RABBI BERKOWITZ: To be sure, I am a great proponent of the Hebrew language—however, no less of Yiddish. I have felt for a very, very long time that one cannot understand Jewish civilization and cannot be a total Jew without an appreciation of the Yiddish language. In fact, many rabbinical students today who come from a non-Yiddish-speaking home are taking courses in Yiddish because they need the knowledge of that language to serve fully in a community. And so, ten years ago when I founded in our congregation an all-day school, a private school, I included in the curriculum, in addition to Hebrew, the Yiddish language. Now as far as I know, no day school in the Conservative movement has introduced into its curriculum—in addition to English, mathematics and science, and other languages—both Hebrew and Yiddish, as we have here in Congregation B'nai Jeshurun.

MR. BIKEL: I must tell you that one of my greatest experiences was in Mexico City, where the Jewish community is a phenomenon in Jewish survival, whether by necessity or choice is a moot point. But 79 percent of all Jewish children in Mexico receive a full-time Jewish education; it starts from kindergarten and goes right through the university age. They have a faculty of sixty teachers who teach subjects and twenty-five teachers who teach only Jewish subjects, both in Hebrew and Yiddish.

When I went to Mexico, they called an assembly of all the kids in a large hall, and a little girl aged eight, who I later learned was fourth generation Mexican-born, greeted me in perfect Yiddish. Later, an older child made another welcoming speech in Hebrew without reading it from a paper. This was an extraordinary experience.

In Argentina, I understand the percentage of Jewish children who receive full-time Jewish education is 17 percent. In the United States, if figures were available, we would be lucky if we could point to 4 percent of all Jewish youth who have a Jewish education.

RABBI BERKOWITZ: You have traveled a great deal in Israel. What meaning does the State of Israel have for you personally, and what meaning do you think the State has for the American Jewish community?

MR. BIKEL: To me personally it has extraordinary connotations. For one thing, I spent part of my formative years in what was then Palestine—which, of course, is Israel now—and it is extremely important to me to know that that center of my people not only exists but also thrives. Apart from anything else, my parents live there. I have so many personal ties that I could not even begin to enumerate or analyze them.

For the Jewish community what is vitally important is this—we have always had a Jerusalem, a Jerusalem of the spirit, of heaven, and we have always fixed our eyes on the spot in the synagogue on the eastern wall and called it for ourselves, "Jerusalem." Later, any center of great learning was a kind of Jerusalem. Now, in addition to this spiritual Jerusalem, we have an actual geographic center whose soil is just as important to us as its soul was and is.

A while ago, I overheard a conversation between a renowned rabbi and a member of the Israeli delegation to the United Nations. The question was asked of the rabbi: "How would you explain, in your wisdom, the fact that in our lifetime Jews went to their death practically without fighting, yet years later they were fighting like devils? What happened during these years?

The rabbi gave an extraordinary explanation which had

never occurred to me, and I was startled. He said, "When they attack our faith, even when they attack our bodies, we do not have to fight. We can die and know that the faith survives. During the Spanish Inquisition they attacked our faith—no question, one had to die there. In the case of the Nazis, they were not interested in our faith, they were interested in doing away with our bodies—there one could either fight or not fight. But when it is a matter of the soil of *Eretz Yisrael*, the holy earth, then we must fight. The holy soil has been attacked; we have to fight."

RABBI BERKOWITZ: I had the privilege of visiting this very same rabbi on that day when they celebrated the emergence of the founder of the Chabad Movement from St. Petersburg Prison. It was really something to behold; the Hassidic rabbi giving Torah and the Hassidim dancing and singing.

MR. BIKEL: Let me also tell you a story about the Hassidim. Not all Hassidim are adverse to going into the Jewish community and making converts. While we discourage making converts in general, there is no law in the book that says you cannot proselytize your own. I was on a boat to the Statue of Liberty. We had two boatloads of Jewish kids going there to have a protest meeting about Soviet Jewry. It seemed a good place to do it and it was a Sunday morning. Two Hassidim approached me and said, "You are Mr. Bikel," and I said, "Yes, and you are Lubavitcher Hassidim." They asked, "How do you know?" and I said, "If you weren't, you would not be here. Other Hassidim don't go around among other Jews." They said, "Mr. Bikel, have you put on *tefillin* this morning?" I replied that I had not. They asked me to put on *tefillin* so that the kids should see me doing it. I said, "I don't mind putting on *tefillin*. I have not done it for some time, but would it not be dishonest? In your book I am probably not what you call a kosher Jew. I am not as strict as you. The theater has not stopped performances on Friday night. I go on airlines and who knows what kind of food they serve. For all these reasons, would it not be dishonest if I put on *tefillin* out of the blue?" They said, "Not really," and when I asked why, they answered, "The rabbi has evolved the theory of the partial *mitzvah.*" They explained it this way. There are 613 *mitzvos* in the book. *Tefillin* is just one of them, but if you start with putting on *tefillin* and you do it regularly, eventually you are going to end up praying. Their answer amused me, but it also made sense. So I took off my coat and put on *tefillin*. And now comes the American part. They brought out a big yellow button, like a campaign button, but twice the size, and pinned it on me. The button said, "I put on *tefillin* this morning, did you?"

RABBI BERKOWITZ: In what way, aside from the usual philanthropic ones, can American Jews be of assistance to Jews in other lands? What can we do, as important as it is, in addition to writing checks?

MR. BIKEL: First of all, the Israeli leadership and intelligentsia are not cognizant of the fact that world Jewry and Israel need to have a partnership. I do not mean this in the sense that we keep giving money and they keep giving their bodies and bones. But a partnership, in the sense of a two-way street, of exchange of information, of examining what unites us and what divides us, for there are feelings that divide us also. Israel, too, has a Jewish problem. Not all things that world Jewry does and thinks are consonant with what Israel does or thinks. In some instances what Israel does is even inimical to some aspects of world Jewry. For example, not that anyone would have it otherwise—every time that Israel has an added success, Soviet Jewry smarts, because they are further oppressed every time that this happens. Soviet Jewry would not have it any other way. They are happy to take that upon themselves if it is part of the price of the success of Israel.

I am not suggesting, nor is Israel, I am sure, that everyone should go to live in Israel. But I am asking people to go as pilgrims, to learn and observe—not merely on bus tours, but to go out among the people. This must be done far more than it is being done now. One must go. It is an essential experience. It is going to be made less expensive and therefore more possible. It is really most important.

RABBI BERKOWITZ: What can American Jewry learn from their brethren in other countries? Is there anything to learn from other Jewry that would contribute to our own way of life?

MR. BIKEL: First of all, I believe that Jewish survival in this country depends, as I said before, on study. Also, analyzing the meaning of the holocaust may furnish some clues. Germany was a fantastic parallel to America. The Jewish community there was rich, affluent, and considered itself more German than Jewish, or at least as German as Jewish. They were a community that came to grief because of their failure to comprehend the Jewish content of their lives. We consider ourselves as much American as Jewish. Now, many segments of the Jewish population in America are secure in the knowledge that at the moment nobody, at least in appreciable numbers, wanders the streets of Manhattan or Los Angeles yelling for Jewish blood—that's gone. It's not our time, it's not here in America. But if your Jewishness, or the extent to which you declare yourself a Jew, or have decided to live as a Jew, is to be determined by the presence or absence of anti-Semites in the streets yelling for Jewish blood, then that in itself is an evil because you are giving them the key to your soul. There should be a positive determinant of your Jewishness without the necessity of anti-Semitism.

We learn from the experience of Germany, of Argentina, of all other countries, but we have very little contact with other communities and very little knowledge of them. What do we know of other Jewish communities? Despite a constant preoccupation with Jewish affairs, I can, with difficulty, name six French Jewish leaders. The average Jew in the streets of New York probably cannot name even one.

RABBI BERKOWITZ: Mr. Bikel, speaking as an individual and serving as you do as vice president of the American Jewish Congress and chairman of its Arts Division, what are the reasons for Black anti-Semitism, and how should Jews react?

MR. BIKEL: This is an extraordinarily complex question today. The man in the street, black or white, reacts to simplistic stimuli, as psychologists can testify. The black man who is emerging now, either gaining or grabbing for his freedom, is a man in the street. He also wants shortcuts to that freedom. The villain that is painted for him—that he knows to be his oppressor—is "Whitey." Whitey has oppressed him for four hundred years. He has brought him to the state in which he is less than a citizen. But Whitey is a very unmanageable villain numbering about 200 million. But if you boil him down to a more manageable size, it becomes easier. Then we have to realize that, especially in the ghetto, four out of five white people that the average Black ghetto dweller meets are Jews—the shopkeeper, the landlord, the teacher, the social worker and the cop. With the exception of the cop, the others more often than not are Jews. Thus the villain who once was all the white people and the white power structure—which always has been and still is the WASP structure—has now been boiled down by the ghetto dweller to the much more manageable villain in his mind—the Jew.

The point is, group libel is something that we cannot afford any more than the Blacks can. Now, any responsible Black leader—the Bayard Rustins and the Roy Wilkins'—will tell you that there are many individual Jews who have committed wrongs against many Blacks, but they will never in a hundred years allow themselves an anti-Semitic word because they believe anti-Semitism to be as wrong as racism is against Blacks. There are others who seek to cash in on the prevailing mood. They look to what is called "confrontation" and that is usually done with clubs, not with words, and sometimes with incendiary bombs and other kinds of weapons.

Anti-Semitism exists in the Black community. We can work against it, we can fight against it, but not with the same weapons which it uses. If we were to reply with indiscriminate racism against the Blacks, rather than act against those who are hoodlums, we would be guilty of the same irrational, unintelligent behavior as racists always have been through the ages. I recently had a cab driver who had a concentration-camp number on his arm. He came to this country after he had lost his entire family in Germany. He had just come out of the hospital because he had been mugged by three Black hoodlums, and he said to me, "Do you think I go around hating all Black people? If I did that, would I be better than the worst Nazi in the world? I hate those three punks that hit me, I hate them, no question about it. But I am not going to take it out on the first Black person that I see in the street and run him over because he is Black. I'm a Jew. I can't do that."

RABBI BERKOWITZ: A few years ago we had the question of reparations to the Black community. How did you feel about that?

MR. BIKEL: Well, James Forman, whom I know very well from the days when we used to hold hands and sing "We Shall Overcome," in which there is one verse which says "Black and White together"—he no longer sings such songs.

He used to go around wearing an African dashiki—not that I minded that, except that he wanted to deny me the right to go around in a Jewish dashiki—demanding reparations from the churches and synagogues of the country for the wrongs that have been committed by the community. I only questioned whether he was the right Black demanding amends from the right whites. Yet it would be very facile for all of us to say that the Black community does not deserve special and extraordinary consideration for the extraordinary hardships they have experienced and are still going through.

The fact remains that we must work—the Jewish community must work—again with the responsible leadership in the Black community in an effort to keep the cities quiet, not to have them burned. Part of this is, for instance, to enable the Black community to take over the shops and the buildings of Harlem. If we can make that possible, we will help avoid and avert bloodshed, holocaust, name-calling, all kinds of things. Even the slaves in the Bible had to be set free after forty-nine years. We are still keeping slaves or are content to let other people keep slaves and to say that it is none of our business.

I don't know how different we are. I remember when I was a little child in Vienna the Nazis pulled our people out into the streets, many of them never to return. I remember very well that there were some very nice, well-meaning Gentile people next door. They were well-meaning and decent. I call them decent because they were not Nazis and never became Nazis, they never joined, never were members, but they never called a halt, either. And today neither you, nor I, nor history, absolves those nice, decent people of duplicity and guilt. So if we see the WASP structure from Darien, Connecticut, and from Wall Street oppressing Black people, we cannot afford to comfort ourselves with the knowledge that we are nice, decent people. Silence is guilt, and nonaction is in itself an act.

RABBI BERKOWITZ: A while ago a man came up to me after

services on a Saturday morning when I spoke about the JDL. He said we needed more Jewish Defense Leagues throughout the country. What is your opinion?

MR. BIKEL: We have always maintained that we are law-abiding citizens, that the law here is sufficient. One does not take the law into one's own hands. I think that since the days of the Wild West, people who walk around armed, whether it be with guns, bicycle chains or clubs, must be called what they are—vigilantes. Vigilantes by tradition and attitude hit first or shoot first and ask questions afterwards, if they ask them at all. Therefore, I cannot subscribe to the notion of Jewish vigilantes any more than I can subscribe to the KKK, whose vigilantism is directed against Catholics and Jews and Blacks. I cannot abide, as a Jew, as a citizen, as a human being, the notion of people roaming the streets with weapons in their hands, bicycle chains or guns. I cannot do it.

The law of the land is the law. The JDL activity is an extralegal activity. If you tell me that the people who attack us are also extralegal, I grant you that. But do we fight fire with fire, murder with murder? Do we become murderers? No! Never, a thousand times no!

Let me hasten to add, I do not entirely disbelieve in self-defense. Don't mistake me. But self-defense is being conducted entirely differently by intelligent people. Take for example a biracial patrol. Jewish and Black, four people in a car, and they drive through the streets, a radio patrol, and when they see trouble they radio and let the law take over. They detect trouble in order to shut it off. That is permissible, they are allowed to do that. And if it is biracial, it makes more sense than if it is only Jewish.

RABBI BERKOWITZ: Mr. Bikel has given generously of his talent and energy to help the cause of the poor and the oppressed so that he has become one of the most respected performers of our country as social-justice activist. He has, through song and through the written and spoken word, expressed his devotion and commitment to the ideals of Judaism. By taking part in the many movements and issues of our day, Mr. Bikel has given added meaning to the word "performer"—that of the artist who actively performs with people as well as entertaining them.

ROSE N. FRANZBLAU

RABBI BERKOWITZ: Dr. Rose Franzblau has received many degrees and honors. I believe, however, that she is proudest of the fact that she is respected and loved as a guide, mentor and teacher in the field of human relations. *Human Relations* is also the name of the syndicated column that Dr. Franzblau writes for the *New York Post* and is, of course, our theme for discussion.

We cannot, of course, expect to solve individual problems or those of the world in one session. What we can do is to touch on a few of them and attempt to gain some insights and deeper understanding of some of the things that trouble us.

One of the paramount issues of our day is that of marriage and divorce. Dr. Franzblau, does the tradition of romantic love provide the best basis for a marriage partner?

DR. FRANZBLAU: I would say that romantic love is only one half of marriage because true love is made up of two parts, romantic love and tender love. Tender love means being considerate, mindful and respectful of the other partner. If there is only romantic love—which is, of course, expressed in sex life—there is only one half of love, and it does not last. Also, if there is only consideration, sweetness, kindness and respect, it is not enough, because the couple then live like two very kind, mutually considerate roommates. There must be both parts to have true love.

RABBI BERKOWITZ: How has the emancipation of women affected marriage?

DR. FRANZBLAU: The emancipation of women is nothing new in the life of the Jews. They have never had to be emancipated and liberated. They have always had special standing. The wife was shown respect, was listened to. Also—and this is interesting in our faith—did not the rabbis of the Talmud tell women that it was their responsibility to look attractive, dress themselves up, use cosmetics and be beautiful so that the husband will feel that the wife loves him enough to want to look attractive? It was her way of showing that she wanted to be loved and show her love. This is all in our tradition; it is nothing new.

The American woman today is fighting for liberation and respect, and she will not be denied. In our culture more and more women are going to college and are becoming professionals. Many are working mothers, since running the house is much easier in some ways than it was before, and the children go to school and have a full program. To stay home at this time is like being retired from life. They want to be liberated to work for causes, to go back to school, to go back to work—to do something.

RABBI BERKOWITZ: Are Americans, generally speaking, getting married at a younger age and are they having more children?

DR. FRANZBLAU: At one time, if a girl was not married by the time she was 22 or so, that was the end of it. And if a girl did not marry shortly after graduating from college, she was an old maid and was stigmatized. That is no longer true, which is a very healthy sign. Girls now get out of college and want to wait a year or more. And many attractive, brilliant and popular girls are waiting to make sure that they do want to get married and that they will find the right husband. Many early marriages of yesteryear were really escapes from home and were not healthy marriages. They were not necessarily motivated by love but were a means of breaking away from home and parents.

RABBI BERKOWITZ: What do you think of early dating? Parents are pushing children, boys and girls, at the age of twelve, thirteen, fourteen, to have dates. By the time a girl is seventeen, she is quite advanced.

DR. FRANZBLAU: These are usually the mothers of girls, not boys. Boys can wait, you know, but a girl has to show her popularity early. Most parents do not really want them to date, they want them to socialize. They do not mind if a twelve-year-old gets a phone call from a boy and they talk for a few minutes. That is not called dating. They like it when their children go to dances at temples, churches, schools and community centers. I would say that when parents push their children and make their daughters of twelve or so feel that they have to date and if they do not they are failures for life, the parents have a problem and they create problems for the children. Now, what do you call dating? A boy in a suburb will ring the doorbell and take the girl for a walk around the block—that is dating. They go steady for ten minutes and then they break up.

RABBI BERKOWITZ: How do the customs—dating, courtship, sexual experience —in college differ from those off the campus? What can parents do to provide guidelines? How protective can parents be without creating resentment and rebellion?

DR. FRANZBLAU: The values that children learn are taught long before they go off to college. By that time, if a boy or a girl wants to misbehave he or she does not have to go to college to do it. They find various ways right in the city to violate the morals they have been taught. As to what is happening on the college campuses today, there is a conflict between authorities. I think this is something we have to face: the authority figure—parents, teachers, heads of schools—each saying that it is not his job, it is the other fellow's job. The school is a school, not a home. They say they cannot supervise the kids in college, establish laws and watch the students. They have to teach them, and that is their only responsibility.

Incidentally, this is one of the reasons why we see such rebellion. I have worked with adolescents all over the world, and in meeting with them, they always say to me, "My mother says when I am twenty-one I can do anything I like." In other words, as one said, "I can become a delinquent when I am twenty-one, but I am going to accelerate and I am going to get there earlier." Also, our authority figures, in politics and elsewhere, violate the morals that youngsters are taught. And so the youngster says, "If he can do it, why can't I?"

I know you will be happy to learn that psychology being taught in college is now teaching the youngsters about sex, premarital sex, and what happens, and how it affects a marriage. This is having an effect, and more and more it is becoming chic to be a virgin. The girls are taught, and they know, that boys kiss and tell. They tell how they "made out" with this and that girl, to show how masculine they are, and sometimes nothing really took place. Girls have become aware of that. They have become aware of what makes a girl go from boy to boy and what makes a boy go from girl to girl, and that it is not love but a bodily function. They recognize that. And once they are taught the psychological background and the reasons for the morals and values that our religions have taught us, then it all begins to make sense to them.

RABBI BERKOWITZ: Almost any magazine you pick up, any newspaper, seems to reflect the very opposite of your belief that there is a more wholesome attitude. What is wrong with the media that they are not picking up this very interesting observation you are making about our young people?

DR. FRANZBLAU: I can only say this: several years ago I was asked to talk on "Sex Education in the Mass Media" at the Berkeley Medical Center in California. This is one of the things I talked about on television for two days with a number of people discussing the problems. I said that the mass media has to take certain responsibilities for itself and its audiences, or we are going to have a return of censorship. They do have to learn how violence affects the youngsters, and once they become more aware of this, I think that they will be increasingly more careful.

RABBI BERKOWITZ: One of the factors that can make for a poor marriage is the problem of interreligious and interracial marriage. Before I go into some of the specifics, do you find today that it is more a matter of interracial or of interfaith?

DR. FRANZBLAU: At times, you can almost tell the wave of the future by the letters I get. About eight or nine years ago I received a great many letters about interfaith dating, then about interfaith marriage, and then interracial dating, and now it is interracial marriage. Parents are concerned, and the answer is that the greater the similarity of background, in training, in life style, the better the chance for a good lasting marriage. Where there are great differences, sooner or later the marriage breaks up, and even if it stays together, it is still broken up emotionally. The sad part is that the children of such marriages are the victims—the youngsters from broken homes. I can tell you that in a study on delinquents, over 90 percent came from broken homes. A home can be broken up emotionally or legally, and the children are the ones who suffer most.

RABBI BERKOWITZ: By the way, how many letters do you get a week and what subjects do they cover?

DR. FRANZBLAU: The letters vary from two hundred and fifty to eight hundred a week. And it is very interesting, the questions are determined by the seasons of the year. In the springtime I get "beating" problems. In olden times they used to beat the rugs and pillows in springtime; now they beat the kids. In September it's always sex problems. "Dear Dr. Franzblau: I have a sex problem. I have been married seventeen years. . ." All of a sudden there is an emergency. The children are now old enough to be sent away to camp. The couple go on vacation. She cannot plead weariness and he cannot plead fatigue, and suddenly they do not have the sex life they had in their early years. So it's "Dear Dr. Franzblau"—an emergency, they have a sex problem.

Then in December I get letters about: "It's an emergency, my son has a severe reading problem. Please help me; he is fourteen and a half." Suddenly he has severe problems. She knows the report card is coming in January and now she wants me to solve the problems between about the fifteenth of December and the fifteenth of January.

Before holiday times, like the Jewish holidays, Christmas and Thanksgiving, there are very few complaints. Questions are asked, but after the holidays the complaints start.

Now, which do I pick from these for my columns? When I

get a great many letters on a particular subject, I pick a letter with which most people can identify, which would be an answer to the other letters.

RABBI BERKOWITZ: What are your views on interfaith and interracial marriages?

DR. FRANZBLAU: There may be a change and there may be an adaptation to change, and what I say now may no longer be true in twenty-five or fifty years. But as of today, interfaith marriages or interracial marriages do not work out too well for the great majority. Unfortunately, some such marriages are entered into as a form of retaliation, a form of escape, and not from any real love of the partners for each other. When young people or parents have come to me about this problem I have suggested that the couple seek psychological counseling or therapy. If they are not really in love with each other and want to marry for the wrong reasons, it is better that they find it out before they are married. If, after therapy, they feel they are really meant for each other, they will have a good marriage. Also, marrying after some counseling or therapy, they feel less guilty about entering into a marriage that is hurting their parents because they have done everything to make it a good one, and the parents are more accepting of it.

RABBI BERKOWITZ: Parents who oppose interfaith and interracial marriage often pressure their children. What are the youngster's reactions to such pressures? What happens to relationships between the parent and child, once parental pressure is applied?

DR. FRANZBLAU: Once the pressure is on, it only pushes the youngsters closer to each other. Most of the time it has just the opposite effect to what is intended. Again, if the pressure is exerted for the wrong reasons it does not have the effect it would have if done for the right reasons. The parents' motivation may be good, but the way they express themselves may be wrong. That is why the youngster will not listen. The youngster's motivation in doing this is retaliation or rebellion against the parents.

RABBI BERKOWITZ: So what are they to do, throw up their hands in despair?

DR. FRANZBLAU: No, they are to tell their youngsters that they have done everything, that they want happiness for him or her and that they really mean it. Then they tell the child to get some counseling. And they may say this to the youngster, "If you are really sure of your love, you won't be afraid to go for counseling. You have nothing to hide, so you don't have to fear that anything will be found out that is terrible." Usually, the young people will then go.

RABBI BERKOWITZ: The divorce rate has been increasing in the United States. Between one-quarter and one-third of American marriages end up in divorce. The divorce rate is increasing among Jews as well as non-Jews. Why is this so?

DR. FRANZBLAU: Your statement that between one-quarter and one-third of American marriages end up in divorce repeats an oft-quoted but incorrect statistic. It is based not on the ratio of marriages which last a lifetime, or end in divorce, but on the figures for any single year. It compares the number of divorces granted each year with the number of marriages performed each year. It leaves out all the people already married who stay married. For example, in 1971, 75 million people were married and only 4 million divorced. In 1971 the divorce rate was not one in three or four, but 3.7 per 1,000, even though it had climbed from 0.8 per 1,000 in 1901, and from 2.4 per 1,000 in 1951. Whenever there is a spurt in growth—and this happens with a child as well as with a culture—there is a period of adjustment. For every advantage there is a disadvantage for a while, until people adjust to the new good in life.

For instance, we Jews now represent 30 percent of the population of New York, and we contribute a little less than 4 percent to delinquency. But in 1907, when we had the largest wave of Jewish immigration here, we represented 20 percent of the population, and for the one and only time, we contributed 20 percent to the delinquency. With our great affluence, our increased life span and all the rest, people take a while to adjust to these very good changes. At first it appears almost too good to be true. In this period of adjustment there are breakdowns. There are outbreaks in children's behavior, upset marriages and so forth.

People are living together longer. The age of menopause, which not so many years ago was forty-five, is now fifty-five. Nowadays people of forty-five are parents of grown children and often are grandparents at that age. They have parents who are sixty-five and seventy. They are caught in the middle of this great, wonderful, longer life, this better life. But they become like the middle child. They are parents and grandparents and still they are treated like childen by their own parents. Now, at the age of forty-five, their sex life naturally continues, and for more than ten years. They have to adjust to this. They think of what they are doing as grandparents and fear that they might become new parents again. It is at this time that you find men going off to have sex with women outside rather than with their wives.

RABBI BERKOWITZ: The average American male has a life expectancy of sixty-eight, the female seventy-three. At the turn of the century, the figure was just a little over forty years of age. In 1967 there were 18 million people over the age of sixty-five . In 1980, 24.5 million will be over sixty-five. What are some of the problems, boons and blessings of the aged?

DR. FRANZBLAU: Let me remind you that religion is the parent of philosophy and the grandparent of psychology. Almost everything we are learning in psychology today has been said by our religious sages throughout the ages. This has been part of our tradition and our way of life, and now we have found that three things make for a better adjustment and longer living. One is that which we have always emphasized: learning—learning for its own sake. Whenever we were exiled from land to land, people could take our material things away but not what we were taught and what we had in our hearts and minds. No persecutors could take that away from us.

Another was that we always emphasized loving. Loving started in the family and the home and extended also to our fellow man. This has been our tradition, our Jewish way of life. Then giving—we have always taken care of our own and we have also taken care of others in need. We never discriminated in our giving.

We have found that in homes for the aged, where residents are senile, when they are given classes in subjects which they had always dreamed about studying, they can study and do not have to apply what they learned to earn a living. They can just learn for the love of learning. When they make toys or things for underprivileged children, they feel privileged because they can do something for the handicapped and less fortunate. They are permitted to hold hands, to sit with their arms around each other when they watch TV and to kiss each other good night. There has been a great increase in marriages in homes for older citizens. They marry at seventy-five. They move out of these residences. So he may have a little heart attack and she an increased blood pressure, but they go on living. They have some romantic love in their own way and this is good. We have found that learning, loving and giving makes for longer living and this is what we have always been taught by our religion.

RABBI BERKOWITZ: The period of adolescence seems to be a

very troublesome and tense time for those who are going through it. Is it worse now in our time than before?

DR. FRANZBLAU: Several years ago at a national psychoanalytic meeting, a whole day's panel was devoted to adolescence. There were four panelists and the chairman. Before introducing the panelists, the chairman said that he would like to read a description of the adolescent. He described him as "disrespectful to his elders; never standing up when an older person comes into the room; interrupting conversations; never listening, messy, irresponsible;" and saying, "if this continues, our civilization will come to an end." And then the chairman added, "This was written by Socrates in 410 B.C.E."

This is part of growth. Rebellion is the road toward independence. The way a youngster rebels depends, of course, on the home, family and environment, but also on the times. Youngsters send up warning signals that they have really serious problems, but these warnings are sometimes ignored or never noted. Youngsters of twelve or so, when they begin to shoplift, have a problem. Also when they are truants and when they run away from home. These are the usual warning signals. Nowadays, instead of running away from home they run off into space because of drugs. This is the modern version of truancy and running away. But this is not to say that because it is the modern version, it is a healthy way of rebelling. It is not. It shows that youngsters who go on drugs in this way have a serious emotional problem. These kids would have had a problem fifty years ago, but fifty years ago they would have acted it out differently.

RABBI BERKOWITZ: Do you approve of children being encouraged to go away to school or do you feel that children are much better off—I am speaking of the college experience—if they live at home?

DR. FRANZBLAU: Usually, it is good for youngsters of the age of eighteen or so to go away to school if the parents can afford it, and if the youngsters want to go. It is a sign of faith in them, which the youngster wants to live up to. But they should not be *"sent away"* to school, like youngsters who are sent to camp and feel that they are being sent away because their parents want to get rid of them for a while. Youngsters who feel that their parents are sending them off to school to get them out of the way have a problem which they will act out when away at school.

RABBI BERKOWITZ: What about the problems when they are away at school? Parents have come to me and said, "Our biggest mistake was to let our daughter go away to college; this and that happened." They feel she would have fared better at home.

DR. FRANZBLAU: The child wanted to go away, maybe to get away from the parents, and the parents wanted her to go away with the hope that their daughter would meet nice boys. In a co-ed college she would have more of a social life. With the boy who did not go out very much, the parents feel—the father in particular—that he is too dependent on the mother and that he may become more of a real man if he does go away and become more independent and social.

Like marriage, going away to school is supposed to be a miracle cure for certain things. But when it did not perform the miracle the parents wanted, they felt that going away to college caused the problem. However, the problem was there beforehand. As I said, any girl who wants to act up is going to do so; she need not be away from home to do it. She can do it in her own home when her parents are away.

RABBI BERKOWITZ: What about affluence? Is affluence a significant factor in today's student unrest? We have read about more than one girl from a middle-class home winding up in the East Village taking drugs.

DR. FRANZBLAU: When people blame affluence as the reason for all of our problems, they are really asking us to go back to the cave-dwelling days. Affluence is good, and it has nothing to do with breakouts, violence and other things taking place. Youngsters are dependent on us for a longer time now, and this is something we must all adjust to. More kids are going to college now, for instance. Twenty-five or fifty years ago they went to work at eighteen or so. When they graduated from high school and became independent, they earned their own living and felt fine about it. They did not have to fight their dependency on their parents. Now they go to college until they are twenty-two, and if they go on to graduate school the parents are delighted if they can afford to support them. However, the feelings of dependency, of having to come to the parents to ask for money, upset them. At the same time, parents ask, "Why does he run around, why doesn't he get a job during the summer? Not that the money matters, but he should learn the value of a dollar." But it is this prolonged dependency that is causing some of the problems, and it is something to which we have to adjust.

RABBI BERKOWITZ: What are some of the problems of graduate students whose affluent parents support them in their studies?

DR. FRANZBLAU: Some youngsters accept it, but others do not. They resent their parents' affluence and the way they use it. For example, a parent will send a child through medical or graduate school and pay for everything—tuition, support—they feel it is so wonderful to have a son or daughter go to medical school. But if the son wants to get married, they say "Nothing doing." He must wait to get married when he can support a wife. If he disobeys them, they will stop supporting him. There is no reason why a man going into the rabbinate or into medicine, where he is going to serve mankind, has to wait until he graduates to marry. The parents are seeing their own child through school anyhow. If the kids find someone they really love and it is a good choice, and both sets of parents approve, why cannot both sets of parents continue to support their youngsters?

Making young people wait for graduation before marrying is asking them to restrain their desires when they meet someone they love. There is no reason for it. We are not making our children dependent and we are not making them irresponsible when we say, "You have found someone; go ahead and get married, and we will continue to make the same contribution we always did." The combined amount can make for a better way of living for each of them, and it doesn't cost each set of parents any more.

RABBI BERKOWITZ: Why do children feel rejected when parents feel that they have given them love?

DR. FRANZBLAU: Parents who have given real, healthy love never make their children feel rejected. But parents think they are giving love by giving in to whatever children want or by giving them material things instead of attention and concern. Parents who are too permissive are seen by their children as not caring enough to say "no." Usually such parents give in, and the youngster sees that the parents are more concerned with themselves and will give anything just to avoid a fight or to avoid tension. This does not make a child feel loved.

RABBI BERKOWITZ: Should parents sacrifice for their children?

DR. FRANZBLAU: I do not know what you mean by parents "sacrificing" for their children. Parents who love their

children do whatever they can. If we do a thing out of love, it is no sacrifice, it is the greatest gift that God can give us. In former generations parents could not save for the future and worked really hard to see their children through school, particularly among us Jews. But our forebears did not feel it was a sacrifice.

RABBI BERKOWITZ: Is the American family too child-centered?

DR. FRANZBLAU: I do not think so. At one time it may have been, but I think that parents are now becoming more aware of what makes for a good parent-child relationship and know better how to rear a child so that he or she will be happy and adjusted. Parents in this country are more aware of this whole matter than in any other country. They are learning more, but they also have to know how to put what they are learning into practice. You do not find parents' associations and our kind of adult education in almost any country in Europe.

RABBI BERKOWITZ: Professor Mordecai Kaplan has depicted our society this way: ". . . enjoying a religious boom and moral bust." Dr. Louis Finkelstein has said: "The problem is not so much whether civilization will survive, but whether there will be a civilization worth saving." Are we really confronting a new morality, or are we battling old immorality in modern dress?

DR. FRANZBLAU: I think you said it beautifully; we are battling old immorality in modern dress, and the modern version of it—morality whether it is called old or new—makes for good living and for self-fulfillment. It is basic. It is the immorality that is acted out differently from generation to generation. But the things that make for a good life are eternal values which never change. There are no fashions in values. Values are always in fashion. Morality, decency, truthfulness, love for another, self-love and self-respect do not change.

RABBI BERKOWITZ: Do you feel that there has been a breakdown of morality in our day?

DR. FRANZBLAU: I do not think so. I have been hearing about it for a long time. The difference is that it is now coming out in the open and it is getting the coverage it never got before. We now hear more about unwed mothers, premarital sex, and so forth, but this has been going on for hundreds of years in different ways.

Men in politics who are acting the way they do are nothing new, but their behavior is getting more coverage now, as it should. We think it is something new and that it has never happened before. It has happened before, perhaps to much greater degree; only now whatever happens is brought out into the open.

RABBI BERKOWITZ: As an illustration of our modern morality, I heard recently of the gift of a year's subscription of *Playboy Magazine* to a Bar Mitzvah boy.

DR. FRANZBLAU: May I say that anyone who gives such a present has no *saychel*, emotionally or otherwise. And as I have said, because of this wonderful extension of our life span, with people staying younger longer, the middle generation now, instead of keeping up with the Joneses, is keeping up with the kids. They think that if they give them *Playboy* they are "in" and are going to bridge the generation gap.

RABBI BERKOWITZ: What do you think of shows and movies that exhibit nudity? Is this a breakdown of morals?

DR. FRANZBLAU: It is really not a breakdown of morals and

ethics, but again an indication of the kind of people who want to see these shows. It is revealed as a form of exhibitionism on the part of the performers and the producers. What they are really doing is making sex and the body something ugly, dull and boring. The people who want to see and get any kind of stimulation from that have a problem. Years ago in Paris, they used to go to houses where they watched other people having sexual intercourse and they got some stimulation from it. That was as much sex as they wanted—viewing instead of doing—and the same is true here.

RABBI BERKOWITZ: Do you feel that our civilization has a sick concentration on sex in the movies, in television and in advertisements?

DR. FRANZBLAU: It is not sex. It is similar to what is happening in education, but happening in a different way. You remember at one time the approach was very punitive, and they used to beat children. Then we had a change, and education was modernized, but while giving up the punitive it became overpermissive. The kids chose their subjects, called teachers by their first names and at home they called their mother by her first name. Then it was soon recognized that going from one extreme to the other was not any way to solve the problem, and they returned to the normal and the sane.

It is the same with sex education. Once it was not permitted. It was a dirty word. It was beautiful when one engaged in it, but to talk about it was awful and parents did not know how to tell their children about sex. Now sex has become an accepted form of expressing love, and adjustment to this new freedom of talking about it openly is making people go to extremes. When sex education became an acceptable thing, parents did not know how to teach the children, so they walked around in the nude, showered with the children, and thought this was the way kids would learn the differences between the sexes. All the children have to do to know the differences between the sexes is to take one look; that's enough.

RABBI BERKOWITZ: Both adult and children's education are issues that we often argue about. What about sex education? Should it be taught at home or in the school?

DR. FRANZBLAU: I feel that sex education should begin with the parents, first of all, and I mean that very seriously. I think that parents must be taught how to bring this about and become aware of their own feelings and feelings of others. The home is the first schoolhouse, and the parents are the first teachers. If sex is going to be presented as a cherished act of love, the teaching has to come from the parents. Children begin to ask about sex in their own way when they are very young.

About fifteen years ago in some of the temples and churches in Boston something very creative and innovative was done for adolescents. Permission was gotten first from parents to have the youngsters come on Sunday afternoons to discuss boy-girl relationships and sexual growth. The girls met separately with the psychiatrist, then the boys. Then a rabbi or minister met with them. There were questions and answers, and then the rabbi and psychiatrist together would have a dialogue with the youngsters. Then the boys and girls met together with the psychiatrist and minister leading the discussion. At that age they want to discuss not facts, but rather feelings, whether they are normal, and how they can control these feelings, what the boys will think if the girl is too responsive and vice versa. This is sex education. Then they have a meeting with the parents, and there is a parent-youngster discussion with the rabbi and psychiatrist

This is the way to present it. But I think that parents who are the first teachers in the child's life need to be taught how to handle this subject. Just as parents have training before they have a baby, I would say that after the child is one year old, it is equally important to begin to have classes for young fathers and mothers so that they can learn about the first questions that youngsters will ask about life, sex, etc., and how to answer them.

RABBI BERKOWITZ: In our times we are being told to trust our feelings and emotions and that the suppression of emotions leads to illness. What do you think of this kind of freedom to express our emotions and what does it do to the individual?

DR. FRANZBLAU: It makes him more confused than ever, that is all. If we expressed every thought we had, and every feeling and emotion, it would really be troublesome. It is part of growing, learning to say no to ourselves. Just having a feeling, or having an emotion, does not mean that it is right or should be expressed at any time, or that this is the right time.

RABBI BERKOWITZ: Suppose one has a thought or emotion and does not carry it out. Should one feel guilty?

DR. FRANZBLAU: No, one should not feel guilty as long as one does not act it out. For instance, a friend of yours has a beautiful ashtray, and you say to yourself, I wish I had one like it. I could take it and no one would be the wiser. This is an adult version of a little boy who has a friend who has a toy and he wants to take it away. Just because you want something does not mean that you should get it. We have to learn how to say no to ourselves. We have angry wishes towards others—that is normal. But as long as "You're a this or a that" is just a thought and we go no further, it is all right.

RABBI BERKOWITZ: As you pointed out so well earlier, the wisdom of religion and the structure of religious education give a frame of reference, a sense of guidance and understanding in terms not only of controlling appetite and thoughts, but sublimating and acting constructively. Opposed to this is the concept of hedonism; that is, since we cannot be certain of the future we must live for and enjoy the present. Does this explain the mood of "Eat, drink and be merry, for tomorrow we die"?

DR. FRANZBLAU: It was written a long time ago. Every generation feels this is the end, this is the worst, and this generation is doomed. It is hard growing up, adjusting to a new life, and sometimes the acting out is worse. We have made great spurts and great movements—the adjustment makes one breathless—but there is no question that we will adjust. And just because life is going on longer and it takes a little longer to adjust does not mean that people should die earlier or that mankind is nearing an end.

RABBI BERKOWITZ: We speak a great deal about the blessing and the curse of leisure time. I am a great believer that boredom is a great illness of our age. It is estimated that one million new people join the labor force each year, but only 33,000 new jobs are created yearly to meet these swelling ranks. What are the problems created by greater leisure time and earlier retirement?

DR. FRANZBLAU: This has been taken care of for the past eight or ten years. The big companies are now working with the psychiatric faculties of various medical schools, planning for people who are retiring. One of the problems is mandatory retirement at sixty-five, when a man is going to live to be seventy-five or eighty. They have nothing to do to fill up their time. Then they just wait for death to come.

This is a great waste of human talent and experience. It is ridiculous. Here an executive or a professor has made great original contributions and all of a sudden is not wanted. He feels rejected and excluded. Nowadays smaller colleges in the West and Middle West and East are hiring the retired professors. They could never get these men before. But now that they are retired, the smaller schools are getting them. The academic status of these colleges is going all the way up.

In big business many men are not retired now. They work part-time as consultants to the firm, and if they want to spend the rest of the time as consultants to another firm they can do so. Sometimes in retirement they make even more money, and this is the best thing for them.

Some women today feel that after the children are grown, they are on their own, just as their children are. Then they want to fill up their time, and more women are going back to school or to work, or are working for causes. This is the way to be fulfilled. I would say that twenty-five years from now, people are going to work as long as they are physically able to do so. Retirement is not going to be determined by their chronological age.

RABBI BERKOWITZ: What has your Jewish feeling, life and commitment done for you?

DR. FRANZBLAU: I am very proud of my background and my religion. It has been a source of great comfort to me. My mother died when I was thirteen and my father when I was fifteen. I had four little sisters, and I stayed out of Hunter College High School for a year until the youngest was old enough to go to school. They skipped me in class. But with this was the message that if I didn't pass the Regents, I'd have to be put back. Then my religious teachers got me jobs and I worked my way through high school and college, teaching religion and Hebrew. Every Friday night my friends and some of our Hebrew teachers would come to my house for Shabbat talk and to sing hymns, etc. A high school teacher sometimes also came. Only in America could this happen. It was my religion that sustained me. I am both grateful and proud of my forebears and their teachings, which made for a good way of life.

RABBI BERKOWITZ: What would you say is the meaning, the essence of being happy and achieving fulfillment?

DR. FRANZBLAU: One has to be fulfilled as a person, in love and marriage and parenthood, and if a person—male or female—feels fulfilled and has a happy family, he has the formula for a good and long life. We have also found in the field of psychology and in studying delinquency that two things make for the continuation of civilization. These are a happy family and religion in the home. When either one of these begins to deteriorate, the culture is coming to an end.

There has been a return to religion, which pleases me. The young Jewish professionals — the doctors, psychologists, psychiatrists, engineers and others — are becoming active in the Conservative and the Reform Jewish movements. My husband is national chairman of the Committee for Psychiatry and Religion for the American Psychiatric Association, and it is fascinating how the young psychiatrists are returning to religion and going to church and synagogue and taking their children. They realize how much security it adds to a child's life. It is a beautiful thing to behold.

RABBI BERKOWITZ: This upsets another myth, that psychiatrists and psychologists are antireligious. There is a definite upsurge, as we have been told.

In the field of psychology and psychiatry there are few that have the gift of being able to express clearly and succinctly the many and complex ideas and theories of these disciplines. There are, also, too few who can translate the theoretical concepts of these learnings into simple, practical advice. Dr. Rose Franzblau has these outstanding abilities and has used them to help many, as she has helped us understand more about the problems that we meet in our daily lives.

ALAN KING

RABBI BERKOWITZ: Alan King is, in a sense, Everyman. He is annoyed by the things which annoy us. His biting, incisive comments against the Establishment and everything that plagues all of us are as much social commentary as they are comedy and are major contributions to American entertainment. His many other contributions, mainly to American philanthropy in all of its aspects, are evidenced by a wall hung with plaques, scrolls and testimonials.

The reason for his deep involvement in humanitarian causes is the same as the reason for his success as an entertainer. He is primarily interested in people. He is endowed, obviously, with a gift from God, a sense of humor. He has the parallel gift of a deep sense of compassion.

As a humorist, musician and writer, Mr. King is known to millions and has met and mingled with the greatest, but he has remained a great humanitarian and a very deeply committed Jew.

In the daily course of life we try to communicate with one another and try to reach understanding. We try to elicit from people their problems, sorrows and the comedy and tragedy of the day's work. You constructively distract people and communicate with them with your great talent in the art of comedy. Has what people once laughed at and what people laugh at today changed through the years?

ALAN KING: You say that I "constructively distract" people. But if there is anything I do *not* try to do, it is to distract. I try to make people open their eyes to the reality of things. I may do it comedically, but that is just my way of doing it. I try to make people aware. I have seen many things change in my lifetime. Some things disturb me, but one thing that concerns me greatly is that I think we have largely lost our sense of humor. I think that we have become a polarized nation. In the past few years we have chosen sides, and the ability to relax has become much more difficult.

I am disturbed by this. Since the 1930s, which is about as far back as I can go in terms of subject matter, we have developed many sacred cows because of our insecurity. Subject matters like birth control and the pill—they tell me I cannot make fun of these. Why not? I researched a radio broadcast by Will Rogers in which he discussed the farm problems in the thirties, and he talked about teaching hogs birth control. Everybody laughed at that in 1934.

I have come to the conclusion that perhaps people at that time had a better sense of humor, or perhaps had more to laugh about. This is part of the change—not being able to make fun of as many subjects as we could in the thirties.

RABBI BERKOWITZ: A comedian once said that there is a deep vein of melancholy that runs through everyone's life, and that the humorist is perhaps more sensitive to this in himself than others are and therefore compensates for it. Another cliche is that tragedy and comedy are just a hair apart. Can you comment on this?

ALAN KING: I don't think they are a hair apart. I think they are intertwined. I think that I have to go back to my Jewishness. There is a big difference between being Jewish and being a Jew, and I will discuss my Jewishness. The ability to survive two thousand years, the pogroms, the Holocaust. We are the people of the Book and we ask, "What is knowledge?" With knowledge comes wisdom, and then comes wit, which is a derivative of wisdom. I think the ability to laugh against adversity may be one of the greatest contributions the Jew has made. I think this is a reason we have been able to survive.

So I would say that anything which is tragic is funny; it is just a question of interpretation. If a man slips on a banana peel, this is not funny, but if it is described properly it is funny. I have always said that the man who slips on a banana peel is not funny, but the man who slips on the banana peel and laughs *is* funny.

The ability to laugh at ourselves, at all the sorrow, the grief and the aggravation, is good. We know that grief and aggravation are not Jewish monopolies, but the ability to laugh at these is one of the great contributions of our people.

RABBI BERKOWITZ: The vast majority of the comedians today are of a minority religious faith—Catholics and Jews, and now the Blacks, like Bill Cosby, Flip Wilson, Nipsy Russell and Godfrey Cambridge. It would appear that persecution, poverty and prejudice are still the breeding grounds for most of America's laugh makers.

There seems to be a theory that in order to be really funny a comedian has to come from that kind of background.

ALAN KING: The records show that this seems to be true of

the time. I don't think that a comedian has to be from a minority, or that he has to be poor or have been oppressed or suffered adversity. I think that what is more important is that he must be *aware* of poverty and oppression. What makes a comedian successful and humorous is the fact that he cares. I am not talking only about the professional comedian—the so-called standup comedian that you see in the films and television; I am thinking also of authors. By far the greatest contribution to humor has been through the written word. A person can come from a very wealthy background and still be able to interpret people's problems if he cares enough. This is the important element—the fact that he cares. I do not think that he has to be poor, although it helps. I know a lot of people who rose from poor backgrounds and were persecuted, who do not give a damn. The basic qualification is to be involved, to be aware, to care.

RABBI BERKOWITZ: I agree heartily that it is important to care. This is the basic factor in communicating with people and achieving results, whatever the field may be. One may not succeed, and suffer because of failure, but at least one has the satisfaction of having cared and acted because of it.

I would like to put two questions into one. I have heard people say that so-and-so is such a gifted humorist, why does he have to resort to smut? Why, indeed, do some comedians use such material? The second question involves the role of ridicule in humor. There are comedians who use ridicule which is cruel and unkind. What about smut and what about this kind of biting ridicule, even when it is sometimes mixed with kindness?

ALAN KING: When you say "smut," this term takes on a certain connotation. I happen to feel very strongly about words—that is how I make a living, whether they be written or spoken. The word "smut" is a very good indictment against words. I believe that the English language is terribly limited. It takes so much time and so many words to say and describe something. What you consider smut, some people consider obscene, and others consider profanity.

Now, I don't know why we have to have the so-called language of the streets and why we have to have the language of the so-called intelligentsia. Harry Truman got so angry at a critic of his daughter that he called him a son-of-a-bitch. That was the President of the United States. I don't understand what is "dirty" or "smutty." It is a question of how words are used. If a word helps to communicate and describe a situation—if you can do it in one word—then I think this is the word that should be used.

About ridicule. Humor, it has been said, is the period at the end of the sentence. This means that you can discuss something on every level, but when you ridicule and make fun of it, there is no place to go. That's the end. This is the power of humor. An example of this is when Governor Tom Dewey ran for the presidency of the United States against Harry Truman, and a woman said that Tom Dewey looked like the little man on top of the wedding cake. That was ridicule and that was a powerful weapon against Mr. Dewey that could not be answered. When Mr. Nixon ran for the presidency for the first time against John Kennedy, Democrats showed his picture and asked, "Would you buy a used car from this man?" "Tricky Dicky"—that's ridicule, that is humor. In a free society you cannot take this away.

A comedian who used ridicule could not exist outside of our society. Comedians and humorists are only products of the times. There must be a need for them. You see the popularity of a show like *All in the Family* right now. This is the greatest example. I think a society must be loose and free enough to have this. One doesn't have to agree. If one doesn't like ridicule, one shouldn't listen to it.

I remember, as a young man, Lenny Bruce, whose so-called biography appeared on Broadway. Lenny and I were kids together; his mother was a burlesque comedienne and I worked with her. I thought Lenny Bruce was a giant. He had a great talent, yet I was offended at that time because I wasn't sophisticated enough to appreciate him. When I went to see Lenny and I heard his language, I used to say, "Lenny, you are hurting yourself. You have a message but you are turning everyone off by using these words." Lenny and I argued a great deal. As a matter of fact, during the last few years of his life we were not friendly; I debated with him one night on the David Susskind Show. In retrospect, when I realize how many things he tore down, how much prejudice he put down, by telling it like it is, I feel differently.

There is no danger in language. The danger is inhibiting speech and language. I understand dignity, but I would say that as long as man is able to speak freely, I don't give a damn about what words he uses. I know that freedom of speech does not mean that you can shout "Fire" in a crowded theater. But anything is important that gets us closer to the core of the meaning and kicks away everything that is nonessential. I think that ridicule and what you may consider smut are terribly important in communication.

That is a very long answer to a very short question, but I think it is central to our society.

RABBI BERKOWITZ: Jews a long time ago understood human behavior. The rabbis said that there are ways of behaving: *B'tzina,* which means "in private," *B'ferhesiah,* which means "in public." I feel very strongly that there are enough words in the English language to express oneself in the way one wants. Also, there is always one word that is associated in my mind with you—you may not like it—but it is my reaction—and that is the word "wholesomeness." There is something very wholesome about your humor; you don't ever have to use those words. You have me laughing because you are drawing from my own experience.

ALAN KING: This is something that we can spend an hour and a half on. What I am saying is this: it took excellent courage to do what Lenny Bruce did. What Lenny said, at the time that he said it, made things easier. I don't use the same words that Lenny did, but the fact that Lenny used them made it easier for me, and to people of all walks of life in extreme situations. I consider it a breakdown of prejudice. Nobody ever walked out of a room after hearing a so-called dirty word and committed a crime.

The Bible says "begat" and "begat" and "begat," and what do you think "begat" is? Somebody was sleeping with somebody else and they kept begatting and begatting. But there are a lot of people who don't know what "begat" is.

Again I say, language is tough enough. Just as an example, in television—and, of course, this is what I deal with—one finds the greatest bigotry and censorship. Do you know that when I started writing for radio I could not use the words "piano legs." This may sound ridiculous, but I could not use "piano legs"—"legs" was dirty.

Do you remember when Claudette Colbert and Clark Gable, in *It Happened One Night,* slept in the same room? This was considered revolutionary.

Things change and the world changes, I hope, for the better. I just don't understand the belief that if you don't say something it does not exist. I think that the contribution of the young people today is that they are pulling these barriers down.

RABBI BERKOWITZ: Every great comedian seems to present a total, familiar personality and does this over the years, a personality which the public knows and accepts. Do comedians consciously build up a stage personality?

ALAN KING: I remember that years ago Jack Benny created a characterization by accident—being cheap. It was charming. Conditions were not the same as they are today and the world wasn't moving as quickly. Being cheap was a comedic device. Jack Benny is not cheap. In fact, Jack Benny has told me on many occasions, because he is a good friend, that when he goes into a restaurant now he has to tip twice as much because everyone expects him to be cheap.

Don Rickles was a comedian like most of us. When he first started out he tried telling stories about a Jew who got on a trolley car. It did not work. Out of deep frustration, he began to insult the people in the audience and they started to laugh, so that characterization more or less evolved. But Don Rickles is the kindest person—a very kind, considerate and loving guy. His type of comedy may be a combination of various things: it may be something in his Id, which is terribly deep and Freudian, stemming from his childhood as a result of his father's death when he was very young, or it may be due to his degrading experience in the Navy. The point is that now, all of a sudden, it works.

I have always been angry about things; it is part of my whole being and background. So I am often disgusted, but not discouraged. There is a streak of anger in me about injustice, oppression, poverty. At first I was a boxer, a prize fighter. This was an outlet for all my anger. Then in one fight in Hamilton, Ontario, I took an awful beating, and all of a sudden I was not that angry any more. I said to myself that there must be another way that does not hurt physically. I started telling jokes because I had the ability to entertain. At first, I was stealing everybody else's act, but it did not fit. It was all right, it was funny, but there was no cushion behind it. Then when I first got married I started telling jokes about my wife. Of course I did not originate wife jokes, but I started telling jokes about my wife that were almost personal.

In a sense my success created a monster. I realized that

there were people out there who were frustrated and who could not give vent to their frustrations. I said to myself that perhaps this is my way: to say out loud the things that bother everybody. At first they laughed about wives. So the next thing I did was about kids, and then the suburbs. I started to talk about taking out the garbage, and so on. It evolved as I realized that everyone has grievances against the insurance company, the doctor, the airlines and so on.

It is basically different from, let's say, Rickles, who is a Jekyll and Hyde. When on stage he does one thing and then is something else privately. With me, my public character is much closer to my whole personality, because I am instinctively angry about things. The fact that I am able to turn this into laughter does not make my anger less powerful.

RABBI BERKOWITZ: You have satirized the telephone company, insurance company, consumer products, airlines, marriage, suburban life. Recently you turned to political humor, and I am curious to know what kind of reaction you had to that, particularly in regard to your appearances on the *Tonight Show*.

ALAN KING: You see, with success you seem to get a little more freedom. When I started to talk about political figures, politics and government, when I started saying things about the President of the United States, when I started to tell jokes about Mr. Agnew and Mr. Nixon, I had to do it in such a way that the audience realized that I was not just picking on these particular individuals, but that my job as a humorist was to make fun, to keep sticking pins into the sacred cows. I have been saying these things about five Presidents, and this is what some people seem to forget. This is not partisan politics. Although I am terribly partisan in my politics, I am not in my humor. I have to disguise it, because I am a professional. I made fun of Harry Truman and of Eisenhower. I made fun of

John Kennedy and Lyndon Johnson, and I will continue to make fun of Mr. Nixon, or whoever follows him.

Right now, with the polarization I mentioned, a few people become offended, so I have to use a gimmick. I invoke the name of Will Rogers, one of the great American humorists, who did the very same thing, and that takes the edge off.

Today, who cares about a guy who went to a race track with his mother-in-law, and when she bent down to tie her shoe, threw a saddle over her and she came in third? Who gives a damn about that today? That is humor that was funny twenty-five to thirty years ago. People today are aware of their problems and in order for humor to sustain and to grow, it must keep up with the times. I don't do this to offend, and if some people are offended, that's the name of the game.

If I didn't get hate mail, I would not think I was doing my job. I am sure that all the humorists throughout the years—for example, Mencken, Mark Twain, and Will Rogers—all got hate mail. I am not putting myself into the same category, but I am doing in my way what they were doing. I may not be as subtle, but I am trying to tell it like it is.

The fact is that my success has grown and is growing. People line up to see me. I ask myself, why do they come to see me? The reason, I believe, is that I am, in a sense, saying what they are thinking. I am saying something in addition to entertaining them. If I talk about Mr. Nixon, and there are Republicans in the audience who happen to believe that Mr. Nixon is a great man, they say, "Wait a minute, Alan King is against the Arabs and he is against the telephone company, and we are against the Arabs and the telephone company. The fact that he is against Mr. Nixon can't be all bad." If I just came out and just talked about Mr. Nixon, that would be another story. But what I try to present is the entire picture.

RABBI BERKOWITZ: I found it very interesting that you said: "The shape of the world changes with my moods. Sometimes

I feel in such pain and sometimes I feel there is little hope. Instinctively, I do not think man wants to destroy himself. You talk to college kids and every once in a while they restore your hope. But you turn and you look around and you see that the liberals of the thirties are the conservatives of the sixties—some of the labor unions, for instance." The whole tenor of this statement is on a hopeful note.

ALAN KING: As I mentioned earlier, I am disgusted, but not discouraged.

RABBI BERKOWITZ: I am concerned, every parent is concerned, society is concerned, about the effect of television on children. In your experience has television become better or worse? Who determines what the programs will be like—the advertiser, the producer, or the public?

ALAN KING: Television has not gotten worse because it was never very good to begin with. Those who do what I do would like to think that they are participating in an art form. Television is—and in the forseeable future will remain—an advertising medium. The name of the game is numbers—the cost per thousand of listeners. Saying this, I know I am biting the hand that feeds me. We listeners and artists are sheep, and the fact that you get television entertainment for nothing allows the advertisers and TV executives to continue this dishonesty. They are interested only in the market. They are not interested in your intellect, they are not interested in your feelings, they are not interested in your needs, they are only interested in selling a product. No matter how they disguise it, TV is a medium that lives and dies at the cost per thousand.

Every once in a while, because of some uproar—some Senate committee hearing or some other influence—they express a feeling of conscience. They say, "Well, we'll give them the ballet, and then we will still give them a blind cop, or a chief of police in a wheelchair, or Doris Day."

Now I am not saying that there isn't room for these types of shows, but when they become the overriding concern, when it is *the* thing that television is, then television is not doing anybody justice. News, sporting events, political conventions, the inauguration, this is what television is, these are the great moments of television. But that is only one speck of what you see on television.

I get the argument from the people I work for that they have to fill 20 hours a day, so how can it all be good? I want to know where it is written that they have to fill 20 hours a day. I just think that we've been had, and we will continue to be had. And as long as we allow this to happen, you will continue to get the type of entertainment and quality that you are getting. It's not only bad, it's outrageous.

You cannot tell me that when they give you sixty minutes of the New York Philharmonic that that is going to make up for all the other hours of garbage. I remain in it because, first of all, I am a hypocrite. This is the way I make a living. I try to bring my own degree of truth to television; that is the best I can do. By not going on television, by saying this is not the medium for me, I achieve nothing. It's like being a politician. . . the first rule is, you have to get elected. In order to make changes, in order to do something, you have to get on TV and then you deal.

"Compromise" is not such a dirty word. I worked for Kraft cheese for three years and Kraft wants to be all things to all men. In the three years that I was on Kraft cheese, the advertising people said that I got away with more than anyone in thirty years of Kraft broadcasting. The reason I was able to sneak it in was that the success of the show allowed me a little more freedom. But television is not something about which people have anything to say.

RABBI BERKOWITZ: In terms of improving television, you

are speaking of the power of marketing and advertising people. Don't those who build television shows always claim that they are giving the American people what they want?

ALAN KING: I don't think that is true. I have much more confidence in the people. Watching television has become a religion, and people have become so indoctrinated and so channeled into one level that they resent it when you break in with an important item about a crisis when they are watching a football game. I think that television has a responsibility to bring out the best in people, and what we are doing is bringing out the worst. The fact that viewers were upset by the interference of the news of the Cuban missile crisis during a ball game was the reward of a medium that has brought out the worst. I think that people are much more intelligent.

I am not making a blanket indictment against television. One thing that television *has* done is to bring everything to everybody at the same time. I am talking about public events. People in Des Moines, Iowa, know about a news event at the same time as those in Chicago, New York, Miami and Los Angeles. I go to places that you just could not even believe. We play country fairs and we tell the same jokes that we do in the cities. That is the one thing that television has done. It is a great equalizer. It has made everyone aware of the same things at the same time.

I just feel that television has a greater responsibility than this. I think that the only way that we can bring television along is to hear the voices of the people who watch, not only those complaining about interrupted ball games, but those watching good shows. When the ballet was on television, the researchers figured out that the ratings were very poor. When you look at the ratings, you see that two million people watched the ballet while twenty million people watched the Ed Sullivan show. Does that mean that twenty million people were not sophisticated enough and that two million people do not count? And even in terms of cost-per-thousand viewers, big companies like Xerox, Kodak and others which represent the best are not looking for that overall marketing. They are still reaching two million people, a pretty good number to whom they can sell their products.

Selling the product is the overriding issue, and that is why television will never become an art form.

RABBI BERKOWITZ: You have been an active and innovative producer with "The Long Winter," "The Investigation" and "Something Different" to your credit. You have acted on Broadway and you also—quoting your own words—have been "constructively an angry man about the theater." What about the theater of today?

ALAN KING: I don't think there is any theater of today. I used to go to the theater, and now this is my profession, this is my business. Fifteen years ago I found myself going to the theater once a week. Last year I went to the theater nine times. This year it might even be less.

I think that the theater has become nonexistent here. I know there are many angles to this and I know the problems. There is the cost. Some blame it on the unions, but whatever, the prices of the tickets are high. Whatever the reasons may be, the theater is no more.

There is no room any more for real theater, for controversial theater. That is why I stopped producing plays on Broadway. You have to charge $15.00 a ticket, and then you have to sit and wait for one or two critics to tell you whether it is good or bad.

I think that the movies have become what Broadway was 20 years ago. I think that the experiments in form are now taking place in the movies and not on the stage. The movies are going through a phase now. There was censorship for so long, then all of a sudden the movies have been freed. A lot of charlatans have taken over, and they are using themes just for shock value, but eventually, when people are no longer shocked by the sight of the nude body or by dirty words, those charlatans will be out of the film industry and then the art form will come into being. Even now, you cannot make just a dirty movie and expect it to be a success.

The motion picture, with the demise of the big studios, is in the hands of the independent, the young and the creative people. If there are fifty or a hundred movies and you do not like any of them, you don't go to see them. But the fact is that you now have a choice. This is where the excitement is now in my business.

RABBI BERKOWITZ: We are going to turn now to Jewish themes and ideals. If you could go back into history and select three people you would like to meet, who would these three people be, and why would you want to meet them?

ALAN KING: I would like to think that in the scope of my new-found intellect there have to be a couple of thousand that I would like to meet. As a matter of fact, I think back on some people I knew who are no longer with us and say that I know more about them now than when they were here. While they were here I never took the time to find out the make-up of the man; we sometimes accept others on a very superficial level.

I would have to take three, but in what category? I would like to have met Jesus, because if I were a Catholic I would believe that I was going to meet him anyway. For me, there is the chauvinistic charm—the fact that Jesus was a Jew. There are many religions and there are many people who deny Jesus's existence completely. We know that a rock brought back from the moon is three million years old. We know that a skull found somewhere in Africa goes back to the Neanderthal man. We accept this scientifically, and we cannot deny that a man did walk who preached what his religion advocated. I think that Jesus may have been a revolutionary of his time, a man who never denied the Ten Commandments. I think the teachings of Jesus were used for many reasons after his death. I am not concerned with what I am told of his healing the blind or of his resurrection. I do not believe that he was the son of God. But that is not important. What is important is that he was a common man. You see, our religion was first the religion of the kings, then the religion of the priests, and finally the religion of the people. There was a great deal of evil in the world at the time. There was a lot of oppression, and I think that a little carpenter who walked among the people and told them that there is faith, that there is hope, that there is goodness, was important. I am fascinated, absolutely fascinated by the goodness of what the man preached. What became political and commercial does not interest me.

RABBI BERKOWITZ: Who are the other two?

ALAN KING: Perhaps Sigmund Freud. It is so difficult to answer because I am talking only about men who really interest me. Anyone who has enlightened, anyone who has brought new thoughts to humanity, interests me. Freud saw man's problems, as did all great men in history, and brought something new. There were so many broken lives, so many unhappy people, and one little Viennese came along and said there was nothing abnormal about being in love with your mother; nothing wrong with many feelings that we have that we thought were taboo. The ignorance of our society over the years has always been lessened by men like Sigmund Freud.

As to the third person, I don't know—I can think of so many people who came out with a new idea, with a new concept that changed the face of the world. Karl Marx and his philosophy, which again, as in the case of the teachings of Jesus, was misused and abused. His thought was corrupted. There is nothing corrupt about thought, it is what society does later that causes damage.

I would like to see someone like Clarence Darrow, a man who stood against all ignorance, a man who stood for what he believed in—the rights of man. He defended Leopold and Loeb, who were accused of the most dastardly crime committed in this country. He defended them despite what people said about them. They called Darrow the "attorney for the damned," a man who took on all the unpopular causes, particularly in the labor movement. And Darrow said, "Even the rich have rights." He said, "I may hate the sin, but never the sinner." Men like that, who had courage, are the kind of men I would like to meet.

RABBI BERKOWITZ: You were recently given a humanitarian award. The citation read: ". . .Tribute not only to a well-deserved reputation as to his skills as a performer but for his many achievements and accomplishments on behalf of his fellow man, extensive charitable work and devotion to good causes." You have said that your philanthropic motivation is Talmudic. What do you mean?

ALAN KING: I think it is mystical, and I think that this is part of the Talmud. There is a line between studies of the Talmud, which can be interpreted every day as they are, and the absolute—the written words. You cannot argue with the words of God. The Talmud was written by men. Interpretation, constructions, change all the time. I was taught as a young boy, "Cast thy bread upon the waters." My father used to say this to me all the time, and, if anything, my father was not communistic. He may have been a socialist, which was understandable. My father's interpretation of this was: "You have to give a little; you've got to pay back."

I think we are all motivated selfishly, in a sense. I wish more people were motivated selfishly in that way, because if you have and others have not, and if you don't do something about those who have not, eventually they are going to rise up and get it. They are going to come and get you, because it is the nature of man. He can only be suppressed so long. Eventually he rises up against those who oppress him.

The man who gives a million dollars to a charity is not necessarily philanthropic. The question is what motivates him to give. I will tell you a story about raising funds after the Six-Day War. There was a little man in the music business. This little guy was in his eighties, crippled with arthritis and barely being subsidized by the music industry. He got up and said "Five hundred dollars," and there was more applause than if someone had given a million. And then we had to go around again, because we were short for money. You know, you never reach the goal. No matter what happens, we are always short a few dollars, so we went around again. We realized that if this elderly man had given $500 it was probably his burial money. We decided that someone should get up and say "One thousand dollars in memory of my mother." I did not want to stop at the table where this little fellow was sitting, but when we tried to pass him by, he got up and said "One hundred dollars in memory of the five hundred dollars I just gave."

I am very fortunate to be able to give, and what I do give does not take away from my children. They are in the best schools. But I think that whatever philanthropy I am accused of practicing is not so much in dollars, because that is easy. Giving time is what my philanthropy is. It means nothing for a guy to stand up and say, "Five thousand." It is tax deductible. We need the money — nobody says we don't need it, or that it does not serve a purpose. But the real business of giving is giving of yourself. You become involved in the charity itself, whatever the cause may be, and that is where it's really at.

To me philanthropy is not only giving your money but giving of your time, yourself, your involvement.

RABBI BERKOWITZ: What is the pull that moves you to take such an interest in the State of Israel? Even though it may be obvious from places such as the Alan King Diagnostic Medical Center in Jerusalem. You were recently honored by the Hebrew University for American students. What does Israel, as a state, as the revitalization of the Jewish Commonwealth, mean to you?

ALAN KING: When I was a kid and started working in show business I remember once receiving a review in a trade paper that I was "too Jewish." I was very upset by that, and I spent the next ten years trying not to be too Jewish. Then one day I woke up and said, "What does it mean, being too Jewish?" Being too Jewish is like being too smart, too healthy, too rich. I realized that for me, as an individual, being Jewish did not merely come out of the fact that my father was a good storyteller and that I had heard of his ability to tell stories. It did not come from my grandfather. No, it was that four thousand years of heritage that had brought me to a point in my life, that in a sense made me what I am. A lot went into it, but all of the years and all of the generations that preceded me brought me to the point where I was able to see things through my Jewishness. All of a sudden I realized that it was terribly important for me to perpetuate and to sustain this kind of feeling.

Now, for two thousand years we Jews never had a homeland. The State of Israel came into being in 1948, and I found that what I called "quasi-Jewish" people, who were not overtly Jewish, all of a sudden became Jewish after 1948. We had more Jews in 1956, and then after the Six-Day War still more people who were not Jewish became Jewish. I never needed something that was material to give me pride in my heritage, but all of a sudden here was something tangible.

The Torah and the Talmud were not enough for some people, but all of a sudden they could identify — there it was.

Now we were considered a state, we had a personal dignity in a sense — not that we ever lacked dignity before. I thought it was good; aside from the fact that I was emotionally involved, intellectually it was good.

I was not heroic enough to go there and join a kibbutz, but I realized the fact that there are many Jews in the world who are not as fortunate as we are here in this country. And I felt that I had to do something tangible to perpetuate and sustain their country.

I was on British television and someone asked, "How can you, as an American, have loyalty to two nations?" The United States is the only country in the world where one cannot have dual citizenship. Charlie Chaplin was literally run out of this country because he made millions here and was a British subject. That is chauvinism. Yet we have hundreds and hundreds of people who live in other countries, who have made millions, and who have never given up their American citizenship. So when I am asked how I can have loyalty to two countries, I answer, "For the same reason that a man can love two women." Of course, people wonder, What the hell does that mean? I equate Israel with this: a man can love two women, three women, ten women. I love my wife, and I love my mother, and I love my daughter. The United States, my country, is my wife, and Israel is my mother. So it gives me great satisfaction to know what I have known all my life, and what Jews have known for thousands of years, and what the rest of the civilized world is just beginning to know, that we do have this ability to build a land, that we are not all *schneiders*, that we don't all walk around with long beards, though there is nothing wrong with having a beard, and nothing wrong with being a *schneider,* either.

I remember being in Israel when there was a demonstration by the ultra-orthodox, because according to their interpretation of the Bible, they could not allow the Israeli defense forces through their sections because it was the Sabbath.

They lay down in the streets and would not allow the troops to come through. So the soldiers put their cars and trucks in reverse and went another way. At that time General Rabin was the Chief of Staff. I was angry, and in the heat of the moment I said, "The troops should have run them over." Because by having to put the column in reverse and having to go around, how many young men were not saved? General Rabin said to me, "We have been an oppressed people since almost the beginning of time, and we have fought for our right to be different. And now that we are in our homeland we must allow them the right to be different."

That is the way they interpret it, and that is the way it must be. It was this kind of feeling, call it what you may, that sustained our people. That is what they believe in, and if that is what they believe they have the right to believe it. I cannot get that out of my head.

RABBI BERKOWITZ: You have expressed an ideal which is the basis for a very secular humanitarianism which is popular today, and which to me falls short of real tradition—"You do your thing and I'll do my thing; I won't ask you to fit my pattern and you won't ask me to fit yours." This could be a shallow thought, but the way you express it it has a truly pious basis. You have the ability to lift the mundane up and give it meaning.

ALAN KING: We all have moments that wrap up our feelings in something we really can put our fingers on, and Israel inspires us. I must tell this story. My grandfather was a very pious man. He was also a man literally filled with smut, because when my grandfather cursed somebody, Lenny Bruce in his wildest imagination never used adjectives like my grandfather. The fact that they happened to be in Yiddish or Polish had nothing to do with it. When I was a kid during the Depression, we lived with my grandfather. Every Seder, when family would gather, my grandfather used to say, "Next year, Jerusalem." Being a child and not being aware, I did not understand what this was all about. To me, it not only was spiritual, it was mystical.

In 1955, my grandfather—who lived to be ninety-four years of age—had a stroke at the age of about eighty-six or eighty-seven. He was taken to the hospital, really only a vegetable of a man. I was going to California to make a movie, and my mother said, "You had better go to visit your grandfather and in a sense say goodbye." So I went to visit him in the hospital. At this time, he could not speak, but he showed me that he was beginning to move his arms. I sat and visited with him, and then I went to California.

I was in California for about two weeks, and I spoke to my mother two or three times a week on the phone. My mother said, "You wouldn't believe it, Daddy's gaining. He will never be the same, but it looks like he might beat it." He did live, he lived on for many years after that—of course, in the nursing home, and his speech came back to a certain degree. I was in Israel with my wife when I got a telegram that my grandfather had died. I was disturbed and I was sad, but I wasn't distraught; he had lived his life. So I put a call through to my mother. I had just arrived in Israel, but I asked, "Shall I come back?" My mother told me that there was no reason to. I agreed; there was no reason for me to go back. I was with some government officials, and when we went down to the dining room I said to one of the officials, "It is a strange thing; my grandfather who was such a pious man has just passed on, and here I am in Israel. I would like to do something, say a prayer, something." The holiest place in Israel at the time was David's tomb, because Israel did not have the Wall. They said that we ought to go to King David's tomb and light a candle and recite a prayer. My wife and I went to the tomb of David, and we walked into this very dark, cavelike room where there was an altar and candles. There was a rabbi, a custodian, in a white coat; he had a beard and he looked exactly like my grandfather.

My wife said to me, "Isn't this strange. It's mystical. Look at the rabbi." He was a Rumanian Jew, and my grandfather would never have tolerated him.

My host, the government official, went up to the rabbi and explained the situation. The prayer was said and we lit the candles, and as we were leaving the rabbi came out with us. He was a man well into his eighties, and he spoke Yiddish. I told him the story about my grandfather. It was strange, having been raised by a man who always said, "Next year, Jerusalem," and there I was in Jerusalem when my grandfather died.

The rabbi looked at me and said, "He is now in Israel." My wife and I did not shed a tear when my grandfather died, but at that moment, as we walked out I thought this scene typified the millions of people who went through life with this one dream, and here it was—a reality. To deny it would be to deny everything that came before us.

RABBI BERKOWITZ: Let me paraphrase that last sentence. . . To deny it, to deny the millennia of the Jewish experience, would be to deny the very reason that we are here. You have, Mr. King, provided us with an unparalleled curtain line for what has been an unforgettable performance. You have given us the opportunity to explore together some of the questions which are constantly before one who is in the public eye in a special role and have shown us a few of the many facets of that role. I think that none of us—after this period that we have had together—will ever hear the term "Jewish comedian" without a deeper appreciation of what it means. . . an appreciation which we have gained from the insight which you have given us.

ARTHUR MORSE

RABBI BERKOWITZ: The murder of six million Jews by the Nazis is the most cruel, sadistic and bestial crime in the history of civilization. Many have written about this, but few have investigated and documented the guilt of the democracies in the mass murder of Jews. In a book entitled *While Six Million Died,* this aspect of one of the world's greatest tragedies is seriously and deeply investigated. Arthur Morse wrote this volume after years of research, which included a period during which he worked in a locked room in the National Archives in Washington. In addition to interviewing more than a hundred participants, he studied records in London, Paris, Rome, Stockholm and the Roosevelt Library in Hyde Park. The culmination is a volume that has been read and discussed by many thinking and sensitive people in which the nations of the world are accused of indifference and apathy while six million died.

Why did you write *While Six Million Died,* Mr. Morse?

MR. MORSE: I am not really sure that anyone can honestly explain his own motives. He can guess at them, but he may not be quite accurate. I am a journalist. I spent some years at CBS in documentary television and in writing magazine articles about social questions. It seemed to me that the Nazi destruction of the European Jewry, or the attempted destruction of it, was the most significant event of our times if one is interested in human capabilities—in the possibilities for human error, on the one hand, and human nobility on the other. It also seemed to me that if we are going to prevent genocide in the future, no matter who the killers may be, no matter who their intended victims, we have to know how it happened in the past. There has been very little literature about this question.

RABBI BERKOWITZ: How does one go about writing a book like this?

MR. MORSE: The techniques I had used in television and in writing for magazines were not very much different from those used in the book. The problem was to get the material. Much of it was classified as secret, although it is difficult to understand why this was so classified so many years after the event. It would not seem to threaten national security. But to get to these secret archives I had to have clearance—and this took eight months.

You may be interested in a personal anecdote in this connection. My family lived in Stamford, Connecticut, for a while, and we had some very pleasant neighbors, people we liked but with whom we had very little social relationship. Some months later, after we had moved to Westchester, I met my former neighbor, who asked rather hopefully, I thought, "Are you in some kind of trouble?" I asked "Why?" and he said, "Well, a man came to our door and flashed a badge and asked me questions about you and asked me if I thought you were loyal to our form of government. I told him that I thought you were loyal but not very sociable." So if you are going to try to get clearance from the State Department be sure your relationship with your neighbors is sociable.

Once you have clearance, the State Department, though wrong in many ways—I think it is fair to say that it is the villain of my book—is very generous. It is more generous than the State Departments of other governments in opening materials. In most countries one cannot get any material for fifty years after the event. In the United States, generally, it is twenty years after the event.

RABBI BERKOWITZ: How long did it take you to write the book?

MR. MORSE: About two and a half years to research and slightly over a year to write.

RABBI BERKOWITZ: Has it appeared in other languages and in other countries?

MR. MORSE: It was published in Germany with the German title, *Die Wasser Teilen Sich Nicht,* which means, I gather, "The Waters Did Not Part," which seems to be a rather eloquent title. It has been published in eight countries up to now.

RABBI BERKOWITZ: The book documents an involved, long and complex chapter of human indifference and lack of involvement in the rescue of millions of innocent men, women and children. You write: "In the years between 1933 and 1944 the American tradition of sanctuary for the oppressed was uprooted and despoiled. It was replaced by a combination of political expediency, diplomatic evasion, isolationism, indifference, and raw bigotry which played directly into the hands of Adolf Hitler, even as he set in motion the final plan for the greatest mass murder in history."

How do you explain the fact that our American tradition of sanctuary was reversed during this era?

MR. MORSE: In general, this period from 1933 to 1944 was marked by a departure from the American past in the field of immigration. We absolutely reversed the whole tradition of this country as an asylum for the oppressed. It was also marked by the fact that for perhaps the first time in American diplomatic history, we made no overt diplomatic intercession in order to aid people who were suffering through no fault of their own. Between the time that Hitler came to power—in January 1933—until December 1942, there was not a single American protest to the German government about their treatment of the Jews. This is utterly at variance with the way in which we responded to similar problems that occurred in the past. Many times in American history we interceded; the Czarist pogroms against the Jews, the Kishinev massacre which led to Theodore Roosevelt's intercession, the Turkish persecution of Armenians in 1915 which led to strong American protests. We broke the treaty of 1832 with Czarist Russia because of Russian pogroms, even though that meant a loss of income to the United States government. The House of Representatives voted 300 to 1 to abrogate the treaty of 1832. There always had been a past pattern of American humanitarian intercession.

I am not speaking of the ordinary people but of the government. Almost every aspect of government, it seems to me, violated our tradition during the 1933-1944 period. Of course, there were reasons which we cannot go into. Unemployment, as you will recall, had its impact on immigration. Congress was dominated by fairly extreme reactionaries, and there was an increase of anti-Semitism as well. But, nevertheless, during that period we turned our back on our tradition.

RABBI BERKOWITZ: Some time ago the entire world was stirred by a play that appeared in America and Europe, called *The Deputy,* an accusation of Pope Pius XII. In your book you comment on the role—or lack of role—of the Pope. "The apathy of Pope Pius XII became the subject of numerous dispatches to Washington from Myron Taylor." Further on, you say, with regard to the Pope, "The self-imposition of the most delicate reserve begins to look very much like abdication from his leadership." Do you want to add to these comments?

MR. MORSE: During this period, approaches were made by Myron Taylor, American representative to the Vatican, in collaboration with a number of other governments, to induce the Pope to take a position threatening the Nazis with excommunication if they continued their deeds. All of these efforts were of no avail. The Pope refused to take action. The evidence, which I have seen in American archives, seems to me to bear out in large measure the accusation in *The Deputy*. But having said that, one must also add that we cannot extend the apathy of the Pope to the whole Catholic Church or the whole Catholic population, because the history of Europe during this period is filled with examples of heroism on the part of churchmen, of nuns, of many Catholics who sheltered Jews.

We may say that there should have been more of them, but nevertheless we cannot forget that there were many. One of the things my book does is to reveal for the first time the role of Monsignor Angelo Roncalli, who became Pope John XXIII. He rescued at least 50,000 Jews by issuing baptismal certificates to Jews in Budapest. He was then the Apostolic Delegate in Istambul, and he was approached by Ira Hirschmann, who represented the American War Refugee Board. Mr. Hirschmann described the plight of the Jews, and Monsignor Roncalli, who was aware of it, said that since the Germans were not killing anyone carrying a baptismal certificate, he would issue a great number of them for the Jews in Budapest. He said that he hoped they would accept this in the spirit in which it was offered, as a method of saving lives, and not as a way of recruiting converts. Hirschmann said that he thought they would accept it. Some 25,000 of these certificates were distributed in Budapest. In addition, the future Pope John, who had been the Apostolic Representative in Bulgaria before the war, learned that Hitler had ordered the King of Bulgaria to send the 25,000 Jews of Sofia to Auschwitz. Monsignor Roncalli sent a letter to King Boris saying that if he sent the Jews to their doom, the King would face eternal damnation. King Boris, who, by the way, was not a Catholic, dispersed the Jews of Sofia into the Bulgarian countryside, where they lived in safety for the rest of the war.

There were others who helped during these episodes, but the man who was to become Pope John XXIII was indeed a most significant friend to the Jews.

RABBI BERKOWITZ: In this period, there was one great personality, a towering human being, physically and spiritually, who is not remembered too often. I wonder how many of us recall the devotion and dedication, the dynamism and commitment to the Jewish people of Dr. Stephen S. Wise?

MR. MORSE: During this period, Rabbi Wise was president of the American Jewish Congress and spiritual leader of his own congregation. He was in the forefront of every effort to try to awaken the United States government to its moral obligations and was constantly badgering the President, albeit in a respectful way, to accomplish this. He led delegations repeatedly to the White House. He helped author a document called "Blueprint for Extermination," which was a very detailed report of what was happening to the Jews based on materials coming in from occupied Europe. It seems to me that in every respect he worked tirelessly. Unfortunately, it was a very lonely effort. Nevertheless, if he had been listened to, I do not think that all that happened would have occurred.

RABBI BERKOWITZ: In the book, you write that in November of 1942, Sumner Wells summoned Rabbi Wise to Washington and that the Secretary showed the Rabbi the affidavits from Switzerland which supported the revelations of the leader of the World Jewish Congress. Just a few weeks before, the President had made an important announcement that the United States would join Great Britain and the other allies in establishing a War Crimes Commission. What was the War Crimes Commission?

MR. MORSE: That War Crimes Commission, which I think originated in 1942, was one of a whole series of facades—facades with nothing to back them up. The War Crimes Commission was first suggested, oddly enough, by Roosevelt to Winston Churchill in Washington. The idea was to set up a group of legal specialists who would begin the work of sifting the war crimes and who would establish the judicial requirements for treatment of war criminals. The hope was that publishing this would inhibit the criminals from carrying out their actions. What in fact happened was that the United States, which had first proposed the idea, was so dilatory, it had not sent a representative to London six months after the first meetings were held. Finally, the President chose a man named Herbert C. Pell. Roosevelt chose him because he had been a loyal political follower.

To me, as a writer, the evolution of Herbert Pell is a fascinating illustration of the possibilities of human development. Judging from the manner in which he was chosen and considering his background, one would expect him to be ineffective. As a matter of fact, once he got to London and to the sessions of the War Crimes Commission and began to read about the Nazi atrocities, he became more and more inflamed. He realized that the War Crimes Commission really offered the possibility of punishing the Germans for their mistreatment of the Jews, because there was no precedent in International Law for punishing a country for the way it treated its own citizens. He also realized that the worst perpetrators of these crimes could go free if this continued. So he began a personal crusade, growing angrier by the day, and as he did, he aroused the antagonism of the State Department, which was opposed to this sort of action.

It was fascinating, because eventually Herbert Pell was told that there was no longer any money in the budget to have him continue as a member of the War Crimes Commission. At this point he said that he would serve for nothing, but he was told there was no precedent for that. His firing led to a wide public awareness because all the newspapers picked up the story. This led eventually to the later American position and a determination in the War Crimes Commission that Germans could be punished for the mistreatment of other Germans.

RABBI BERKOWITZ: In discussing Roosevelt's Secretary of State, you write: "Hull had neither the time nor the conviction to go deeply into the refugee problem. He became short tempered and rigid when faced with opportunities for rescue. For example, in 1940, a refugee ship carrying Jews that had escaped from France before the German occupation was turned away from Mexico. Mexican authorities ruled that the passengers' visas had been sold illegally, and the Jews were ordered to return to Europe for certain doom. When the ship made a brief stop for coal at Norfolk, Virginia, a delegation of American Jews, encouraged by Eleanor Roosevelt, visited Hull. Among them was one of Rabbi Wise's colleagues, Dr. Nahum Goldmann, a persuasive and toughminded Zionist. Goldmann urged the Secretary to grant the refugees asylum, although they lacked U.S. immigration papers. Hull swung around in his chair and pointed to the American flag behind him. 'Dr. Goldmann,' he said, 'I took an oath to protect the flag and obey the laws of my country and you are asking me to break those laws.'

"Goldmann reminded Hull that several weeks earlier, a number of anti-Nazi German sailors had leaped overboard as their ship departed from New York. Since the United States was not as yet at war with Germany, the Coast Guard had picked up the sailors and had given them sanctuary at Ellis Island. Goldmann suggested that Hull might send a telegram to the refugees in Norfolk and ask them to jump overboard. 'Surely,' he said, 'they will not be allowed to drown. The Coast Guard will pick them up and they will be safe for the rest of the war.'

" 'Dr. Goldmann,' said Hull sharply, 'You are the most cynical man I have ever met.' Unabashed, Goldmann replied, 'I ask you, Mr. Secretary, who is the cynical one? I, who wish to save these innocent people, or you, who are prepared to send them back to their death?' Hull dismissed the delegation, refusing to shake Goldmann's hand, but in the end he yielded to Mrs. Roosevelt's intervention and the refugees were admitted."

Would you comment on Hull?

MR. MORSE: Cordell Hull, from my studies at least, was not generally an ill-intentioned man. He was a Tennessee lawyer, a very significant force when he was in the Senate because he was used by Roosevelt to bring together the recalcitrant Southern senators with the more liberal Eastern senators. However, he was totally focused on questions of reciprocal trade and ending tariffs. He had very little time for the question of humans in distress. There was some conjecture that the fact that his wife was Jewish played a psychological role in his attitude. I cannot say whether it did or not, but it is an interesting thought.

In this connection, when the German ambassador returned to Germany in the thirties, he sent a note to his colleagues in the Foreign Office saying, "You know, we are made to look ridiculous in the United States because we accuse all important Americans of being Jews. There are enough important Americans who are Jewish so that we can be accurate about them." He made up a list—Herbert Lehman, Henry Morgenthau, and so on, who were Jewish. The name of

Cordell Hull had an asterisk next to it, and at the bottom of the page next to the asterisk was a note that Mrs. Hull was Jewish. But I do not know how important this was in Hull's life. In any case, the most charitable thing one can say about Cordell Hull is that he was a man of very narrow vision and grasp, and that he was disinterested in the problem. I am certain he never regarded himself as anything but a friend of the Jews. He could not relate this problem in any way to the American tradition.

RABBI BERKOWITZ: You mention, in your book, the names of people responsible for the evolution of the American policy. One was Robert Borden Reams, another Breckinridge Long. Who were they?

MR. MORSE: Breckinridge Long was a product of very socially prominent Virginia-North Carolina families—the Breckinridges and Longs. He married an extremely wealthy woman and used his money to cement his own relationship with the Democratic party. One hears he contributed $130,000 to the Democratic campaign. He was not the most perceptive of men. I might mention that his thesis at Princeton was entitled "The Impossibility of India's Ever Becoming Independent." His career from that point on was an unbroken series of misjudgments. He was the American ambassador to Italy and wrote that line which people think is apocryphal—the one that says that Mussolini made the trains run on time. Of the Italian-Ethiopian war, he wrote: "This is a war in which there is no moral question that I can find out." With that background, Franklin Roosevelt appointed him Assistant Secretary of State in charge of every division of the State Department dealing with refugee problems.

Among his subordinates was Robert Borden Reams, a graduate of Allegheny College. He had been a hotel clerk in

Washington and had taken the foreign service exam, passed it, and had become a Foreign Service officer. He was put in charge of the "Jewish Question." All matters dealing with refugee problems passed under his benevolent supervision. I interviewed him for several days, and in response to my questions he said, "Well, you know I was only a master sergeant." That may have echoes for you of a certain trial in Jerusalem. In fact, there was something in that—he was a very zealous master sergeant. He was important because he read all the incoming cables from American diplomats. When an American ambassador, such as Anthony Drexel Biddle, who was the ambassador to Poland and a fearless, eloquent opponent of Nazism, sent in his telegrams, they were initialed by all of the men who saw them. If you were to go to the U.S. Archives, as I did, you would see the initials of all the people who read them. This man had read and initialed all the documents coming in from occupied Europe, and yet, whenever he was asked whether there was, in fact, a Nazi plan for the extermination of the Jews, he invariably replied, "That information comes from Jewish sources," tending to cast discredit on it.

In one instance, the President of Costa Rica, shortly after the beginning of the "final solution" in 1942, sent a telegram to Cordell Hull asking whether it was true that a Nazi plan existed for the extermination of the Jews and was being carried out. If this were true, he said, his government wanted to make a formal protest, but he was not in possession of the information. Hull forwarded the telegram to this same person for reply, and he, in turn, sent a telegram to the President of Costa Rica, saying, "The source of that information is a Jew in Geneva." In fact, the source of that information was a wide variety of people of all faiths all over Europe.

These were two of the people who were on a lower level. Before we castigate them too severely, we must remember that they were carrying out American policy, carrying it out more cruelly, I am sure, than the President realized, with more duplicity than he realized—but they were carrying out official American policy.

RABBI BERKOWITZ: Let us go to the higher level, the very top level. From 1933 until he died, Franklin Roosevelt was a favorite of the Jews. What role did President Roosevelt have in all of this?

MR. MORSE: Let me say that this was one of the more painful parts of my research, because I always related people who had nasty things to say about Roosevelt to the extreme hate-wing in the country. I do not have nasty things to say about Roosevelt. I use the documents. I use his own words and try not to give my own interpretation. Having said that, I think it only fair to say that however great he was in many other aspects in life—and he was certainly great—one does, in measuring Roosevelt's performance in this particular crisis, find him wanting. On this behalf, however, one must also put this in the context of his times.

One must recall the years when this country was engulfed in a terrible depression and there were more than 20 million unemployed, when Congress was dominated by men like Martin Dies and Senator Robert Reynolds of North Carolina, people who wished to eliminate all immigration. One must remember that our quota permitted at least 150,000 immigrants a year, although we never really fulfilled it. And one must realize Roosevelt's problems in marshalling this country's resources to overcome the depression, to make it aware of what was happening in the rest of the world, to rearm a country which was isolationist in spirit, and at a time when anti-Semitism was, I think, more prevalent than today. His role was an extremely difficult one.

It is certainly not my intention in my book to imply that Roosevelt was an anti-Semite or that all our appraisals of Roosevelt are incorrect. I think it was probably Mrs.

Roosevelt—and you will be happy to learn that none of your feelings about her will in any way be disturbed by this book—who put it perhaps most accurately when she wrote: "Franklin often fails to fight for those things in which he believes because he considers the political realities. That was the reason he never opposed the poll tax, or fought for anti-lynching laws, although certainly as a human being he was opposed to those."

Roosevelt was a political animal and operated as such, and I do not use the word "animal" disrespectfully. To me, a very touching example of the ideological split between the President and Mrs Roosevelt was in 1939, when there was a proposal before the Congress to admit 20,000 German children and not to charge the numbers against the quota. There were thousands of American families who were willing to adopt these children, and a Quaker was going to be in charge of this nationwide program. It was beautifully organized, the labor unions were assured that the children would not compete for jobs, and so on. There was not a word from the White House in support of this bill. The President was off on the cruiser *Houston* on his birthday, and Mrs. Roosevelt sent a telegram, which I will have to paraphrase, but it was something like this: "Happy birthday, darling, hope you are having a lovely cruise. Can I tell Sumner (Welles) that you favor the child refugee bill?" There was no answer and there was never any presidential support for the bill.

RABBI BERKOWITZ: In the Roosevelt era, there was another great personality, a man who in later years became exceedingly active in the Israel Bond organization, a very distinguished person, Henry Morgenthau. What was his role in helping to rescue refugees?

MR. MORSE: Perhaps I can begin this with an anecdote which I thought was charming, told to me by Morgenthau's former secretary. She was a Jewish woman who was very disturbed because the Secretary of the Treasury was not really interested in Jewish Affairs and she tried to proselytize him.

One day, a distinguished-looking rabbi, who shall be nameless—a tall, imposing, bearded man—came into the anteroom of the Secretary's office without any appointment and demanded to see the Secretary on important business. Mr. Morgenthau's secretary said that he was going off on vacation, and since the rabbi did not have an appointment, he could not be seen. At this point the rabbi began shouting that while these terrible things were happening to the Jews of Europe, the Secretary of the Treasury, himself a Jew, was going off on vacation and did not have time to see a rabbi bringing the story to him!

The shouting of the rabbi brought Morgenthau out. He was a very delicate man who did not like disturbances. He immediately summoned the rabbi into his office and tried to explain to him privately that he really could not see him that day and would see him within the next week or two. At this point the rabbi put his hand to his head and fell on the floor in a faint. Morgenthau was desperate. He summoned the Treasury Department doctor and his chauffeur, and he had the rabbi escorted down the corridor by the rabbi's young assistant.

Now, Morgenthau's secretary did not look Jewish. She was following them down the corridor when the rabbi turned to his assistant and said in Yiddish, "How did I do?" The secretary decided not to tell Mr. Morgenthau the story because it would only make things worse, and she said that this was the one secret she ever kept from him.

From this quiet beginning, Morgenthau, in late 1943, became a tiger, and the incident which touched off his wrath and played a very profound and positive effect on American policy had to do with what I think is probably the most disturbing episode in this disturbing book. In March 1942, the

Dictator of Rumania, Antonescu, deported 185,000 Rumanian Jews to a terrible group of concentration camps in the Ukraine. These Jews, riddled wth typhus and hunger, clothes ripped off their backs, brutalized by the Rumanian police, dwindled down to 70,000. In 1943 the German armies were in retreat before the Soviet counteroffensive, and in the path of the retreating Germans were the 70,000 Jewish survivors. Suddenly, dictator Antonescu became a humanitarian. He realized that if the Jews were killed, with the tide of war now turning and an Allied victory in prospect, he would be regarded as a war criminal after the war. He therefore let it be known to the United States and the World Jewish Congress that he would be willing to bring back the surviving 70,000 Jews from the Ukraine, provided the United States sent food, medicine and clothing. There was no bribery involved; this would go to the people. The money could be placed in a blocked Swiss account, where it could not possibly fall into the hands of the Nazis. It was to be repaid after the war.

This offer was reported to the U.S. government. It took nine months for the United States to authorize the transmission of the first payment of $25,000, because a license was necessary in order to send money overseas. This license had to be authorized by both the State Department and the Treasury Department. The Treasury Department agreed immediately to the license; the State Department refused.

As a result of the State Department's refusal, three officials of the Treasury Department, all of whom happened to be Protestant—Randolph Paul, Josiah E. Dybois, Jr., and John Pehle—drafted a detailed documentary report on these nine months of indifference. They entitled this report "The Acquiescence of This Government in the Murder of the Jews." This report is printed for the first time in "While Six Million Died." They gave the report to Morgenthau, who read it and was shocked by it. He retitled it "Report to the President," and made an appointment to see Franklin Roosevelt. He and the three authors of the report went to the White House on January 16, 1944. They handed the report to the President and sat there while he read it. That day President Roosevelt set up a rescue mechanism, the War Refugee Board. It was January 1944, eleven years after Hitler came to power, seventeen months after the United States had definitive information about the Nazi order for the extermination of the Jews. The War Refugee Board, without diverting a single American serviceman, without firing a shot, without sending a bomber or a fighter, without spending taxpayers' money because they used the funds of Jewish philanthropies, were able to rescue about 400,000 people within the next nine months.

RABBI BERKOWITZ: In connection with the War Refugee Board, you mentioned a number of names, among them Dr. Nahum Goldmann and Ira Hirschmann. What was Ira Hirschmann's work in connection with the War Refugee Board?

MR. MORSE: The War Refugee Board sent representatives to each of the neutral nations. Ira Hirschmann was sent to Turkey; Roswell McClelland was sent to Switzerland; a Unitarian minister, Dr. Robert Dexter, was sent to Portugal. Regrettably, the American ambassador to Spain, Carlton Hayes, refused to allow a War Refugee Board representative to serve in Spain. He was the one American ambassador who refused.

Ira Hirschmann was responsible for the release of the 48,000 Jews who remained in the Rumanian camps. He did it very simply. He called on the Rumanian Minister to Turkey and said, "If you do not release the remaining refugees from these camps, you will be executed after the war as a war criminal." The Rumanian Minister asked if he could get a visa to the United States, and Hirschmann said he would try. And the Jews were released. That's how simple it was to effect rescue in this case.

RABBI BERKOWITZ: One name often in the news at that time was Joel Brand. What does your book say about him?

MR. MORSE: You may remember the proposal that Eichmann was supposed to have made to Brand to trade one million Jews for ten thousand trucks. That story is rather widely known. It is a tragic story because we will never know whether or not Eichmann had the power to keep the bargain. Joel Brand said repeatedly before his death that it was not crucial to him whether Eichmann could do so, but what was important was to keep the dialogue going in the hope that lives would be saved in the course of it.

Joel Brand was captured—that is a strange word to use, but that is exactly what happened. He was captured by the British and was imprisoned in Cairo. All the while he felt that he was responsible for the lives of millions of Jews. He was not sent back to Budapest, so that one is unable to tell whether or not any lives might have been saved. Actually, even during the period that he was engaged in discussions with Eichmann, there was a slowing down of the transports to Auschwitz.

What is new information in my book, I believe, is that we have never understood why this dialogue between Brand and the Germans was terminated, because there seems to have been no objection on the part of the United States to the deal. We know that the British captured Brand, but there seems to be more to it than that. The mystery seems to be cleared up by the fact that Andrei Vishinsky told Averell Harriman, the American ambassador to the Soviet Union, that the Soviet Union would not countenance any discussion regarding the rescue of the Jews between representatives of the German government and Joel Brand. It was that message which was sent to the U.S. Secretary of State which terminated the dialogue.

Ira Hirschmann, in a very heroic bid, went to Cairo and forced his way into the office of Lord Moyne, the British High Commissioner, and demanded the right to see Brand. He was able to see him and he submitted a character report on him which matched the report which Moshe Sharett, whom the British had allowed to come from Palestine, also sent about Brand—that he was a man who seemed to know what he was doing, of great courage and very pragmatic, a man who realized that Eichmann's offer was probably a trick but was willing to go along with it to delay the proceedings against the Jews. The Brand case, of course, is a tale of failure. Nevertheless, the idea of a dialogue with the Germans was continued by a man named Saly Mayer, representing the Joint Distribution Committee. With the help of the War Refugee Board, he conducted negotiations with the Germans on the Swiss border, never giving them anything, but always showing and negotiating with Swiss bankbooks. The Germans did not know that Mayer could not release funds without the signature of the State Department. Yet, Mayer was so skillful that many lives were saved during the course of these negotiations with Germans who thought they could get rich by releasing Jews.

RABBI BERKOWITZ: What is very distressing and disappointing is that one gets the feeling that we just want to block out this period. We are not interested in hearing about those atrocities, or concerned enough. Perhaps this stems from an awareness that we did not do enough. I don't know, but I do think that what we are doing here—reminding and reawakening ourselves—is very important and necessary. There were other attempts to negotiate with the Germans in trying to save lives. What were the discussions with Hjalmar Schacht?

MR. MORSE: There were attempts during the thirties to see if freedom might not be bought for the Jews from the Nazis, which is really what it amounted to. It posed a terrible problem, because the Jewish organizations which were prepared to raise a great amount of funds were not prepared at the same time to fuel the Nazi war machine. This put them in a very difficult ethical dilemma. It soon became clear that what the Germans were asking for would only strengthen Nazism and Hitlerism, and so the problem became an extremely sensitive and difficult one. In addition, one could never be sure whether the Nazis were really serious and would carry out their agreements.

In the thirties, complex negotiations were carried on with Dr. Hjalmar Schacht, who was Hitler's financial chief. At one point we seemed to be getting close to an understanding which was feasible—that in return for substantial sums of money, but not sums of money which would have made that much difference in terms of Nazi power, Jews might be released after actually undergoing training in Germany for Palestine and other areas of resettlement. But when it appeared that Schacht was close to coming to an agreement with a man named George Rublee, an American who was the law partner of Dean Acheson, Schacht was suddenly removed from his job and another man put in his place. All these efforts came to naught, and to this day there is no reason to think that any of these plans were really feasible.

A distinguished delegation of British Jews visited the United States in the thirties. They agreed to put up a third of an enormous sum to rescue the German Jews, although British Jews represented one-twelfth of the number of American Jews, but it came to nothing because always at the critical moment the Germans introduced some new element. One cannot be sure that any German offer was really serious.

RABBI BERKOWITZ: You wrote that in May of 1939 the Gestapo permitted representatives of the German Jews to visit London to plead for immediate action with the Intergovernmental Committee. Why was this done?

MR. MORSE: The Intergovernmental Committee was one of those endless committees set up with a noble charter and no resources, with the people at the head of this group really having no interest in what they were doing. What had happened was that discussions between Schacht and representatives of the Jewish organization went stumbling along month after month. The Gestapo became disturbed by the fact that there did not seem to be enough interest on the part of the Jewish community and allowed representatives of Berlin Jewry to come to London to this meeting. It is a terrible story, because the representatives of the Jews of Germany in the privacy of a room with the two Englishmen who headed the Intergovernmental Committee said, "You know that you don't have the funds and we know that the Germans may not mean it. All we ask is that you give us a note to the Gestapo saying you are interested in continuing negotiations and are serious about them." And Lord Winterton, who was the leader of the Intergovernmental Committee, said, "You will not tell us how to conduct our business." They refused to give these people even a note and simply sent them back empty-handed to the Gestapo.

RABBI BERKOWITZ: With all that was going on, you said, "One factor which enabled Roosevelt to maintain his discreet silence without losing political support was the disunity of American Jewry. This was reflected most sharply in the conflict between the American Jewish Congress and the American Jewish Committee."

MR. MORSE: Perhaps it is my fault in writing it that way, but if you take these individual sentences out of the body of the work, it leaves one with a false emphasis. It was clear to me that all of the Jewish groups, however differently they responded to the problem, did respond in their own way and they did respond sincerely. Influential, well-to-do, highly placed Jews in this country chose to work more behind the scenes to influence the President, whom they knew socially.

This was their way of trying to help. Others, more militant people, were not afraid to demonstrate and hold rallies.

My own idea is that while it was true that for part of the period there was disunity, most of this ended in 1938 with the *Kristallnacht* when the Jewish organizations did come together. The feeling I have is that, given the attitude of the government at the time, it probably would not have mattered much whether the Jewish community was totally united or not. Apart from that, my own conviction—with which you may disagree—is that Jews, the same as everyone else, are very different from each other. They perform differently and their notions of how to operate under given situations vary. They are not a homogeneous mass. At that time they had different political attitudes, on foreign affairs and everything else.

I do not think this is the critical part of the problem. I do not think that people should beat their breasts now and say, "If only we had done differently," because it appears that all the cards were stacked against a successful approach. I really believe that.

RABBI BERKOWITZ: Isn't it true that part of the cards stacked against the Jews was America's immigration policy of that time?

MR. MORSE: Before I comment on that, I do want to make a point which is out of sequence in our discussion. I am acutely aware that when we talk about the book as we are doing now, what we have is an endless saga of despair. We say, "My God, how terrible, how awful! Nothing but blackness!" Because of the nature of this discussion, we do not have time to go at length into the work of the War Refugee Board, although we touched upon it. I would like people to remember this: the War Refugee Board demonstrated that when the government of the United States makes the decision to take a positive approach to a problem that seems difficult, it can overcome the most incredible obstacles, and we did at that late period. It seems to me that we must always keep this in mind. This is the only thing that will prevent despair from overwhelming everything else.

The question really is, How does one get the government to do what it did in 1944, and did not do in 1936 or 1937? I think that is the lesson for the future. It is important for us to know how apathy and indifference and government failure lead to the loss of innocent people's lives. Yet we must not forget, and I would not want this saga of despair to make one forget, that when this government decided what it wanted to do, it did so exceedingly well.

Now, your comment about immigration demonstrates the reverse of this. Here is an example of how we missed the opportunity. Between 1933 and 1943 we admitted 1,200,000 fewer people than even our restricted immigration quotas permitted. In 1933, when Hitler came to power, the quota for Germany was 26,000. We admitted 1,700 of all faiths, not just threatened Jews. A year later, as the lines lengthened around the American consulates in Germany, we admitted 3,000. In 1935 we admitted roughly 4,000. Not until 1938 or 1939 were we even filling the German quota. At one time we had five times as many applications from Germany alone as we could give to the whole world. So this country of immigrants and sons and daughters of immigrants completely turned its back on its own tradition during that period. Every time we turned away a refugee ship, one could always find within a day or two the German press asking, "Who are the beasts, we or you?"

Some of you may have had terrible first-hand experience with this. As examples of how people were rejected, I was able to get some of the immigration case histories. Let me read you just one, which is, I assure you, similar to so many others.

This is a report of the American consul in Rotterdam, who in 1933 received 74 requests for visas to the United States. Sixteen were granted, and of the 58 refusals, 57 were based on the public charge provision of the immigration law—that is, that no one was to be admitted who was likely to become a public charge. Let me read to you about one of these likely "public charges," a thirty-three-year-old German physician and his thirty-year-old wife. They had $1,600 and three affidavits of support from a sister, cousin and friend in the United States. It was claimed that a second sister in the United States owned $70,000 worth of property and had $12,000 additional resources. This was the consul's analysis of that case: $1,600 was insufficient; the greater part of the resources listed on the affidavits was unproved; and the number of dependents of the cousin, sister and friend signing the affidavits was unstated; the cousin, sister and friend had no direct obligation to the physician and his wife. The couple was refused admission to the United States on the grounds that they were likely to become public charges, and this went on and on. The public charge provision was misused, and so were so many other provisions, some of them written in the late 1800's to prevent the immigration of indentured servants and so on. These were later used to justify the rejection of Jews who, in every respect, fulfilled American immigration requirements.

RABBI BERKOWITZ: There is an important point that you stress in your book: "Of course, not all the actors in this drama practicing silence and inaction were bad guys wearing black hats. There were both nations and groups who wore white hats. There were the Danes, the Swedes, the Bulgarians, the Dutch, most of the French clergy, the American Quakers."

There are some individuals you single out for their role in helping or trying to help. One of them was Prince Johannes Schwarzenberg. Who was he and what was his role?

MR. MORSE: Prince Schwarzenberg was an Austrian nobleman who escaped from Austria at the time of the

Anschluss, went to Switzerland and became an official of the International Committee of the Red Cross, which, I might add, had a dismal record during the war. But Prince Schwarzenberg broke the International Red Cross tradition. He decided that there was no way to get through to the concentration camps and he, through great resourcefulness and ingenuity, built up a list which began with 16 people in Oranienburg and later was extended to more than 55,000 people who received food packages.

RABBI BERKOWITZ: Who was Roswell McClelland, the Quaker?

MR. MORSE: He was the representative of the War Refugee Board in Switzerland, a man of enormous courage and resourcefulness, responsible for getting materials to the German underground and for working with Saly Mayer on the Swiss border. He is now an American Foreign Service officer stationed overseas.

RABBI BERKOWITZ: Raoul Wallenberg?

MR. MORSE: Raoul Wallenberg, one of the most extraordinary characters of this period, is a member of one of Sweden's great families, the Wallenbergs, a great family in banking, military and clergy. They are not Jewish. He was sent by the King of Sweden in 1944 to throw a Swedish protective umbrella around the 100,000 Jews in Budapest. He rented, borrowed and begged for thirty-two apartment houses and placed the protection of the Swedish crown over thousands of people who had no remote connection with Sweden. He later was captured by the Russians, allegedly our allies at that time, disappeared in the Soviet Union and is presumed to have died in prison. His family still lives in Stockholm.

RABBI BERKOWITZ: I would like to read a tribute that was offered to Raoul Wallenberg: "The time of horror is still fresh in our memories when the Jews of this country were like hunted animals and thousands of Jewish prisoners were in the temples preparing for death. We recall all the atrocities of the concentration camps, the departure of trains crammed with people who were to die, the suffering in the ghettos and the attacks against the houses that had been placed under international protection. But also we remember one of the greatest heroes of these terrible times, the Secretary of the Royal Swedish Legation, who defied the intruding government and its armed executioners. We witnessed the redemption of prisoners and the relief of suffering when Mr. Wallenberg came among the persecuted to help. In a superhuman effort, not yielding to fatigue, exposing himself to all sorts of dangers, he brought home children who had been dragged away, he liberated aged parents. We saw him give food to the starving and medicine to the ailing. We shall never forget him and shall be forever grateful to him and to the Swedish nation, because it was the Swedish flag that guaranteed the undisturbed slumber of thousands of Jews in the protected houses. He was a righteous man. God bless him."

You write about another man, an American and a Jew, whom you admired, Eddie Cantor.

MR. MORSE: Eddie Cantor was one of the most active people in the plan to adopt children. He told the United States State Department, "Don't worry about finding homes for the children, I can find 10,000 myself." Unfortunately, not much attention was paid to him in the White House. There is a sad little note which the President sent to his secretary, saying, after one of Cantor's innumerable letters to the White House about the adoption of children, "Send him a nice letter because he is very important in the National Foundation for Infantile Paralysis."

Nevertheless, Eddie Cantor was one of thousands of Americans, of all faiths and from all over the country, who were prepared to do anything to help. They had no power to bring children out of occupied Europe. They could only express their willingness to shelter them.

RABBI BERKOWITZ: Are there modern counterparts of the Nazi era today? If so, what can we do about it?

MR. MORSE: I think that unfortunately there are such counterparts and that there are things that we can do. I think the lesson of the Nazi period can serve us in good stead. In fact, perhaps this is really the way to memorialize the people who died, to determine what can be accomplished now. Consider the fact that the United States of America had the power, imagination and resources to feed the children of Biafra, and did nothing. I think it is a disgrace that we in this country, suffering more from overweight than any others, were unable to figure out how to get food to them when we knew one million innocent children would die in that country. I know there are all kinds of political problems, but when one thinks about it, the political problems are much simpler than they were in other periods of history. It was unbelievable that the Nigerian government could stand before the world and literally try to shoot down American planes bringing only food. I am sure that if some other government had threatened to shoot our planes down if we brought food supplies to a hungry population, we would not have reacted as quietly as we did to the Nigerian threat.

A second thing can be done. The United States is one of only two major powers on earth which has not yet ratified the United Nations Genocide Convention. This is the first attempt to consider genocide an international crime, to define it, to provide provisions for the return of genocidists who try to escape from one country to another, the first step toward an international court to treat cases of this kind. We actually helped to draft that convention in 1948, and no American President since Harry Truman in 1948 has called upon the United States to ratify it. The Genocide Convention should be ratified. There is a move afoot in this country to stimulate public support of the Genocide Convention. It is another concrete way in which we can try to see to it that legal provisions are adopted which would at least make such an event in the future less likely.

RABBI BERKOWITZ: I think the great value of your work is what I mentioned before: that this was one of the tragic eras of Jewish history, but that the reminder of how things were in those time can be valuable to us if such recollection can help us to spot the danger signals and avoid another such human catastrophe.

It is inspiring, I feel, to see a person gifted in a craft such as yours devote his abilities to the benefit of his people. For two and a half years or more, television and the printed page suffered a loss while you used your skills as a researcher and writer for this important work. It has proved to be a small loss, for the information which you uncovered and the lesson which you point up will be valuable for generations to come. You have indeed added to the literature of our people.

ALAN F. GUTTMACHER

RABBI BERKOWITZ: May I begin this dialogue by reading the following: "I am indignant that the liberal side of the socio-medical issues we discuss is rarely ever portrayed to the American reader by a physician. I am indignant that organized American medicine is more interested in its own economic security than in the social health it serves, and I am indignant that the church wields such stultifying powers in certain areas of medical care."

These few sentences, thoughts that are provoking and stimulating, were written by our distinguished guest, Dr. Alan Guttmacher. Dr. Guttmacher was the Director of the Department of Obstetrics and Gynecology at New York's Mt. Sinai Hospital, was a member of the faculty of the Albert Einstein School of Medicine, and retired in 1966 as member of the faculty of the Columbia University College of Physicians and Surgeons and the Harvard University School of Public Health. He is the editor of many scientific and popular books. He serves as chairman of the Medical Committee of the International Planned Parenthood Federation and was a member of its managing and planning committee.

Dr. Guttmacher, your name is renowed in the field of medicine and science and is known by millions throughout this country and throughout the world. Yet, I wonder how many know that the Guttmacher name is also renowned in American Jewish religious and social life.

DR. GUTTMACHER: I grew up by accident in Baltimore, Maryland, because my father was a rabbi. When he had a pulpit in Fort Wayne, Indiana, he was asked to come and try out for two different pulpits, one in Richmond, Virginia, and one in Baltimore. Baltimore came first, and Father gave a sermon there on the Sabbath. Apparently, he satisfied everyone sufficiently so that they told him not to bother to leave. By that accident, I was born in Baltimore and not in Richmond. Actually, I am proud to say that my Jewish origins go back to the great man named Eli Guttmacher, who was a very distinguished scholar and rabbi. He lived in eastern Germany, or perhaps Poland, and was born in 1796 and died in 1874. My grandfather was a merchant. My father was one of five children, and at the age of eighteen came from Germany to the United States because at that time they had conscription in the German Army, and he was not particularly anxious to become a soldier. He studied at Ohio University for a few years as a young man and then went to rabbinical school in Cincinnati. He was graduated there and had his first pulpit in Fort Wayne, Inni. At that time, it was expected that if the president of the congregation had an unmarried daughter, the rabbi would marry her. Father did his duty, and they later went to Baltimore.

Most people think of their parents as exceptional people. I think this of my own father. I can say that he was an accomplished scholar, but above all he was a wonderful human being, a man with a very warm heart, and deeply appreciated by the whole community.

I like to tell a story about the National Democratic Convention that met in Baltimore in 1912 and nominated Woodrow Wilson. They chose for the first day's prayer the leading prelate of that community, a great Cardinal, who was not given to succinct remarks. His prayer was dreadfully long. It was a hot day in an un-air-conditioned armory. William Jennings Bryan was there, with his shirt open and a big palm leaf fan. Many other well-known men were there, and they suffered through this prayer which probably lasted for five minutes. The next day they decided to have a leading Protestant Bishop. He felt that the Cardinal had omitted certain people in his prayer, so he added a bit, and his prayer was about seven minutes. I never saw such a sweating, restless group of people in all my life. My father was asked to give the prayer the third day, and I remember it because it was so short. He said: "May the Lord God bless your deliberations." The delegates got up, cheered, marched with their banners, and thought he ought to be nominated for vice president. Perhaps this will give you some idea of the kind of man he was.

My mother was the youngest of eleven children, which is a bad advertisement for Planned Parenthood. Her father had come as a peddler to American in 1833, and he was the second white settler in the little community which later became Fort Wayne, Indiana. My mother, I think, went to a Catholic school, though her father later was president of the congregation, and when she was very young she married my father. I always thought she was a remarkable woman. I did not realize it until later in life, but she was very dependent upon my father. There was a thirteen-year age difference, and she lived her life for my father and seemed to have very little independence. However, after his death, after mourning for five solid years, she finally took hold of herself and became a very distinguished social worker. She became director of the Jewish Children's Bureau and was appointed by Governor Ritchie as chairman of Montrose, a huge school for girls in

Maryland. A large hall in Montrose is a memorial to my mother. These were remarkable parents. There were three children in my family, my sister who died a few years ago and my twin brother who died just last year. We were not raised in luxury. I did not have quite as much spending money as most of the other children, but we did not want. We had a very pleasant home life, and I never had any idea of going into business. There is nothing wrong about business, but my father had no business sense and no business interest. His main concern was his fellow man. Therefore, I knew that I was going to do something which had nothing to do with business. Actually, I was going to teach English and History. Later, I changed my mind and studied to be a doctor.

RABBI BERKOWITZ: I do not say that you would not have been an excellent English or History teacher, but I am just glad that you are a doctor. Tell us something about your relationship with your twin brother. To me, this is a beautiful relationship and should be known.

DR. GUTTMACHER: One of us was born twelve minutes before the other, but we were never quite sure which one it was. Because my parents were very fond of music, Mother and Father went to hear the Boston Symphony and put us in charge of the nurse when we were five weeks old. The nurse gave us a bath; one of us had a pink ribbon and the other a blue. When my parents came home the twins were without ribbons, and the nurse was in tears because she could not determine which child belonged to which ribbon. Mother and Father and the nurse had a consultation, and I was chosen as Alan and the other boy as Manfred. Actually, I might have been Manfred and he Alan. We were indistinguishable, except to dogs and other children, perhaps because both have a strong sense of smell. I don't know, but everyone got us mixed up except dogs and children.

My brother and I followed the same career. We went through high school and college together and then both decided to go into medicine. We attended the same classes, ate at the same table and slept in the same room, but later, of course, our ways separated completely. I practiced in one town and he in another. His field of medicine was above the neck and mine below the waist. His field was psychiatry and mine was obstetrics-gynecology. He produced four sons and I produced three daughters, so we were quite different.

RABBI BERKOWITZ: Referring to your home and parents, you have said: "On this basis of social consciousness, untrammeled by rigid religious dogmas, many other forces left their mark." Please elaborate on some of these other forces.

DR. GUTTMACHER: All of us are subject to powerful forces in our formative years. I think back on several. Perhaps the earliest and most powerful force in my life was a simple man who was a shepherd in a park about three blocks from my home. Almost every afternoon after school, my brother and I went to see this shepherd, his flock and his two sheep dogs. This man was unschooled. He had come from Manassas, Virginia. During the Civil War he had been too young to enter the Confederate army, but he had stolen cattle from the Federal troops and herded them into the Confederate lines. Later he came to Baltimore and tended sheep. He was a remarkable naturalist and knew biological behavior, and he interested me in biology and the reproduction of life. So you can see that he was a powerful force in my life.

Then, when I grew up, there were teachers in school who influenced me. I remember one man who had just graduated from Harvard and who had a broad range of interests, which at my age was very important. Then I had the good fortune to be the 20-year-younger friend of one of Baltimore's most distinguished citizens, an outstanding judge. We would get together on weekends and take hikes and trips. I also remember another Baltimorian who had a great feeling for books. He collected old books, and he handled the incunabula with much tenderness and reverence. I think I learned a lot from him.

In medical school I had two great teachers. One, a historian, who is still living, whom I followed for two years, teaching where he taught. The other was a very great teacher and a very dramatic man. He was both narrow and liberal at the same time in some of his views. He had a paternalistic feeling for people. Particularly for the ward patient, he had a strong feeling of obligation rather than one of equality. He had great depth of feeling and a sense of strong moral rectitude. He was a man who would never allow any kind of faking or chicanery. He was truthful, and he expected all the people around him to be likewise.

I like to think also that Henry L. Mencken had an influence on me in my feeling for words. Henry had a brother named August Mencken, and from 1930 to 1942, the two Menckens and the two Guttmachers drank beer every Monday night from nine to twelve. I developed quite a feeling for Henry. I have always admired his writing even though I could not always admire the man. The year 1942 was actually when we stopped drinking beer together, because, as you remember, he was rather pro-German. He was pro-German in the first war (he was American-born but of German ancestry) and in World War II, so obviously our paths separated then.

RABBI BERKOWITZ: The late Dr. Abraham Heschel, who was professor of ethics and mysticism at the Jewish Theological Seminary, delivered an address before the American Medical Association in which he said, "Doctors should voluntarily set a maximum income, and when they reach that maximum they should spend the rest of the year doing research and taking care of the poor patients, or something of a similar nature." What do you think of this suggestion?

DR. GUTTMACHER: I think it is impractical. I do not think that one can take six months of practice and then quit. What I think he means is that a man who has one aim in mind, a large income, should by no means go into medicine. The man who has this goal will be a poor doctor. This I believe strongly. Of course, all good doctors spend a great deal of time in "investment," as we might call it, but they get just as much in return. I do not believe that any patient has gotten more from me then she has given to me.

The trouble with medicine, from my point of view, is that it is neither a profession nor a business. A doctor makes a very good living and at the same time he wants the same kind of respect that goes to the clergyman and to the teacher. This is one of the difficulties. Some of us try to take the middle course and look upon medicine as a source of an adequate living and, of course, also as a source of adequate service. This is probably what we ought to do. Unfortunately some start out idealistically and get sidetracked into seeking the dollar, and the dollar and good medicine do not get along together.

RABBI BERKOWITZ: It has been said, "Sometimes the drug cures, sometimes the smile cures," which, of course, refers to the patient-doctor relationship. Do you think, Dr. Guttmacher, that this is being neglected today with increased depersonalization, especially with one doctor in one room and another doctor in the next and the patient going from one to the other?

DR. GUTTMACHER: I am sure that it is. Medicine has become depersonalized. The laboratory has taken over clinical observation to a large extent. The doctor used to sit by the bedside and observe the patient; now, very often, he sends the technician in to take samples of blood and urine and spends very little time with his patient. While this results in a much keener diagnosis, I am sure, because medicine has made great progress, we are sacrificing the relationship between patient and doctor.

RABBI BERKOWITZ: Is it worth that sacrifice?

DR. GUTTMACHER: No, not really. Of course, if doctors were not so fiendishly busy they could still do both. But it is very difficult to establish this relationship in large cities, where travel is difficult for physicians. The office is a cold place, you are a number, someone is before you and someone is behind you. In the earlier days of medicine I could spend some time with the patient and his family, and we had a much warmer relationship then we do now. I am not blaming modern doctors—it is probably modern living as much as anything else.

RABBI BERKOWITZ: It has been said that doctors have become hardened and insensitive.

DR. GUTTMACHER: I do not think that doctors have really become hardened. Some try to put on a veneer showing that things do not really affect them. In talking to another doctor I quoted the distinguished teacher I mentioned before, who claimed that when he left the clinic at five o'clock in the afternoon he was able to close his mind until nine o'clock the next morning, unless he was called during the night. I said that I have never been able to do this. I can remember many sleepless nights that I spent worrying about patients. I think this is true of most of us. The doctor in times of tragedy feels the tragedy almost as much as the people involved. Some doctors have to defend themselves by being brusque and indifferent, but I think that nine out of ten men and women in medicine do not act this way.

RABBI BERKOWITZ: In modern medicine today, how has the increase in insurance—Blue Shield, Blue Cross and other such plans—affected the practice of medicine? What has it meant to the patient and to the doctor?

DR. GUTTMACHER: Medical insurance has probably raised the level of medicine in terms of the average individual, but for those who are financially better off, it probably has decreased the quality of medicine. In other words, a much larger pool is now in the treatment group, and perhaps the doctor has to divide his time more fairly. You might ask yourself: "If I were sick in 1930 and if I am sick now, would I get better care then or now?" The answer is obvious. With the improvements in hospitals, laboratory techniques, medications and the training of physicians, the patient is, of course, infinitely better off today. Perhaps patients do not have the warm relationship with the doctor, but comparing the brand of medicine practiced in the United States with that in other parts of the world, except for England and the Scandinavian countries, I would say that medicine is far superior here. The brand of medicine we are selling here is a very excellent one. You might say that the patients don't always get tender loving care, but when it comes to results, we have a high brand of medicine.

RABBI BERKOWITZ: Jewish law and tradition have long been concerned with the question of medicine and the physician. For example, Maimonides, the doctor and the philosopher, insisted that every man has a duty to take care of his health in order to serve God with all the strength of his body and the power of his mind. He said: "No code ever existed among Jews which prohibits curing," and "The physician's right to heal is a religious duty, and he who shirks this responsibility is shedding blood," and "Prayers for the sick are not meant to take the place of medical treatment."

A final observation from Maimonides is very interesting. He said that when a child is stricken one must not read a Scriptural verse, nor place a Scroll of the Law over it, for the words of the Torah are intended not to heal the body but to heal the soul. Against this background, let me ask you to comment on some very fundamental issues, for example, euthanasia.

DR. GUTTMACHER: We are confused about euthanasia. In theory I am in favor of it, but it is rather difficult to put into practice. Certainly, I think that all doctors are in agreement that a person mortally ill should not have his life prolonged unnecessarily by therapeutic procedures. At the same time, I think many of us have a compunction against taking a human life. Frankly, I have not been faced with the issue and therefore have not had to make the choice. In my field of obstetrics and gynecology, we, of course, are much more concerned with the abnormal infant when it is born than we are with the older patients who resent being kept alive. The latter is a much more important issue than a doctor's responsibility to a seriously malformed child who has no chance for a happy life. Each of us has to face this responsibility according to his own conscience.

RABBI BERKOWITZ: How do you feel about informing the patient that his death is certain?

DR. GUTTMACHER: I see no reason for doing this. I remember an experience I had when I started in medicine. A young man came into the hospital where I was the resident. He came to see about certain glands in his neck. Shortly after his arrival they took specimens to submit them to microscopic examination to make a diagnosis. I happened to be in his room when the physician in charge of the case entered. The young man was a dentist and knew what swollen glands in the neck might mean. He knew that they were potentially cancerous. He said, "Well, I suppose that now you have the diagnosis, doctor." The doctor said that he had. The patient said, "I am 27 years old and this is no time for foolishness. I want you to put it all on the line, Doctor. I want you to tell me exactly what the diagnosis is." So the doctor asked, "Are you sure that this is what you want?" To which the young man replied, "I couldn't be more certain." The doctor told him, "You have a carcinoma." The man asked if it was fatal, and he was told that it was. He asked, "Do you think I'll live six months?" The doctor said, "I think that is a good estimate."

This young man got rid of the doctor and secured another physician. This one told him that there could be some misdiagnosis in these cases and that doctors were not always aware of all the possibilities. About six months months later the young man died. But his life had been made utterly miserable, and after that experience I have never told a patient that he was going to die, except in a few cases in which I found it necessary. I do not think much is gained. I suppose that for a man who may be president of a bank who has to make peace with his creditors, it may be necessary. But for the ordinary person I do not think there is much advantage.

RABBI BERKOWITZ: How about the choice between the life of the mother and the life of the child at birth?

DR. GUTTMACHER: In Judaism there is no choice; the life of the mother takes precedence. There are many similarities between Orthodox Judaism and Catholicism in the area of reproduction, but this is one area in which there is no similarity. The mother's life is of inestimable value compared to that of the fetus.

RABBI BERKOWITZ: In other words, you are indicating the Jewish point of view.

Some question has been raised about the matter of autopsy in Israel. Can you comment on this?

DR. GUTTMACHER: Yes, I realize that, but I see no good argument against it. I suppose it all depends on how one views the body after death. The body is a totally insensitive thing. It does not know what is going on. I do not see how autopsy does any harm at all. I feel it is completely justified.

RABBI BERKOWITZ: Justified on what basis?

DR. GUTTMACHER: Justified on the basis of all that we have learned by autopsy on humans. We can learn many things from animals, but we cannot, unfortunately, learn about human disease from animals. Perhaps not every autopsy leads to a medical discovery, but cases are similar with similar causes, and autopsy often leads to the discovery of the cause of a disease. So I think that autopsy has much merit.

RABBI BERKOWITZ: You have said, "There are basic issues that cut across all countries, races and creeds. World peace is doubtless the most important. Equally important to the solution of the problems of the twentieth century is the question of population explosion." In your book, you have a quotation from Huxley which reads: "The problem of population is the problem of our age." In your own words: "The bursting pressure generated by the unrestrained growth of population may be the agent of man's destruction." What is the estimated population for the year 2000 compared to about 3 billion now?

DR. GUTTMACHER: About seven billion and about twenty-one billion in the year 2050.

RABBI BERKOWITZ: When did you first begin working with Planned Parenthood?

DR. GUTTMACHER: I began working with Planned Parenthood when I was the house obstetrician at Johns Hopkins. Our obstetrics department was so arranged that on the fourth floor we had the carriage trade, that is, the private patients who, back in the twenties and early thirties, had one, two or three children. On the second floor we treated Black patients, who averaged a child every year. I was very puzzled by this, so I went to the library to find out about ethnic and social differences in fertility. I came across a text by a man who had done some studies in West Virginia showing that the differences between white and Black reproduction were simply sophistication in birth control. And when I began to question my patients, I discovered that this was the fact. Now, it struck me that it was cruel and totally undemocratic to compel these people to have children through ignorance while the white private patient had the choice of family size and spacing. I felt that the Blacks had good reason to have exactly the same advice and knowledge. So I came to Planned Parenthood simply because to me it was an urgent, democratic form of medicine. I was not interested in population because, as you probably remember, when I went to school we were talking about race suicide. Some nations were actually shrinking in size, and we were concerned that perhaps we were not growing fast enough. My concern was simply that every American should have the same democratic opportunity of having families according to plan. To me it was simply a basic human right.

RABBI BERKOWITZ: Please describe the Planned Parenthood Federation.

DR. GUTTMACHER: Margaret Sanger established the Birth Control League in 1914. In 1941 we changed the name to Planned Parenthood Federation. This was done as a euphemism because we thought that the American public would be much more likely to accept the idea of planning rather than the austere concept of birth control. This is a negative-positive concept, not merely controlling fertility but also trying to cure infertility. Therefore, we changed the name. This organization has grown, of course, so that now it is in about 170 cities, and about 150 of these have clinics. We have hundreds of thousands of patients. I think we operate about 408 clinics in the United States. Our goal is a very simple one: wanted children only, and children born to parents who are responsible and can take care of them properly. So it is "wanted children born to responsible parents."

RABBI BERKOWITZ: We read about the world population explosion in relation to countries in terms of social, political and economic factors. Specifically, what will be the effects of population explosion on food, water and peace on a country such as India?

DR. GUTTMACHER: First, we have to set the stage by saying that the world population is growing slightly more than two percent annually. This means that it doubles itself every fifty-five years. Food production, worldwide, is growing at the rate of one percent, according to the Food and Agricultural Organization of the U.N. This means that the world is being less well fed by one percent every year. The situation, of course, is far worse in some areas than it is in others. India, for example, has large arid areas, agriculture is primitive, education is highly defective.

I always imagine when I think of India that I am back in the days of Abraham, because when one goes through the countryside one sees people who have lived almost like the Patriarchs for centuries. They have long beards, they often have white robes, they turn their fields with oxen, and they draw water from their wells in jars which the women carry on their shoulders. So one has a glimpse of history when traveling through much of India and is carried back more than three thousand years just by looking around. India has, of course, a tremendous distance to travel to bring it into the modern world. It has some large cities, most of them horrible ones. Close to a million people sit on the streets of Calcutta. They are born there and they die there. They have never had a roof over their heads and they sit by the curbstone, lighting their fires with their primitive fuel and cooking their primitive food. Yet some of the handsome houses of maharajas in the background make it hard to realize that these two very contrasting ways of living exist in the same country or even in the same city.

India is constantly threatened by famine. We have helped to keep the Indians alive by sending grain from the United States but are using up our grain reserves. If India should have a poor harvest and there is a depletion of stores in this country, millions of people will come near to starving, or will actually starve. One of the tragedies of modern hunger is that in former decades, while we had less starvation, people died, but now we move in with penicillin and various drugs to counteract infection, and these empty bellies just stay empty and stay alive longer. Formerly, of course, famine might kill off ten million people, which would mean ten million less to feed. But today starvation does not end in such rapid death, so it is a different kind of starvation.

I do not know if the situation is hopeless in India, for it is very difficult to predict. Our government is highly sensitive to the situation in India, and we are doing our duty to make large sums of money available to them. The United States has given money to the government of India to buy contraceptive materials. India's previous Ministers of Health have been strange women, succeeding each other. They were Gandhi's personal physicians. I knew one Minister of Health very well. She was a very calm, pleasant lady who did not understand contraception or birth control very well and who did not do much about it. Now, of course, India has changed. I know another man who is not only a demographer—an expert in population—but also a public health man, a Minister of Health and Population. He is an activist who has done many things which have not been done before in India. For example, he has established centers for male sterilization at railroad stations, where the VIP waiting room has been turned into a surgery room where men who want to be sterilized can go. He felt that sterilization should not be associated with ill health and hospitals but rather with "reception centers". They sterilized six thousand men in one day recently. This is really not a great number for India, but it will probably increase. They are paying the men twenty to thirty rupees to be sterilized, which is between four and six dollars, a large amount of money in India. And they pay ten rupees to the man who brings in the patient. Contraceptive devices are being distributed through ordinary commercial outlets. A subsidy is given to Lipton Tea, for example, and the man who sells tea also sells contraceptives. I have great enthusiasm for this program, but there is a great deal of feeling against this doctor because he is so much of an activist. The Indians are such gentle people that I am not sure they will take to this kind of bustling activity.

RABBI BERKOWITZ: What about the State of Israel, with the Arab population growing at a much greater rate then the Jewish population?

DR. GUTTMACHER: Israel has a very difficult population problem because the Sabras, the native-born, have 2.2 children per family. The European-born have 2.7 children per family, the Oriental Jew has 5 children per family, and the Arab has 8 children per family. This means, of course, that the Oriental Jew and the Arab are very rapidly outbreeding the native and the European Jew. Israel is aware of this, of course. I think that they are approaching the problem most unrealistically because they are very anti-birth control. They ought to be in favor of birth control because, obviously, the native-born Jew and the European Jew are practicing birth control. As a matter of fact, what they are really practicing is abortion, because this is very easy in Israel. You simply go to a doctor and request it and without much red tape the job is done and done well. It seems to me that they ought to introduce birth control on a very wide scale in the hope that perhaps the Arabs and the Oriental Jews will accept it. But so far I have not been able to convince them.

RABBI BERKOWITZ: Professor Salo Baron, professor of history at Columbia University, once said that all peoples should practice birth control, except perhaps the Jewish people, who lost six million.

What is your opinion of the following statement written by a sociologist teaching at Yeshiva University?

"From whence will salvation come? The Jews in the Western world are hardly reproducing themselves. Our co-religionists behind the Iron Curtain are struggling to survive religious and cultural genocide unleashed by the Communist states. Although the Jewish people have from the beginning survived war by simply surviving physically, even in the free world the Jewish people find themselves in societies that tend to inhibit their rate of growth. What seems imperative, therefore, is a massive educational campaign to persuade the Congregation of Israel to have more children. It is more than a matter of personal decision. In our century it is becoming a historical obligation to assure the continuity and growth of the entire people."

DR. GUTTMACHER: In theory this concept is correct, but in practice, of course, it is very difficult. We Jews have probably the highest contraceptive rate of any group in the United

States, And our families are the smallest, statistically. So there is no question that we are practicing very effective contraception. One of the main reasons is that we, as Jews, place such a tremendous emphasis on complete education for our children. It is quite expensive to care for and educate children and not have them go to work early to support sisters and brothers. Perhaps the deification of education that is part of our tradition—and I am sure that this is a good thing—has a lot to do with our family size.

I feel very strongly that if Israel is to survive, it must grow either by immigration or by a higher birth rate. I wish that we could stimulate the Israelis to have larger families because in that country it is quite necessary. I suppose that here, in this country, our Jewish population could be more static. I am not sure that the growth in numbers is absolutely necessary for our survival. It seems to me that it is a matter of indifference whether the Jewish census grows or shrinks or stays about the same in the United States. We are probably replacing ourselves; we are not growing very much and not shrinking very much. I am not deeply concerned by this. Perhaps I should be.

RABBI BERKOWITZ: Why aren't you deeply concerned?

DR. GUTTMACHER: I think we have a sufficient number to keep our philosophy, our teachings and our traditions alive. I am not one to proselytize religion. I do not believe that my religion is superior to any other, nor is anyone else's superior to mine. By accident, I was born a Jew. I think that if I had been born a Moslem, I would probably be very interested in Islam; if I were born a Catholic, I would be interested in Catholicism. I happened to have been born a Jew, and to me it is the greatest religion in the world and I am proud of it. I do not think that there is any particular reason to increase the number of Jews we have. I think we are doing very well as we are. I do not believe that if we added another million Jews in the United States we would be any better off than we are now. I may be wrong, and I do not expect you to agree with me. I do not feel that I have any special wisdom in the matter.

RABBI BERKOWITZ: Of course, there are two schools of thought, and one is that numbers do matter. There seems to be some historical proof that there is a relationship between larger numbers and commitment.

DR. GUTTMACHER: I have a story I would like to tell you that has to do with this. I was lecturing at the University of California in Berkeley, and I was picketed by a very fine group of Blacks who called themselves "Eros." I was very much taken by this group of people, so I stopped to find out why I was being picketed. I found out that the names "Eros" stood for "endeavor to raise our size." In their literature they brought out the fact that there were only 21 million Blacks in the United States—this was several years ago—and that no Catholic had been elected President until there were 40 million Catholics; so the Blacks must double their numbers as quickly as possible. Now, there are not 21 million Jews in the United States, yet the Jews are quite a powerful group. None have been President, but there have been occasional governors and we have had many professors at schools. I thought that the Blacks should pay more attention to educating themselves and more could be accomplished that way than by just sheer increase in numbers. We find as human beings that if we Jews were greater idealists and paid more attention to our minds than our memories, perhaps it would be better for us.

RABBI BERKOWITZ: What is the population situation in the Soviet Union today?

DR. GUTTMACHER: The Soviet Union has attacked its population increase in a manner exactly parallel to our own.

They are increasing at about one percent per year. They keep numbers down by legalized abortion, which can be obtained on demand in Russia. And they are also dedicated to contraception and they carry out sterilization, so they use all the methods of keeping down population more than we do.

RABBI BERKOWITZ: I know that you are an authority on Latin America. What is the situation there with respect to population growth?

DR. GUTTMACHER: Latin America, of course, is the most dangerous area, because it is growing most rapidly. It is growing at the rate of two percent per year, and that means that in 1990 Latin America will have twice as many people as they have now. There are about 252 million now, and there will be half a billion people in Latin America in 1990.

In terms of income, these are the poorest among nations. They are suffering from extraordinary malnutrition. We are, however, making headway with birth control in Latin America, not remarkably so, but significantly. The interesting thing is that the Church has offered no obstruction. The problem in Latin America is abortion. It is the common method of birth control and a very dangerous one. In Chile there is one illegal abortion for every two children born. In Brazil there is one for every child born. The Church is, of course, aware of this, and it thinks that perhaps birth control is the lesser evil. Therefore, the Church has not obstructed us. It has not given us its blessing, but it certainly has not offered any opposition.

RABBI BERKOWITZ: You wrote: "We are victims in America of the false syllogism that America and the world have never been so prosperous as they are today, and the populations of America and the world have never shown such rapid growth, and therefore the continued growth of population will continue the rapid growth of prosperity." Would you care to amplify and comment on the population growth and its effect on the country?

DR. GUTTMACHER: When that was written we were growing more rapidly than we are growing today, but I am still deeply concerned, because we grow about one percent and we will double our population in seventy years. When that was written, we were growing at the rate of 1.7 percent. Our birth rate has come down. However, many things about the American scene make me quite unhappy. One is the fact that we have such a distorted per capita income. In the United States the average income is $3,100; in Latin America it is less than $200; in India it is $80 per person. There is no country except ours that has over $1,600 per person. So we have twice the income of the most opulent of other nations. And when we create new Americans we create new affluent people. We are using up the world's resources in extravagant fashion. We have one-sixteenth of the world's population, and we are using about half of the world's nonrenewable resources. We estimate that in 1985 we will have one-twentieth of the world's population and will be using 83 percent of the world's nonrenewable resources. This is one of the reasons why it is easy to understand that we are not very popular.

We will not have world peace, I think, until we can equate the use of the world's resources, until we do not have this dreadful contrast of a per capita income of $80 in India and $3,100 in the United States. It is almost impossible to believe that there cannot be jealousy affecting all kinds of relationships.

Further, I think that we are dreadfully overcrowded. This is true of the eastern seaboard, where 38 million people live between Boston and Washington, and of a narrow strip in the West, where 30 million people live in California. All this means, it seems to me, that we have packed into certain areas of America far too many people, more than we can properly take care of, with the added problems of air pollution and contamination.

We find that the impoverished American desires fewer children than we of the middle class. Statistically, they desire 2.9 children and we desire 3.5 children. Now the impoverished American attains about 5 children, and we of the middle class attain just about what we anticipated, slightly less than 3.5. My thesis is that we must make it possible for the impoverished American to have his desire, just as the middle class, and this will help us to some extent. But now, somewhere around 4 million women of reproductive age are medically indigent, which means they must obtain their medicine from tax-supported sources. We do not have effective contraception. This is, of course, what my organization is particularly interested in. This is what I am pressing Washington to do, to try to close the gap, so that we can say that every American couple has the use of contraceptives if they are wanted.

RABBI BERKOWITZ: In your book, you said, "While every effort must be made to increase production to facilitate distribution, to conserve conservable resources and for the 'have' nations to share the good things with the 'have nots' in the world, this alone cannot prevent disaster. Birth control is also necessary on a worldwide scale as soon as possible."

What are the attitudes of the different religious organizations to birth control?

DR. GUTTMACHER: The Protestant community is fairly receptive to all methods of birth control, except abortion, but certainly to contraception and sterilization. They are permissive toward almost all methods of birth control. There is no method which they would exclude, except abortion. As a group they are highly modern. There are some sects and special groups, for example, the Pentecostals, the Mormons, some of the very strict Lutherans, who are against birth control. But these form a very small segment of the Protestant population.

The Catholic community is undergoing a very dramatic change. I remember some years ago, when I was in Baltimore, one of the Catholic papers wasted some of its editorial space in decrying the views of the Guttmacher twins, since my brother was interested in the same things I was. They said it was too bad that our mother had not used birth control before we were conceived. I have had the pleasure now of having arguments with my many Catholic friends. I was on a panel with several Jesuits in Rochester, New York, and we could find no dissension among us. These Jesuits do not approve of the stand of the Pope on birth control. I put the question to them: "What does a Catholic woman have to do who practices birth control methods which are not approved of by the Church? Must she confess?" The audience was composed largely of priests and nuns, although there were some laymen among us. The priests came up with the answer: "No, only if she felt sinful. If she did not feel sinful, even if her method was not the approved technique, she need not confess." This is tremendous progress. Much of the Church feels very strongly that the Pope is wrong, that his stand is archaic and that people are leaving the Church by the millions because they cannot agree with him. They feel that the Church must change. No one is sufficiently omniscient to know when the Pope will change, but he will. But I think that when the Church does change, it will be far too late.

RABBI BERKOWITZ: What is the feeling within the Jewish Community?

DR. GUTTMACHER: You may be able to judge this better than I. From my vantage point as a Jewish physician, there are no restrictions about contraception. I think that the Bible teaches us that we each have the obligation to be parents and that marriage is the proper condition and that when one is married, one produces children. As you will recall, there is some discussion in the Talmud as to whether the obligation is over after a couple has had two sons, or whether a son and a daughter are sufficient. I do not believe that the Talmudic scholars have decided that point. But I feel that we in Conservative and Reform Judaism think being parents does not require having a certain number of children. On the other hand, of course, the very Orthodox Jew feels that a man may never use a contraceptive of any kind and may never be sterilized, although a woman may use birth control if there is a medical necessity for it. I have had extensive experience in treating Orthodox women. I know that if I feel birth control is essential for a woman's health, I write a letter to her rabbi. He will consult with other rabbis, and then he will write back to me and tell me whether I may prescribe contraceptives for this woman. The final decision, then, in the Orthodox view is not made by the physician. It is made by the rabbi after suggestion of the physician. I can say that I have not had my decisions questioned very often. If the woman is normally healthy, birth control is not advised—only when there is a health problem. This factor can be physical or mental, it makes no difference. Therefore, as a whole, the Orthodox Jews have considerably larger families than we in the Reform and Conservative communities.

RABBI BERKOWITZ: You wrote about this in much more detail in a very interesting and informative article in an issue of the scholarly journal *Judaism*. The title of the article is "Traditional Judaism and Birth Control," and some of the areas discussed are celibacy, abortion, conception, contraception, all based on Jewish thinking, law and tradition.

Would you like to clarify another statement of yours?:

"The legal status of birth control in the United States is a bewildering hodgepodge of extremism."

DR. GUTTMACHER: That sentence was written in about 1961-62. Things have changed considerably since then. At that time we had two states, Connecticut and Massachusetts, in which birth control was illegal. The Supreme Court in June 1965 made the Connecticut status illegal. And in January 1966, the legislature of Massachusetts repealed its birth control laws. Now birth control is legal in all fifty states. The abortion laws, however, are different in different states. When it comes to contraception and sterilization, we have equality. There is no difference. So I would say that the hodgepodge has been straightened out considerably.

RABBI BERKOWITZ: The problem of abortion is the subject of technical, legal and emotional discussion. What are your views?

DR. GUTTMACHER: There are three schools of thought regarding this. There is the present Catholic opinion, that abortion is murder and under no condition is justified, not even to save a woman's life. On the other hand, in all of our states we have laws permitting abortion to preserve a woman's life. Therefore, the Catholic has to live with it, but he is not happy with it. Then there is the other end of the spectrum which holds that pregnancy is a very personal thing; the woman has to bear the child, and she is the one who should determine whether she should remain pregnant. If she decides not to remain pregnant, she should be guaranteed a safe abortion. Then there is the school between the two that says we are far too strict in our limitations on abortion, that it is legal to save a woman's life, that health is far more important and that life without health, both mental and physical, is not really life. Many feel, in addition, that if there is reason to believe that birth will lead to a seriously damaged or malformed child, abortion is justified. Others feel that if a child is concieved through a sex crime, rape, incest, if there is impregnation of a child fifteen or less, such pregnancy need not continue. And then, of course, there are others who feel that when parents have three, four or five children and their economic situation is greatly threatened by another unwanted child, such pregnancies should be terminated. I am of the middle-of-the-road opinion.

RABBI BERKOWITZ: In the long history of our people, the physician has held a peculiarly honored position. Not only has Jewish tradition marked the doctor for special *Kovod*, but when the Jewish doctor went out among the nations, he brought distinction and in many cases official favor to his co-religionists. I need cite only such examples as Maimonides, Hasdai Ibn Shaprut, and Judah Ha-Levi.

In our own day, the opportunities for the individual to rise to such peaks of fame are rare indeed, yet we do have among us men who combine the skill and understanding of the physician with a strong feeling for Jewish tradition. History may yet accord them the honor they deserve. If such be the case, Dr. Guttmacher will most certainly be foremost on the list of modern Jewish medical workers.

Seldom have the great Jewish doctors of history been content to practice medicine alone—Maimonides the philosopher, Hasdai the diplomat, Judah Ha-Levi the poet. Dr. Alan Guttmacher will surely be remembered not only for his work as a physician, but as a social thinker and planner whose great concern for the welfare of people has led him into diverse avenues of endeavor. We have had a rare privilege in conversing with him, for not only have we gained some insight into medicine as it is practiced today, but we have been permitted to share the thoughts of a warm human being who is doing great work in helping to alleviate some of the world's ills. And for this we are grateful.

BENJAMIN H. KAHN

RABBI BERKOWITZ: Let me begin with an old Yiddish story which tells of a man who meets his rabbi on the street. After an exchange of the usual pleasantries the congregant tells his spiritual counselor of his despair because of the sad state of the world. "I tell you, rabbi, it's enough to make a man lose his religion." The rabbi, after reflecting for a moment, responds: "It seems to me, my friend, it's enough to make a man *use* his religion."

One of the major challenges which confronts the American Jewish community today is to get people to use their religion; to get young people, especially, to use their religion. In this respect we often give much thought to an important segment of our youth, the Jewish collegian. In every discussion of Jewish survival and American Jewish life, we must take into account this major group, the great and growing number of Jewish collegians. Throughout the United States thousands of college students are preparing themselves for the future, and it would appear that now, more than ever before, they are questioning the values of the traditions of the past.

What is happening to this group? What about their attitudes and feelings and commitments to and knowledge of Judaism? Are they identifying with the Jewish community, or are they moving further away? Few people can answer these questions as well as our distinguished speaker, Rabbi Benjamin Kahn, the former National Director of the B'nai Brith Hillel Foundation and now Executive Vice-President of B'nai Brith. A leading authority on Jewish life on the campus, he is a graduate of Harvard University and the Jewish Theological Seminary of America. He was appointed by President Kennedy to membership on the Peace Corps Advisory Council and then reappointed by President Johnson.

Rabbi Kahn, I would like to begin my interview with the overall theme on how the college student sees himself. Today we speak of a "college crisis." Is there one? If there is, is it limited to one religious or ethnic group? How would you describe it?

RABBI KAHN: You ask whether there is a college crisis in terms of how the college student sees himself. This reminds me of a story about a rich man whose rabbi asked him for a contribution. The man said, "I just can't afford to now. You know that expenses have increased, taxes are up, things are difficult for me." The rabbi responded, "I'd like to ask you to go to the window, look out, and tell me what you see." The rich man went to the window, looked out and said, "Well, I see people walking back and forth in the street." "Now go look in the mirror on the wall." And the man said, "Of course, I see myself." "This is what happens to people;" answered the rabbi, "when they look through a clear vista they see other people, and as soon as they cover it up with a little bit of silver, they see only themselves."

This is an affluent society. A society in which young people, at least our young people, are brought up, most of them, in a culture which is rich and in a family setting which is not poor, in which most of them are able to go to college, and most of them have no financial problems. The question is, Do they face a crisis when they come away from home? I think there is a college crisis, a crisis of many different dimensions. For the young people this is the first time, in most instances, in which they are required to stand on their own. They are face to face with themselves for the first time, because up to this point they have been guided and directed. Now they are separated from the normal influences of home, of synagogue, of community, and they begin to make their way on their own. It is taking the lid off the pressure cooker a little too early because there is a bit of explosion of young people's wishes and ambitions. They have been frustrated for so long, and suddenly they burst out into the open.

This is not unique with Jews, incidentally; this is the crisis of the age—the age in which we live and the age of the college student. You know the old saying, "Small children, small sorrows; big children, big sorrows." This is no exaggeration. Our children come into their own when they move into the later years of their teens and they begin to search for what is known in university circles as their personal identity—the inevitable identity crisis. Sometimes it is prolonged, sometimes they get over it soon, but it is always there. Today American universities have an amazing number of psychiatrists and psychiatric departments available to help young people go through this period of personal crisis.

There are special aspects of this crisis that affect only Jews. In addition to having to find themselves, to know what they are, to become human beings on their own—separate from their parents and family and home—they have to identify themselves as Jews, they have to know what their place is in society. They have to discover the difference between being a Jew and a non-Jew, some for the first time, and especially those who come from a large metropolitan community in which there is a predominance of Jewish companionship.

They have to resolve for themselves the conflict of exposure for the first time to a culture and religion which is different from that in which they have been brought up.

There is a college crisis, but it is a crisis that is shared by all young people—with an added dimension for Jewish young people.

RABBI BERKOWITZ: Someone has said that college is a time of opportunity but, unfortunately, a time of opportunity which is generally wasted. Do you agree or disagree?

RABBI KAHN: I agree and disagree, which is putting it pretty safely. College presents a young person with a tremendous opportunity to learn, to broaden his horizons, to begin to be exposed to disciplines and teachings, professor and classroom opinions. As a matter of fact, most young people come out of college experience very different from the way in which they went into it. This is not only the result of four years in a college or university—it is also the result of exposure to new people, new ideas and postures, and the opportunity to stand on their own two feet. The story is told about a young man who, before he went away to college, had great contempt for his parents' ignorance of things. When he came back after a year of having been exposed to all kinds of opinions he said, "You know, my parents have learned an awful lot in the year I have been away."

A great many young people do not rise to the opportunities and challenges of the university. Many attend the university not because of a love of learning or the intellectual challenges which are inherent in it. Many leave with the same prejudices and preconceived notions that they had when they entered. And many do not take advantage of the opportunity for widening their horizons, for deepening their knowledge, for intensifying their interests in fields other than the ones into which they matriculate. To me, one of the great shortcomings of the higher educational system is that so many students have to know before they become freshmen what they want to be or are supposed to be on graduating. I do not think that most young people at the age of eighteen or nineteen are in a position to know what they want to be, but they have to follow, in the four years of college, a very narrow path with few opportunities in fields outside of their immediate professional curriculum.

One final observation in this area. There are many opportunities outside of the classroom, opportunities to learn from experiences that have nothing to do with books; the experiences of living. Many students are so caught up in the process of memorizing books, concentrating upon examinations, getting good grades, being accepted in graduate school, or preparing for ultimate license examinations that they lose the opportunity to enrich themselves in these other areas.

RABBI BERKOWITZ: Rabbi Kahn, you once said that there are four problems, four areas that basically define the needs of college students: the need for trust, for belonging, for challenge, and the search for meaning. Yet isn't it also true that most upper-middle-class young people of college age seem to hate themselves? Self-acceptance among this group appears to be a rather rare thing in American society. Do you agree with this?

RABBI KAHN: I think that this statement is only half true. It exaggerates the situation somewhat morbidly. There are many young people who hate themselves, but this is an extreme form of relationship toward oneself, and it is part of the search for oneself. That is, before one starts becoming what one is, or will be, one has to stop being what one was. One has to grow out of what his past has been to find his own way. In the process, there is a kind of rejection of what one has accepted on the surface as the norms of behavior or personality. And so there comes a stage in the lives of many young people where they reject that which they have been or the environment into which they have been thrown, not of their own choice, but simply because they were born into a certain family and community. So the process of rejection of that from which they have come acts as a rejection of parents, of community, and of their Jewish heritage, but not, I think, rejection in the sense of self-hate. Rather, it is rejection in the same sense of having to overthrow that which up to this time has been accepted and taken for granted, in order to find their own way.

Now, there are many young people who do not have this necessity to reject, but who are able to move gradually rather than suddenly and sensationally from the stage of adolescence to the stage of adulthood and maturity. There is, I think, lack of trust among our young people, but not so much in themselves as in the society which has been given to them and which they will inherit.

RABBI BERKOWITZ: Why is this so? What forms and what behavior does this lead to?

RABBI KAHN: It leads, in some instances, particularly but not exclusively among Jewish students, to the rejection of the pattern of home observances. This is especially true if the youngster comes from a home that has been relatively observant, since this is one of the most vulnerable areas of rejection. We seem to feel more emotionally involved when a student or a child rejects those things in which we believe most fully and most fervently. So young people frequently reject the traditions of the home to affirm their independence from the home and to set the groundwork for becoming individuals in their own right.

There is a rejection, also, of the ethics of the parent generation which represents a loss of faith in ways of doing things. Young people point to the mess in the world, to our failure to have an ethical society, to the lack of responsibility that they see in some of their parents and friends of their parents. Many reject the concepts of our society and say they have to tear down in order to build up. Part of the activist movement on the campus today is motivated by this lack of confidence in the parent generation.

This was the basis for the saying, "Don't trust anybody over thirty." They do not feel that we have done right by them, by the world. Lack of ethics in government and in human relations bothers them considerably. Basically, our younger generation is a generation of idealists, and when their ideals are frustrated, they have a tendency to reject the total society. Not reject it for chaos, but reject it in order to build it on a firmer foundation.

RABBI BERKOWITZ: Another dilemma that faces young people is their search for meaning. With this, there is a questioning of ideologies. There is, I think, not only suspicion about religous ideology, but about any kind of ideology. They tell us, "Your faiths have failed, you have made a mess of the world. Why indeed should we turn to you for your traditional wisdom, which is in our judgment quite irrelevant?" What is your comment about this?

RABBI KAHN: Part of the activist spirit of our younger people is that they feel that it is time to stop talking and philosophizing, and time to get to work. The leftist movement, for example, is notoriously anti-ideological. This is one of its great deficiencies because without a particular philosophy, without an approach to life or society, one can be very, very busy, but not be going in the right direction. There is a story told about a pilot who announced in mid-air that he had lost his way, the plane was running out of gas, the motors did not sound right, but that the flight was making wonderful time. Well, what is the direction in which our society is going?

What is the improvement in our culture or in our relationship with other people, or in our treatment of minority groups? To what extent has democracy proven itself capable of meeting these needs? Many of the young leftists reject ideology as an activity and want to do something. Sometimes they do not know what they want to do. Sometimes they want to protest, not against anything specific, but as a way of affirming their disgust with the situation and their need to do something, without knowing exactly what to do.

When young people want meaning, they want to have a philosophy of government, of society or of religion which not only makes sense but would take the form of effective relationships with other human beings. Simply to prattle about brotherhood and to ignore the Black slums, for example, makes no sense to our young people. Some of us are inured to the contradictions between these two concepts. But our young people are not willing to accept an ideology and philosophize a problem away or prove that it does not exist. When we speak of a search for meaning that our young people are involved in, it is primarily their search for the meaning of life. Their basic questions are: "Why am I here?" "What is the purpose of my existence?" They wish to be themselves and to know that they mean something.

One caution, however. When we speak of activists, of students on the left, of rebellion and rejection, there is the danger that we think all young people are in all of these categories. I would submit that the best of our young people are in some of these categories.

RABBI BERKOWITZ: An additional dilemma is the quest on the part of young people for belonging, combined, at the same time, with their suspicion of organization. I want to quote one member of the college scene who said, "Isn't it strange that with all this talk about communities and fellowship and belonging, more people are not seeking community in the synagogue and churches?" and continued, "You see, that's why we exist at least in the Judeo-Christian tradition. We are a people, we are a community, we are a fellowship, not an organization in the bureaucratic sense, though we have bureaucracies and organizations. We have far more than that, we are people with roots deep in the past with traditions which should give us vitality and excitement for life in the present."

In this quest for belonging on the part of young people, why is it that with all of our communal resources, we do not seem to be able to create community among our young people?

RABBI KAHN: It has been said that the reason so many Sabras in Israel go out on archeological digs is that they are really digging for their own roots. This is part of the malaise of our times. There is no continuity between generations. What went before seems to have disappeared and the influence of it seems to have vanished along the way. Belonging means not only being part of a horizontal community, belonging among each other. Belonging also means being a part of what went before, of the ancestral tradition, of the heritage, of the history of mankind—in our case, the history of the Jews. Young Jews have a special problem because they do not know the past of their people and they have very little awareness of the Jewish peoplehood throughout the world. They live in a kind of closed community of their own, especially on the college campus.

There is plenty of organization and activity on the campus. A student leader on a university campus can be caught up in dozens of organizations. But this is different. These are his own organizations, not the traditional organizations or establishment. This is the establishment which he himself creates. So when he is looking for belongingness, he is looking for new, not old, institutions, because the old ones are what he is trying to evaluate and sometimes he concludes by rejecting them. I believe this is only a temporary rejection, a transitional state of rejection in order later to draw it back into one's life. This may be an optimistic view that not everyone shares.

When the student looks for belongingness, he does not look to the institutions which he feels are traditional and obsolete. That is why we find it very difficult to establish a bridge between the college student and the community from which he comes.

RABBI BERKOWITZ: The older generation has the opportunity and responsibility to provide challenges for the younger generation. Rabbi Kahn, do you think that we have not been imaginative or vigorous or creative enough in trying to think of new ways to challenge a generation which is really standing around and saying, "Please challenge us."?

RABBI KAHN: Yes, indeed. As a matter of fact, I would go a step further and say that until the last few years we have not even been aware of their existence. It is only recently that the Jewish community, for example, has awakened to the fact that most of its young people are on the college campus, and that they are a generation which has been ignored by the community.

Let me give you an example of what I mean. I do not know of a single Jewish organization in America which, as an organization, as a national organization, invited college students to participate in its activities until very recently. I am not speaking of college homecomings at synagogues. I am speaking of national Jewish organizations. The first organization which, to my knowledge, invited Jewish college students to share in its deliberations was the United Jewish Appeal. UJA became concerned about where Jewish leadership will come from tomorrow. Those of us who are just a step removed from our European backgrounds know the meaning of responsibility to our fellow Jews. The young people do not. Where will they gain the same sense of devotion to our common welfare unless something is done to give them a sense of belonging to the totality of Jewish concern which the organizations represent?

RABBI BERKOWITZ: Do you have any suggestions along this line to make to some of the national organizations?

RABBI KAHN: Much effort is being made in this direction, and I myself was involved in at least a dozen different relationships in which we tried to build bridges between the university campus and the Jewish community. For example, we developed a proposal in some areas for the Jewish community to invite college students to participate in their activities. This is a radical, revolutionary idea! Students will sit on the boards of Federations and serve in every Jewish agency in the community, not only as teachers but as social workers in hospitals, as directors of activities in centers, as participants in the civil rights or anti-poverty programs. I think this is a step in the right direction, as it challenges the young people to do something in which they believe, but to do it under Jewish auspices, as part of the totality of the Jewish community.

So far the response has been excellent and most encouraging. I remember, some time ago, seventy college students participated in a national convention of the United Jewish Appeal. The Council of Jewish Federations and Welfare Funds had a group of college students in the Cleveland area participating in some of their deliberations, giving an opportunity to the leaders of the federations to meet college students, and vice versa. Jewish students may be living in a vacuum on campus, a vacuum which we have to fill. When they leave the campus, they are going to be living where there are Jews and Jewish communities, and they must feel that the Jewish community wants them back as its leaders.

RABBI BERKOWITZ: You said there was a second thought in terms of this challenge. Do you want to pursue this?

RABBI KAHN: The second thought in terms of the challenge is a recognition of the fact that they—at least 80 percent, perhaps 90 percent, we do not yet know—of young Jews of college age go to a college or a university. Notice, I did not say "graduate from," because many do not, but they do matriculate at an institute of higher learning. Within twenty or thirty years the majority of the Jews will be college-educated. This means that the whole quality of Jewish life in this country has to be elevated. Fortunately, Jews of all generations, with or without a college education, are educated because we have a very literate tradition. But the whole quality of Jewish organizational life will have to be elevated to take into account the fact that we have a generation of people who have been exposed to the culture of our time—to the sociology, physics, history, English of academic life.

Our leaders will have to gear their approach to Jewish life—even in preaching from the pulpit, if you will—to the fact that the majority of Jews very soon will make much greater demands, intellectual demands, from the leadership of the Jewish community. The emergence of a generation which has been exposed to university professors has to be met by changing the whole quality of Jewish leadership and the level with which we approach our young people when they return from campuses to our communities.

RABBI BERKOWITZ: There is an issue which concerns the collegian and at the same time the community as a whole. This is the problem of permissiveness. What does permissiveness lead to on our campuses? What can be done—for want of a better word—to contain it, or to channel it into constructive areas?

RABBI KAHN: You remind me of the story of a man who was visiting someone in a suburb and who said, "You have a very beautiful home here; it must have cost you a lot of money." "It did," was the response. "But it cost only half as much as the house my son lives in. He has not only a fifteen-room house, he has a maid, a swimming pool, and a big forest in the back which he can use for hunting." And his friend said, "He must be doing very well." "Oh, very well, indeed," said the father. "Three A's and a B."

I suppose, Rabbi, that what you mean by permissiveness is the fact that we do not make any demands and we find it difficult to say no to children. . . . that we give them too much of their own way. I am not sure if this is the case or not, and I am not sure that I can answer this question with any degree of conviction or intelligence. Let me put it into a little different context so that I will be able to deal with it. Let us say that we do not demand enough of ourselves or give enough of ourselves in things that really count, that we are willing to look the other way when there is a flagrant case of injustice, willing to take the easiest path when it comes, for example, to dealing with a crucial issue in the family, or looking the other way when something not quite ethical has been done. That is the permissiveness which is imitated by, or which is reflected in young people.

In the field of Jewish education, one of the great problems is that parents send children out to learn, instead of following the old tradition that parents learn until they are grandparents, until the day they die. A Jewish education is a life-long process, and what we do in so many cases is to drop the kids off at Hebrew School or Sunday School and go off on our own business. And so the child cannot wait until he grows up and can deposit his child in school and go off on *his* own business. This is the kind of permissiveness which means making no demands on ourselves. We do not make demands regarding Jewish education, or civil rights, or anti-poverty, or in giving adequately for Jewish needs, standing up firmly and vociferously for Jewish rights, protecting the welfare of the State of Israel with a full heart—not only in an emergency, but throughout the year.

This is a kind of self-permissiveness which I think rubs off on our young people. I am not sure that we, as a general rule, despite our tendency to give in to children, are being too permissive with them. With ourselves, I think we are.

RABBI BERKOWITZ: How about permissiveness in terms of the moral standards of our society?

RABBI KAHN: Here I think I can speak a little more firmly, because we have seen on the college campus a kind of revolution in morals. Not that our younger people are immoral or amoral, but they are developing a different philosophy about what is moral or immoral. I am not speaking of drugs, certainly not marijuana, which falls into a different category from, let us say, LSD, but in terms of sexual morality. I do think that the standards of our younger people are changing. I think that the young people are creating their own moral standards even if ours remain fixed over the years.

There is in this country a general permissiveness in morality. We see it in the acceptance of divorce, for example, as the easy way out. In the approach to marriage, as something you can try: if it works, good; if not, "nisht." We see it in the absence of a feeling of permanence in human relationships. I think these do rub off on our young people. And I think that part of the problem of marriages among young people is the casualness about marriage in the adult community. Sometimes, of course, they react just the opposite when they see some of the rigidities of divorce or some of the farces of divorce; they react to what they consider to be hypocrisy in this aspect.

Unless we ourselves have the highest standards of personal and institutional morality, I certainly think the younger generation—which tends in any case to reject restrictions—will find an even less rigorous approach to morality, to drugs, to honesty and so forth.

RABBI BERKOWITZ: I see this in my own work. I see it in the

sense that young people today do not work hard enough at marriage and all that goes with it.

Let me read a statement which sets the tone for our next question: "Ours is basically a competitive society. The competition is now much more sophisticated and takes place within a framework of rhetoric about team spirit and cooperation. But young people are constantly being compared and evaluated—from their size or their weight or both to the size of their funeral at death. They find themselves evaluated and compared with others from the time of the appearance of their first tooth, and the first step they take, the first sounds that can be interpreted as words; then the nursery school, then kindergarten, the kinds of schools they can go to; popularity with their friends, success of their social life; their performance on a vast variety of standardized tests we now have for young people—the college board tests, the graduate record tests. If they go to graduate school, they will be compared with the quality of their first academic appointment and the number of articles they publish. In the business world they will be compared as to how much money they make. They will be compared as to the success of their marriage, success of their children and finally the cost of their funeral when they pass to whatever reward that might be left."

As I see it, this has not been the constructive competition that seeks to bring out the best in young people, but one that forces them to keep up with the other person. What is the effect of this kind of competitive pressure, and what can or should be done about it?

RABBI KAHN: When my daughter was in first grade, she said to her mother and me, "Our teacher told us that if we don't do well in our test, we won't get to college." Now, this is what you are referring to, in part. The educational system in America depends upon a competitive standard; each must do better than the next. And proof of the pressure on our young people is the absence of morality in the classroom. This is one big area, I think, apart from others to which I will refer in a moment, that creates a predilection, a tendency, to look the other way whenever ethics, honesty and morality are concerned. There are many studies of cheating in high schools and college showing that a large percentage of students cheat—perhaps only a little—but still, cheating is regarded as a way of beating the system. They do not look upon it as an immoral act, but as a way of getting around the authorities who are trying to box them in.

This is a tendency in America today in a great many areas. It typifies some of our attitudes about government, even about local rules and regulations, like driving through a red light just because no one is looking, cutting a little corner in one way or another in order to beat the system.

In the educational system the pressure on our young people is not just to graduate from high school, but to be able to get into the right college and then to graduate school. All of these practices create a false standard of what achievement really is. The feeling is that one does not study for the purpose of learning, one studies for the purpose of passing examinations with the highest grades possible. And if one has to cheat a little to make sure he doesn't flunk, that's perfectly acceptable.

This is one kind of competitiveness in our educational system, and it has very serious ethical consequences as far as our young people are concerned. The one thing most of them object to, when you ask them to evaluate communities from which they come, seems to be the material standards that are the criteria by which success is judged. Again and again, when you ask youngsters on the college campus what they remember most of all and what they like least of all about the community from which they came, they almost invariably talk about the enthronement of the dollar or the stress on the material possessions.

What to do about it is, I think, fairly obvious. I would hope for the day when examinations would not be the criteria of a man's achievement. Many schools are moving in the direction of eliminating grading and competition, and providing different levels of achievement that have nothing to do with beating somebody else in exams. Of course, this is a problem that goes far beyond the confines of our discussion. Our standards of material possession would require a reevaluation of our economic system.

RABBI BERKOWITZ: I recall a school where, at the end of a three-year period, we were given an oral comprehensive, and the student was obliged to come in and be examined by a professor who, within a half-hour, would ask a series of questions on a variety of subjects and then give a grade. I will never forget this because of what happened to me. I received a grade of 89.4 and I still wonder how one can get such a mark—89.4—in an oral examination.

I have invited three young people who will present questions of their own choosing to Rabbi Kahn. Through their questions, perhaps, we can go even further into the feelings and thinking of young collegians.

ROBERT: In an atmosphere of academic freedom encompassing a conscious attempt by the individual student to meet other students of various backgrounds—of religion as well as locality—how can such a student be persuaded to join an organization which seems limited to people of a single ethnic background?

RABBI KAHN: When a student goes away to a campus—I exclude a few of the city campuses here, where the majority of the students may be of one particular religious background—he comes into contact, sometimes for the first time, with a society of students and faculty members who are Protestant, Jewish, Catholic, and who come from small towns, big cities, upper class, middle class, lower-middle class. The issue now becomes how he can be persuaded amid this wealth of difference to want to identify himself with his own group. It is a very difficult question because at times a young person goes away to a campus determined to broaden his horizons after the narrow experience in which he was brought up. You know, this was less prevalent years ago than today, the student approach that said, "What is important to me is everybody." This means that I am just as much concerned about the starving children in China as I was about the Jewish refugees in Hitler's Germany. It reflects the need that young people have to be part of a larger, exciting and different group than that which they were used to.

I think we have to admit and accept the fact that many, many college students during the greater part of their college careers will not identify themselves with any single group except nominally or peripherally, and perhaps only once or twice a year. This is a concept, I think, that everyone in America is familiar with, especially us in the Jewish community. We have to accept the fact that some students will go on vacation as Jews for most of their college career, holding their Jewishness in reserve for emergencies such as the Six-Day War, or for a time when they return to their homes and communities.

The second answer is that the community on the campus is a pluralistic community. Before you can relate yourself as a Jew to Christians you have to live as a Jew. Without faith there is no interfaith, and so if you want to relate yourself not just as a student but as a Jewish student to the total community, you have to do it through your own particular religious or, if you will, ethnic society. You have to seek a balance between continuing in the tradition which you know, and in which you were brought up, and remaining part of the total community, which transcends the differences in religion and background but at the same time unites them. Today the university is most hospitable to these differences to a greater degree than ever before in American life. This is one of the plus factors when we think of Jewish students identifying with Jewish traditions while on campus.

ROBERT: In a similar vein, there seems to be in college a general marking of organized religion as an antiquated philosophy. With regard to Judaism specifically, how does one defend the faith?

RABBI KAHN: Most students, even before they go to college, begin to question organized religion and its traditions for two reasons. First, it is the nature of the growing mind to question that which has been taught, even if it is true; and second, most of what has been taught has been presented on an infantile level and has never gone beyond that stage. When we teach the story of the Creation of the world, few teachers in Jewish schools try to relate the theory of evolution to the text of the Book of Genesis. And so we grow up thinking of the Book of Genesis as the way it was, just the way it says—that the world is not a million or two million or a hundred million years old, but just five thousand plus.

When we come to the campus we are suddenly thrown into a stew because in our courses in sociology and the history of science and anthropology we learn a totally different interpretation of the origin of the universe. We are not prepared for it.

The answer, in part, is to include in our system of Jewish education a confrontation, even on the most elementary level, with the critical issues of theology that a student will confront when he gets to the campus, especially since most young people never become educated in the Jewish sphere beyond the elementary level. In effect, general education is moving ahead and Jewish education has stopped "way back there." When these two meet with a clash in the mind of a college freshman—which one is going to give?

PETER: Rabbi Kahn, I would like to direct my questions from my own experience on the college campus and more particularly as an officer, including the office of president, of the Hillel Foundation at City College. Hillel is thought of as the

Jewish student community on the campus and is made up of any Jewish student who wants to affiliate with the Jewish student community. This would, of course, include people who come in with all sorts of affiliations, Orthodox, Conservative, Reform and Zionist. As long as they feel that they want to affiliate with the Jewish community they are welcomed with open arms. Unfortunately, we find that many, if not a preponderance, of those who do affiliate with Hillel come from rather weak Jewish backgrounds, and Hillel by its very nature must be the sum total of the feelings of its affiliates.

How much does the Hillel scope, the Hillel activity, the Hillel program reflect only the sum total of the Jewish students, or is there an added responsibility, an added moral responsibility, if you will, upon the National Hillel to counter this and to enforce more positive Jewish values and goals?

RABBI KAHN: I think you have answered your own question, Peter. We deal with a student body that is varied. Some come from very, very fine backgrounds, some from weak backgrounds, and some have no Jewish background at all. You would be amazed at the number of Jewish students who come to a Hillel director and say, "Can you enroll me in a class because my parents never gave me the opportunity to learn anything." This is a new twist. This is not what we have been expecting. But today there is a generation of young people that is rebelling against the rebellion of their parents. It consists of coming back to what their parents left. This is an old psychological principle; the grandchildren accept what the grandparents threw away.

This is what is happening to a large percentage of our Jewish students today. The problem of the Hillel Foundation is that it is one institution dealing at times with thousands of students and, generally speaking, there is only one man, a rabbi, who has to cut himself into a hundred pieces in order to meet the needs of hundreds of students. So our goal is, first of all, to be able to reach different students on various levels of their backgrounds and intellects, to provide, at the same time, classes in how to read Hebrew, courses for students who know how to speak Hebrew fluently, and classes for those in between.

Let us put it this way. The Hillel program is like a pyramid. At the base are all the students who may never have stepped into a Hillel Foundation, but in the course of their four years in college will know we are there. As one student put it, the Hillel presence on the campus must be there because some day a student may want it and need it. Our job is to try to change those students from simply being there to becoming involved in Jewish life on the various levels of the Hillel program. These involve coming to services, coming to social activities to meet Jewish boys and girls—which is a very important function—coming to a Jewish class, and becoming involved in Jewish leadership. Of course, the higher the intensity of participation, the smaller the number. But this is just as true of the Jewish community as it is in the college community.

PETER: I think we are all familiar with the reaction of American Jewry to the crisis in Israel. But I think, most emphatically, that this reaction was more noticeable on the campuses where many of the Jewish college students who, during their adolescent years, never expressed themselves or ever even wanted to express themselves Jewishly or to affiliate or to show any signs outwardly of being Jewish, suddenly pop out of their shells when Israel is in crisis. As a matter of fact, they feel the crises hitting right at themselves. It is seen by the outpouring of volunteers who go to Israel and those here who volunteer their time here in America to help Israel in any way possible.

What can we do now, perhaps through the Hillel Foundation, to continue with this response and strengthen our affiliation not only during a time of crisis?

RABBI KAHN: I think that the first thing for you to do is to make it very clear that the crisis of Israel's existence is one that will still continue for a long, long time. Part of the programming of the American Jewish community today and of the Hillel program is to intensify the awareness of the crisis of Israel, to establish a continuing sense of responsibility, to elucidate the problems of Israel today. To use continuous propaganda and pressure and education of the American public, and on the part of the Jewish students to be aware of the crisis and to be ready to support Israel at all times.

Next, I think, we learned something: that is, that we have no right to give up our young people as a lost generation. The term "lost generation" ought to disappear from the Jewish vocabulary, because if ever we knew that there was no "lost generation", it has been during the Israeli crisis. I think we have to approach the problem of our young people, our accessibility to them and their accessibility to us, from a positive point of view. We are not here to reclaim you. We are here to give you the opportunity to take a position of leadership in the Jewish community and for the older and younger generation to work together.

Third, we have to have a sense of urgency, not only about Israel but about the Jewish future in America. Our concern is not just the survival of Jews, it is also the creative continuation of Judaism. This has to be tied in with the concept of the totality of the Jewish people. Every Jew is responsible for his fellow Jew, and the fact that he is in Israel, Rumania or Australia makes no difference. This is the concept of "The People of Israel." I think this has become a dominant force in contemporary Jewish life and thought.

PERRY: As is well known, when coming to a college campus, the student is asked to reject traditional observances. How can certain important ritual areas be explained and rationalized to the Jewish college student? For example, how do you get a college student who is away from home to keep *Kashruth?*

RABBI KAHN: That's a difficult question, Perry, and evidently you must have had some experience with young people who go away from home and suddenly cease to be traditionally observant in the way in which they were brought up. Some students are just waiting for the opportunity to get away from home so that they can overthrow some of the traditions. I think that we are going to have to accept the fact that quite a number of students who have been following a certain pattern of behavior will fall away from it when they get away from home, sometimes deliberately, sometimes accidentally. It is going to happen with a great number. The answer to the continuation and the persistence of forms of observance is not what is done when a student comes to the campus. It is our obligation, on the campus, to provide the student with every opportunity to continue traditional forms of observance. We try to do this. But the conviction that observances are worthwhile has to be in the student long before he comes to the campus. That *Kashruth* is a valid and significant experience in the daily life of the Jew has to be something that is believed in long before a person is admitted as a freshman to a university. If he is not convinced that it is valuable, and that it is part of his life, something he wants to do for himself and convey to his children, he is not going to get it there.

On the other hand, there is a special responsibility of Jewish education on the campus: to interpret and to explain through courses, lectures and conversations the significance of Jewish tradition. Not just the observance, but the whole complex of Judaism as a way of life, and to interpret and explain it, and to clarify it in the academic terms that the university uses. For example, if we are teaching customs and ceremonies, which happens to be one of the more popular courses at the Hillel Foundations, we do not teach it as it is taught in books for high school students. We describe it in terms of the anthropology and sociology of the comparative religious traditions that came into being at the same time as Jewish traditions and teachings did. So when we teach a student at this academic level, we approach it as a university teacher would, with full recognition of the fact that the student may reject it. It is our obligation to present it not only with objectivity but with the intellectual integrity a university student has a right to expect.

PERRY: In your experience with the Jewish student at Hillel, has the graduate of the Hebrew all-day school been able to cope better with campus life than others? Has the day-school graduate become particularly active in Jewish activities or generally has he become uninvolved?

RABBI KAHN: I do not think I can generalize an answer to that. Many day-school graduates suddenly drop out of the day-school pattern of observance when they go to a university. On the other hand, there is an increasing number of students, not necessarily coming out of day-school but coming out of a very traditional background, who will form small communities of observant Jews from conviction, not only from habit. And there is hardly a campus in the United States today, except in the South and Southwest, where there isn't a small coterie of observant young men and women, even in places where you would least expect it, or where ten years ago one would have least expected to find Jewish observances. These include not only day-school graduates but many who come out of a Conservative tradition. They also may have gone to day-school, but even if they have not, they still have the conviction of the traditions. I cannot say that by and large there is one pattern for day-school graduates. I can say that their solid Jewish background is more likely to lead them into involvement with the total Jewish community on the campus than if they had come with no background.

RABBI BERKOWITZ: Many years ago, two of the most famous New Englanders, Henry David Thoreau and Ralph Waldo Emerson, both Harvard men, were discussing higher education. Emerson was especially impressed with the fact that Harvard offered courses in all branches of learning. Thoreau's answer to that was, "Yes, in all of the branches, but in none of its roots."

Learning in itself does not suffice unless it is anchored in fundamental convictions about using it for proper purposes. Learning in itself, without application to the enhancement of one's spiritual life and for the betterment of society, can be vain and useless. We need roots to give us the support which will anchor wisdom to meaning and to work. In Rabbi Benjamin Kahn we have that rare combination. Learning and knowledge, not only in the branches but also in the roots. The roots of faith and commitment, the roots from which one draws the inspiration and strength for ourselves and for others. We can all feel better because he helps to translate and inspire this meaningful blending in the hearts and minds of our young people.

MARGARET MEAD

RABBI BERKOWITZ: Dr. Margaret Mead is unquestionably one of the leading figures of our time. She has achieved distinction in many different areas and in her career, or, rather, her careers. She has always been engaged in man's noblest endeavor—the pursuit of knowledge. She has investigated the past, described the present, and has furnished guides for useful and challenging living for the future. To detail her accomplishments would be an impossible task. Let me just say that since her classic book *Coming of Age in Samoa,* Dr. Mead has been considered one of the world's leading social scientists and anthropologists.

How would you define truth? Is truth what the majority believes or is there a better definition?

DR. MEAD: I suppose that one would start out by discriminating between truth and fact, between truth and actuality. What one works with as a scientist is, primarily, actuality. What we really study is the sort of thing that you can photograph with a camera. That is the subject matter of my scientific research. From another point of view, when one talks about truth, one talks about being as truthful as one can. This would be a moral relationship between one's work and one's attempt to convey to the rest of the world what one has found. It involves all sorts of complications because the way one tells what one finds to one group of people would be different, perhaps, from the way one tells it to another. One would not be able to tell the truth to different people in the same way. So one would have the obligation of interpretation, which would be different from the actuality of which one took a picture, or of which one made a tape recording.

But now imagine that I make a tape recording, or give a verbatim account of something in a New Guinea language—and I am the only one, or only one of a few outsiders, who speaks the language. I have to tell you the truth of what I have heard in a language you do not speak. My obligation, then, is to take something that was actually said in the mountains of New Guinea and put it into forms that would truthfully convey to you here in New York what I heard, so that it would make sense to you today. This would be the problem of the truth which I told as compared with actuality.

RABBI BERKOWITZ: It has been said that people and governments learn nothing from history. Are we condemned to keep repeating the mistakes of yesterday? What can we learn by studying the past?

DR. MEAD: I think the main point is that we can learn a great deal from history if we realize that every event in history is different. No man ever steps into the same river twice. Most of the trouble which comes from the study of history is that we insist that what happens today is the same thing that happened before. We had an example of this in England, where the Labour party was so worried about the previous devaluation of the pound that it could not think. They were so afraid that they would repeat the terrible events of the early 1930's that this kept them from thinking, and they probably were much too slow in devaluating the pound. We also had another instance when Anthony Eden got involved in the Suez affair because he identified Nasser with Hitler.

It is necessary as we go on in time to distinguish between an event in the past and another more recent event, and not overidentify the events. When we overidentify them, then we can say we learn nothing from history. We fortified a hill in Vietnam for no known reason, but we used to occupy hills in World War I, so we had to fortify this particular hill. Thus we can say that we learn nothing from history. If we should repeat the Maginot Line, as occasionally we threaten to do, we would be learning nothing from history because we found out a long time ago that the Maginot Line was of no use.

On the other hand, without history, without knowing where we have come from, we cannot possibly know where we are going. One of the interesting things today is that if you compare the answers of children with the answers of their grandparents to questions about the past, the children go further back and further forward. Very often grandparents only go back two or three thousand years, and that's pretty adventurous for them, but the children will go thousands and thousands and half a million years back. And the grandparents are often willing to stop with fifty years from now and on this planet, but the children are often in outer space and a long, long time ahead. The further we have to look forward, the further we have to look back.

RABBI BERKOWITZ: Many have written and spoken about our need to be individuals, to develop our own personality, to do "our own thing." Yet we are also told to be good citizens and work for the good of the community. Can these two ideas conflict? Can the good of the individual and the good of the community be different?

DR. MEAD: I do not think there is any conflict at all between the individual and the community. The individual can only realize his individuality in a good and enriched community, and if the community life is poor and meager and miserable, and its people are starving and uncared for, every individual in that community is to that degree deprived. However, the concept of the state, as distinguished from the community, is something else again, because there are times when those who control the state genuinely want to override the individuality of its citizens and its members. While I would say that there is never a genuine conflict between the individual and the community, it may well exist between the individual and the state.

RABBI BERKOWITZ: Are we ever justified in taking the law into our own hands if there are laws of which we disapprove? Can we as individuals obey what we consider a higher moral law if we feel this supersedes or contradicts the law of the land?

The critics of the United States policy in Vietnam advocated dissent, disagreement or civil disobedience. Opinions ranged from William F. Buckley, Jr., who once said, "The indicated consequence of aggravated civil disobedience seems to me to be obvious deportation" to Noam Chomsky, a professor at MIT, who wrote that resistance to United States policy was justified, and in fact was a moral necessity. John Coe, the editor of *Center* magazine, said that disobedience may take any number of forms, all of them requiring that man-made laws be broken in order that a higher law be upheld.

What justifies an act of civil disobedience? What should be the limits of civil disobedience? What was justified in the case of Vietnam?

DR. MEAD: Taking the law into one's own hands means that one becomes the administrator of the law—for example, shooting the burglar oneself instead of sending for the police. This is an instance of taking the law into one's hands. Now, civil disobedience is a highly moral piece of work. Civil disobedience is a case of resisting the powers of the law in order to underline some evil one believes is being perpetrated contrary to the law that one feels is higher than the law of the state or the land. Personally I agree with the position that it is unlikely that any human political community will ever be able to frame laws which will not in some instances violate individual consciences if these consciences are sensitive enough. But then I think that those who honestly go in for civil disobedience should be willing to take the penalty.

Deportation has never been a penalty in the United States when we are dealing with American citizens. We seem a little confused about this policy of the reversibility of citizenship. But we are faced with a very peculiar kind of civil disobedience, one which we have never had before, namely, that young people were giving up their citizenship as a form of civil disobedience. I disapproved of it. I think people should have stayed here and worked out whatever was wrong here. I have never been in favor of running from things. Suggestions for deportation were a counter-ploy to the people who were deserting the country instead of staying here and fighting it out in terms of their own ethical convictions.

RABBI BERKOWITZ: What did you think, for example, of the burning of draft cards as a form of civil disobedience?

DR. MEAD: It was very dramatic, provided one was willing to take the penalty for doing it. It was a dramatic way of stating the fact that one did not believe in the justice of this particular war and did not believe that the state should force individuals into fighting a war they did not believe in.

RABBI BERKOWITZ: Do you feel that civil disobedience is justified in order to protest something specific, as was the case of the war in Vietnam, or was the civil disobedience a manifestation of a general rebellion?

DR. MEAD: I think that all noble causes are always corrupted by the presence of people with a variety of other motives. This has been true throughout history. There are many pacifists who would like to slaughter the people who do not agree with them; this is obviously contradictory. Nevertheless, I believe in the right of conscientious objection in any war, and I believe that we are moving into a period in history with kinds of wars and kinds of conflict that more and more people are likely to disagree with and disapprove of. When we are not faced with a question of the survival of the nation, I think we should allow selective conscientious objection. I do not believe that we should ask a twenty-one-year-old boy today if he would have fought against Hitler, and unless he can say that he would not have done so, he may not be considered a conscientious objector in another war. I think this is wrong. He ought to be allowed to stand up and say, "Yes, I would have fought against Hitler and I would have fought in the Revolutionary War, but I don't believe in this particular war." I think we should move in that direction.

RABBI BERKOWITZ: Let me say that I agree with you. However, I would like to make this distinction. A leading American rabbi, at the risk of being condemned by his own congregation, advised young people to burn their draft cards if they disagreed with the Vietnam war. I think this is encouraging the wrong kind of action. Let us channel it in the direction of constructive areas in which we all believe and which lead to real progress.

You have done a considerable amount of work with the U.N. People are confused by the many ways in which nationalism is expressed. For example, some who call themselves nationalists oppose our participation in the U.N. or in other international organizations. Native populations struggling for independence and self-government also call themselves nationalists. So does the white ruling party in

South Africa, so did the German Nazis. What precisely is nationalism, and is it necessarily opposed to any form of international cooperation?

DR. MEAD: You know "ism" is a bad ending. Anything that ends in "ism" immediately is pretty bad, and I think we can oppose "nationalism" with "nationhood"—"hood" is a good ending. Brotherhood, motherhood, nationhood, statehood are all noble. Now the difference between "nationalism" and "nationhood" is the crux of the whole matter here. "Nationhood" means taking one's place as a nation among the nations. It means recognizing one's own full position as a member of a particular nation because there are other nations. If there were no other nations, one's own position would be meaningless. "Nationalism" means promoting one's own nation at the expense of other nations.

The very young countries which are trying to grow into nations are overtouchy, overaspiring, and almost everything they do is done in the name of their nation. They talk about "nation building," which I think is also a quite useful phrase. This, of course, gets exploited. I would think that the National Socialism of Hitler's Germany, the kind of nationalism of South Africa at present, goes with any "nationalism" that promotes the self-interest of one nation-state irrespective of other nation's interests.

RABBI BERKOWITZ: I may be criticized for differing with a very gracious lady, a giant of our generation, but I do have to take issue with you about the word "hood" and the word "ism." I can't speak of "Jewishhood" but I can speak of "Judaism."

In an article in the *New York Times* a writer asked the question: "What did we do wrong?"—a question that many parents are asking these days. He says in part, "Modern parents are queasy about using force or threats to make a child do anything whatever. They would rather manipulate the child's desires. Not only do the schools adapt themselves to the child's wishes, but a balanced diet must somehow be more desirable than candy bars, medicine must be tasty, and everything that is good must be fun. One result of this is that the child learns to consult only his desires and diet for action. Another thing is that he never learns to tolerate the least cessation of the steady stream of gratification which he is used to. Someday, of course, he has to learn that duty is not a marshmallow, but it is hoped that by that time he will be away in college." Do you agree with this?

DR. MEAD: We have been going through a period of considerable transition in the way in which we bring up children in this country. Those who set the standards in this country came from Europe, a very old tradition in which parents were very certain of their position and children did not know as much as parents. For thousands of years that was true of almost any society in the world, and we began to think it was an absolute truth. Now when one emigrates to a new country, whether it is a question of coming from Europe to the United States, or going from Europe to Israel as a new country, the children who are born there and grow up there know things that the parents do not know, and an upset develops in the relationship between parents and children. They speak the language, they know that one does not shout over the telephone—which many people who use the telephone for the first time do not know.

And what is true when one goes from an old country to a new country is true when one goes from one period of history to another. A useful figure of speech is that all older people today are immigrants in the world of the 1960's and 1970's—immigrants in time, immigrants in space. The children know things we don't know. Add to this something we have learned which has been true for a long time in this country, but is not true all over the world as people change so rapidly—the harmful effect of extreme discipline on children and the crippling effect, at least in the modern world, of painful punishment. As a result, we have had a rash of confused parents who want to do the right thing and do not know how to do it. I would not say that parents did something wrong, but rather that they did not know how to do what they were doing.

And so we have had a full crop of overpermissive parents, a situation which is still spreading, and which means that the children have not formed any kind of conscience structure with which they can manage their own lives.

RABBI BERKOWITZ: Are there moral qualities that we should develop in our children in our educational system? What are the values that parents should develop in the child so that when he or she arrives on the campus there is a kind of inner strength or conviction, a kind of inner belief that there are certain standards of behavior?

DR. MEAD: I think that we want at each stage to prepare children to go as far away from home as the next educational stage demands. When we send them to nursery school, we want to prepare them to stay there without crying and to enjoy the morning without clinging to their mother's skirt and to be able to conduct themselves like mature two-year-olds. We should move on from there to prepare them so that they can meet whatever the degree of freedom each institution in turn gives them.

RABBI BERKOWITZ: Dr. Mead, are there absolute values in the judgment of moral and ethical values, in what is right or wrong?

DR. MEAD: Answering as an anthropologist, we feel today

that man's capacity to accept the dictum that some things are right and some things are wrong is part of the evolution of human nature. It is one of the most important characteristics of human beings. Now, this is in terms of the distinction between right and wrong but not in terms of the content. The content varies from one society to another. The importance of the distinction between right and wrong is on a completely different level. If we look the world over, there are a very limited number of universals to be found. One of them is murder. Different people may define murder differently—when killing is murder or when it is patriotic to kill. Nevertheless, a distinction between those people whom you can and cannot kill is universal. The prohibition against incest is universal. The people to be included under the definition of incest may vary enormously—it may be tenth cousins or it may be only the immediate family—but the taboo is always there. And there is some kind of respect for the individuality of another person, which may be expressed in the fact that you do not go into a house without knocking, or you do not address him by his own name —in many societies that is a dreadful thing to do—or you do not take his property, whatever it is. You do not violate his privacy. This is found in every society.

The elaboration beyond these universals of specific ethical codes is the special achievement of the great religious systems of the world. Occasionally you will find a small primitive tribe that has done rather well too, but not in a form that can be conveyed to other people.

RABBI BERKOWITZ: I would say that what you have described in terms of universals—moral issues—are not really the challenges, so to speak, on the campus. This is not what educators are talking about. What would you say, for instance, are the moral problems facing young people on the college campus today?

DR. MEAD: One of the principal things, of enormous importance, facing young people on the college campus today, is the matter of cheating. Since we have had one cheating scandal after another in the last few years, I think it is very serious. Another is sex, because the college authorities are almost a hundred percent hypocritical in what they are doing most of the time. I suppose in addition to cheating and sex, another is probably destructiveness, a kind of rebelliousness that is intolerant of the rights of others and of the importance of other people's property, or of the orderly conduct of life.

RABBI BERKOWITZ: How about drugs?

DR. MEAD: I think we have made drugs into a moral issue when it should not have been made into one. Alcohol, tobacco, marijuana should not have been treated as matters of law. If we turn them into matters of law we get exactly what we had during Prohibition. I went to college in Prohibition days and, of course, many of us were endlessly involved in situations which were also illegal. Alcohol was in almost every house all over the country. We have done the same thing today. The moral issue of drugs has been tremendously intensified by putting marijuana in the same class as heroin, for instance.

RABBI BERKOWITZ: Are you saying that if there were a laxity of the law, this problem of drugs would dissipate itself?

DR. MEAD: No. I mean that if we had not and did not continue to pass laws about things we shouldn't be passing laws about, we would not be luring young people into borderline positions that then lead into the kind of drug taking which is exceedingly dangerous.

RABBI BERKOWITZ: I would like your reaction to the excessively competitive spirit which seems to pervade our lives. Do you think that we today in America are following a philosophy that has crept into every facet of living and which can best be put in terms of "You have to be a winner"? Is this not put to the student, driving him and saying, "You have to be a winner"—with its stresses and strains—against a philosophy which says, "You don't have to be a winner, you have to be educated, you have to be well integrated." Is this concept related to the problems of cheating that you mentioned?

DR. MEAD: I think it is more the fact that we are doing very bad teaching and that our whole method of teaching and marking is grossly unfair. Whenever society is unfair and unjust in terms of its own effort, there is law-breaking and every kind of breakdown. We saw an example of this in England during World War II. People believed that food rationing was fair. The food was horrible, but it was fairly divided and there was no black market in food in England. They believed that the matter of children's shoes was unfair, and they developed a black market in children's shoes—among the same people.

Today we have in schools an abomination called the "normal curve" which utterly disregards the distribution of ability, so that if a student takes a course this year, he may be the brightest person in class and get an A; the next year, in a different section, or with a different teacher, he might get a C or even a D. Thus students are not marked and are not judged on their individual capacity or on how hard they work, or on how well prepared they are, but marked according to the accidental aggregations of other people. This is shocking and the students understand it perfectly well. They also understand that the teacher who marks from a normal curve is safe. Such teachers do not really have to teach anything. All they have to do is to mark on a normal curve, and the administration looks at their marks and says "That's fine." But if the teacher gives too many A's, he is immediately suspect. In other words, if he really taught the students something, so that more students could do good work, he is criticized. This is where the cheating comes from. Of course, competition is to blame also. If getting through college meant nothing, or getting through medical school meant nothing, students would not bother to cheat. I believe that if there is a situation that is substantially unsound and unfair and unjust, this is the place where one begins to find cheating.

RABBI BERKOWITZ: In speaking about the college campus, you mentioned "cheating, destructiveness and sex." Would you care to elaborate on the problem of sex on the campus today?

DR. MEAD: We have reached a state of profound hypocrisy, simply enormous hypocrisy, in this country. We preach complete disapproval of any type of sex relations outside of marriage. Such relations are punishable by law in most states, and they are disapproved of from almost every pulpit in the land, not to mention by college presidents and deans of women. At the same time, the same authorities, all of whom express this ethic of disapproval of premarital sex relations, nevertheless wink at them and connive with them in every possible sort of way. For the religious organizations, this means giving very nice weddings to pregnant girls. This is happening all over the United States and at every social level. And I think it makes no sense whatever to have sermons from the pulpit or the college president's podium about the virtues of premarital chastity when they're combined with being perfectly willing to give the kids a fine wedding if they'll just get married.

RABBI BERKOWITZ: But recognizing this as a problem, analyzing the situation as you see it at first hand, do you have any specific ideas as to how to deal with it?

DR. MEAD: We have been dealing with it, but we have several problems on our hands. One, education takes much longer than it did in the past, and to postpone marriage until education is over is no longer feasible. We also have in this country, as a whole, moved from the position that sex is sinful—which is a very heavily endorsed Christian position; I believe this never was a Jewish position. But, nevertheless, we have moved from Puritanism of European Christianity to an attitude toward sex that sees it as simply a part of life having a legitimate part in human relations. Thus, many of the protections against approving such relations have been removed. We have a public opinion that on the whole says that sex is a good thing. In fact, we disapprove of celibacy today; we are inclined to think that it makes people pathologically unreliable in one way or another.

So, we disapprove of celibacy, we believe in everybody being married all the time, not necessarily to the same person all the time, but always married. And we think that the postponement of marriage until the end of education is bad. These are all problems. We are then up against the question of what are we going to do about young people. In the past fifteen years we have been pushing them into marriage when they have not been ready for it. And we have been letting them push us into letting them get married by permitting the girls to get pregnant so that the parents have to support the couple. This is very common now in high schools all over the country. The introduction of oral contraceptives has decreased the fear of pregnancy, and parents whose principal interest in the virtue of their daughters is the fear of pregnancy are altering their position somewhat.

We are now in a position, I think, of trying to consider ways in which we can approve and legalize and sanctify very young student marriages as long as they do not result in children, because they are not old enough for a disciplined and socially approved companionship.

RABBI BERKOWITZ: You have proposed two forms of marriage. Would you care to elaborate on this idea?

DR. MEAD: I proposed that we should have two kinds of marriages. We should have a marriage ceremony that is legal and religious—in whatever terms religious people wish to make it religious—for young people who do not yet want to have children, as well as for older people who are too old to have children. This would differ from a marriage which is primarily concerned with parenthood, where the partners need to have very binding economic arrangements. If young people wanted the first kind of marriage, which does not give them a very heavy economic responsibilty, it would not make any difference who supported them: scholarships, her mother, his mother, or whoever. If they did not want to have children, the girl is perfectly free to work also. Of course, they would have to believe in contraception. A second, much more binding and complicated wedding ceremony would be advisable when they are ready to be parents.

I proposed these a while ago. People overwhelmingly repudiated the idea. They want only one kind of marriage, they want to keep on thinking that marriage is forever, even in the light of the proportion of divorces each year. So we will have to call my first arrangement something else, but I think we are going to have it. We have to have some way to legalize and bless early unions of young people who are not yet ready to have children.

RABBI BERKOWITZ: In Jewish life, not so much today, certainly in the past, there was such a thing as a *shidduch*—in other words, a marital arrangement. A parent went to the *schadchen*, the matchmaker, and he matched his daughter with a suggested young man. This is an ancient way of dealing with the union of two people toward the establishment of a family. Does the American tradition of romantic love provide a better basis for selection of a marriage partner than the old form of matchmaking?

DR. MEAD: In our changing society, where the parents came from a different kind of world from their children, whether because they are immigrants or just because there is cultural change, I think the parents become less capable of selecting their children's mates. That is the reason they moved to this country, for freedom of choice. I do not think there is much romantic love around today. Romantic love was very popular a generation ago, but today young people are very practical. They are trying to find someone who is willing to marry at once, which is much more important. I doubt that we are going to be able to go back to any form of parental choice.

The younger those marriages are, the larger the role of the parents. As we push marriage down below the legal age, for instance, or below the age at which children are independent, we have given back to the parent in this country a tremendous amount of choice. A boy does not bring a girl home to sit on his sofa to watch television every other weekend, and goes to watch television in her house on alternate weekends, unless the father and mother like the girl. So today we are moving back considerably towards parental participation in marriage.

To a degree, this is somewhat narrowing. I would rather see them postpone marriage until the boy can support himself at least. It would be better if they could support themselves on fellowships or scholarships at least. It is inappropriate in our society today for parents to have quite that much power.

RABBI BERKOWITZ: What are the stresses and strains of modern life in marriage?

DR. MEAD: The principal one is that our society has an all-purpose marriage, in which we are supposed to be everything to each other, from having common ideas about economics, politics, schooling, and in which men spend little time with other men, and women spend increasingly little time with other women. The husband and wife are expected to provide all the companionship that used to be provided by relatives and by members of one's own sex. This is terribly trying.

The other thing is that people live so long; they used to die earlier. If you look at the graveyard records of early American colonial life, a vigorous man buried three wives and a vigorous woman buried three husbands. Today nobody dies, so if one marries at twenty he can look forward to fifty years with the same mate. Of course, looking ahead to fifty years when one is absolutely, blissfully happy is fine. The American poet, James Whitcomb Riley, says in his poem, "An Old Sweetheart of Mine": "We should be so happy that when either's lips were dumb/They would not smile in Heaven till the other's kiss had come." But this is the exceptionally happy marriage, in which one can look forward to fifty years of delight.

RABBI BERKOWITZ: We are thankful that the years do extend themselves and that science has helped. But this has its problems, problems of the aged citizen. What should we be doing by now with the senior citizen?

DR. MEAD: I think we should divide them as to grandparents and greatgrandparents, instead of dividing them by ages, as we do at present. We say that we are putting them off all by themselves, when they ought to have the patter of little feet around. Well, that may be fine for grandparents but greatgrandparents may have had enough feet pattering. At present, we are muddled as to very tired, older people, who might like to live quietly with other older people, compared with those pushed away too early, who have not had a chance to be important senior citizens in the community. We are segregating them too much from the mainstream of life, and we are not giving them enough chance to relate to younger people.

RABBI BERKOWITZ: Our age has made great progress in the sciences, yet I often wonder if we are advancing spiritually and morally. Have we really made progress over the years?

DR. MEAD: I have never met any member of the dead civilizations of the past face to face, and I think we make up a great deal about them. We tend to think all Greeks were something like Aristotle or Plato; we know nothing of many of the others.

I have met some people who are like some of our ancestors a great deal further back than the great civilizations of the past. These people are capable only of conceiving of two-hundred, three-hundred, five-hundred other people as creatures like themselves and think of all the rest of the world as subhuman, nonhuman. These are people whose religious ideas are limited to their own ghosts and a couple of rainbow serpents. They live at their own water holes; they do not have any notion of any relationship to God that could possibly be extended to other people. I don't feel that they have reached anything like the heights of ethical, philosophical or aesthetic positions that have been reached subsequently. Now, one of the things that we use the past for, of course, is to take only its high points, comparing ourselves and our next-door neighbors unfavorably with the high points of the past.

RABBI BERKOWITZ: I recall very vividly, at the seminary, one of my professors, a great Hebrew scholar, Professor Shalom Spiegel, whose specialty is medieval Jewish philosophy, poetry and other areas. He made the very same observation in comparing cultures or civilizations, drawing analogies between Greek civilization and Jewish civilization, Roman culture and Greek culture. He said, "You load the dice, so to speak, when you take the best from the Greeks and you take the least from Judaism, or vice versa."

To go back to today. Everyone now is supposed to conform. Anyone who deviates from the social or group pattern is regarded in some quarters as subversive. At times I may, for example, react in a certain way to a certain situation and to people close to me. Instead of answering, they use their hands to make a kind of diagram—which means "square." Is this situation unique? Is this a situation that you have found in your study of the past?

DR. MEAD: People have always conformed, most of the time, to the customs around them. If they did not we would all bump into each other in the street. The only thing that is peculiar about the present day is that we are very self-conscious about it and talk about it all the time, and the mass media and the advertisers exploit it so that we are continuously reminded of it. A junior executive has always acted like a junior executive. Today he will stand up in front of a glass and try on three ties to see which makes him look more like a junior executive. I think this is the difference. Because we have increased in self-consciousness, people think we have increased in conformity. I do not think we have.

RABBI BERKOWITZ: All of us are interested in the problems of cultural accommodation in Israel. You visited Israel as a guest of the Ministry of Health to consider the problems of the integration of immigrants of varying cultural backgrounds into contemporary Israel. What were your impressions of Israel?

DR. MEAD: I was really asked to go there because one of my students was the principal cultural adviser in the Ministry of Mental Health in Israel and in charge of giving advice on the question of immigrants to Israel. The overall policy that guided Israel in the early days of the reception of enormous numbers of immigrants from Asia was primarily to assimilate people as rapidly as possible, which is a good deal like the early American policy. To begin with, they had to learn to speak Hebrew—even if some of them were not able to learn it well, they were able to pronounce it and they had a feeling for it. They had to learn a new language, and they had to learn a whole new style of life in Israel. The general feeling was, Don't let them stay in enclaves because if they did they would keep the old customs, and this young society with its new style wanted to get rid of those things. But this was not primarily directed against European Jews. They were already setting up the new style. The young ones were rebels against the old style, and they were the ones that had broken up the old style.

It was when Israel began to get very large numbers of Asian Jews that this became very much of a problem. They were Arabic-speaking; they shared very little or nothing of the European traditions. Their style of life was quite different—the way they handled the house, the way they handled their children—everything was different, and there was tremendous pressure to assimilate them as rapidly as possible. One of the main ideas was that if they were mixed in enough they would assimilate faster. That is the present theory in Australia, too, to a degree. However, the Israelis found that there were negative aspects to mixing things up. The older people were neglected—not physically, because they were very well taken care of physically—but there was a very sharp break between the old and the young, and many of the young people from some of the immigrant groups became unruly.

One of the things that my friend was working on was how they could permit people to live together and support each other in the old ways, and at the same time to accommodate them to new ways so that the children would learn to think and act in Hebrew and go on to become real Israelis. One of the designs that was worked out was in some of the new towns in the Negev, with a school and a health clinic in the center and a series of little villages, each of which consisted of people who came from the same country and sometimes from the same part of the country. They went home at night and the neighbor's food smelled the same, and the talk sounded familiar, but when the child went to school, he met youngsters learning to be Israelis, and when the young mother went to the baby clinic, she met all her neighbors and was on the way to becoming a member of the new society.

RABBI BERKOWITZ: You said in an article about the study of Jewish self-image that during the 1940's there was a preliminary emphasis on self-hatred, as if this were a uniquely Jewish trait. What do you mean by this?

DR. MEAD: This was the result of some of the studies that were made by social psychologists. They were paying more attention, at this period, to attitudes of young Jewish students than to those of anybody else, and so they were delineating rather sharply what is always the opinion of a minority group. This is a minority group position, in which the minority absorbs some of the attitudes which they attribute to the majority group—whether they are real or not. Women do it, in relation to what men think of them, and if women think that men think they are stupid, a fair number of women then begin to think that they are stupid.

This was a period when we were still very seriously concerned with anti-Semitism and with the possibilities of anti-Semitism for young people who had almost stopped worrying about it, who had been here for two generations or so and felt comfortable. All of their worries were re-established by the Hitler period, and many young people went back to far more observances than they had before and as a result there was a great deal of conflict.

RABBI BERKOWITZ: You say that many useful parallels can be drawn between the establishment of the national self-images of Israel and the United States, but also, you say, there are differences. Would you want to explain?

DR. MEAD: There was no in-gathering of displaced peoples in the United States. The United States was a completely new land, a land no one knew anything about; it had no history. The early explorers did not even know it when they got here. When they came here from England they misnamed practically every tree and bug in the country, because they called them after something that looked like what they had seen somewhere before. The sense of going into an unchartered and completely new land was important here. We could make wonderful religious statements about this, like, "Ay, call it holy land. The soil where first they trod they left unstained what there they found—Freedom to worship God." It was new, entirely new; it represented a new freedom.

Israel was a return, and a return to a place where every stick and stone was known. I have always enjoyed listening to the military conversations where they point out that they never would have won if they hadn't known how the battles were won in the Biblical days. Somebody knew which hill was what and who walked around it. So it was a return to the known, to that which had been cherished long, which is a very different thing. Also, there was the assumption that everyone was the same, although they had been exposed to very different things for a couple of thousand years. And this assumption of unity had a way of receiving everyone who came into Israel.

This is a very different matter from what we had to start with in this country. We had the Indians here, then the African slaves, then the Chinese, who came to build the railroads, and we were not sure that any of them were human. And we had some very serious problems. Now, Israel is not entirely exempt from these problems. European Jews show some of the attitudes of other Europeans about the superiority of the Europeans; some very odd categories developed in Israel. I was always amused by what Israelis call an "Anglo-Saxon," because the category includes a very queer group of people. Besides the British and American Jews, it includes Latin American and Dutch Jews—they are called "Anglo-Saxon," and they do not even speak English.

There was a considerable battle and there still is a considerable battle to accept Asian Jews on the same basis as European Jews. And there are now some reactions to this in Israel; a feeling that the European Jews are overprivileged and the minority feelings on the basis of color of skin and all those things. So there are some very close parallels also.

RABBI BERKOWITZ: You have said that in Israel there has been an understandable tendency to emphasize the successful integration of the young and to write off the old.

DR. MEAD: Well, we did the same thing in many instances in this country. We just let them alone. In the United States we did not insist on their becoming citizens; we did not insist on their learning English. We just left them quietly by the fire and took the children away to schools and Americanized them so that they couldn't talk to Grandma. They have done the same thing in Israel. They have treated the older people magnificently, as far as caring for their physical needs goes. As a matter of fact, they retire them rather young.

The whole emphasis on youth, and on bringing in so many young people, who, of course, came without parents, and then building a kind of new world on young people, kibbutz living in itself—all of these things tended to emphasize the young and turn them into Israelis while taking good physical care of the older but giving them minimum participation in society.

RABBI BERKOWITZ: Let us leave Israel and return to an area where I feel I should at least ask a number of questions. You were the editor of a book, *American Women*, which was the report of the President's Commission on the Status of Women. Did the increased employment of women lead to an increase in juvenile delinquency?

DR. MEAD: I don't know. Many people think it has, but juvenile delinquency has occurred in every part of the world, in old cities and new cities, in the Communist world and in the anti-Communist world, and when I discovered that there was juvenile delinquency in Tel-Aviv, I virtually gave up on the theory of any simple correlation. Tel-Aviv is a new city, it is bursting with ethical leaders, and nevertheless there is juvenile delinquency in Tel-Aviv. Juvenile delinquency is the result of the fact that we do not know how to run a city. We do not know how to care for our young people in cities.

RABBI BERKOWITZ: I have heard this statement of yours made by many women: "Home-making and volunteer work as we now conceive of them are not highly valued activities, and they can do little to give a women a sense of dignity and choice. Only paid jobs can do this." Are we writing off the mother and the home, the raising of children? Does a woman find fulfillment only if she teaches at a university or works at some other job?

DR. MEAD: I was commenting in that article on the report of the Commission on the Status of Women. The report spoke of working women and then it would note, "Of course, this should not interfere with her duties as wife and mother." In the last ten years we have been working very hard to push women, and particularly educated women, back into the labor market. We do it by telling the woman that she is not fulfilled, making it fashionable for mothers to go back to school. This is exactly what happened in World War II; then we put a lot of pressure on women to go to work because we needed them . Between World War II and the late 1950's we lured them back into the home, and we set up concepts that made it impossible for a woman to do anything else because conditions of homemaking in the suburbs were so very difficult.

Now we are trying to push them out again. Currently we are denigrating homemaking and we are denigrating volunteer work. I anticipate that this will pass. It was partly due to the war, but even more due to the fact that automation needs every intelligent person we can find at present to get it going. Once we get it going, we will have so much leisure that we will want women to go back home again to pay attention to their children. I hope they will not have to go back to having to spend their entire time as domestic drudges.

RABBI BERKOWITZ: What did you mean when you wrote: "For a long time in America there was a tendency to make a division between the kinds of values appropriate to men and appropriate to women. And this division weakened our culture."

DR. MEAD: If you give any set of virtues to one sex alone you weaken it, because 50 percent of the society does not have it. In some societies people think that women are incapable of keeping accounts; others think they are incapable of thinking logically, they are emotional creatures, incapable of political responsibilities, incapable of holding political office. If you assign a virtue to only one sex—you can assign tenderness, consideration for other people, sympathy, empathy, intuition—whenever you do this you cut in half the virtues you might have.

RABBI BERKOWITZ: You say, "Men believe that they achieve a sense of their intrinsic masculinity only in those situations in which women know less, earn less, achieve less, and win less recognition." Would you want to make a comment on this?

DR. MEAD: If any occupation is specified as a woman's occupation, men get out of it or they insist on being administrators. On the whole, we have set up occupations so that a man is demeaned if he takes a woman's occupation or is demeaned if he has a woman over him. In education, for instance, any man, if he can be lured into it, is pretty sure of becoming a principal. This means that very often there are very inferior men providing leadership to very superior women, since teaching takes in the best of women and in many instances is not taking in the best of men.

RABBI BERKOWITZ: You have referred to "great gains by American women in literary life, education and health, compared with relatively few positions held by women in industry." What specific gains have women made?

DR. MEAD: American women today have freedom to work at a reasonable level in a great many places in this country. They have a chance to work in many fields, but they do very little in politics compared with those in many other countries. This is consonant with the tradition that women in this country have made one of their principal contributions as voluntary community workers, holding the community together. The country would go to pieces without the work that woman—and as a whole, the older, married woman—gives to maintaining community services of all sorts. I am sure that this is true of Judaism too. Not only this country, but Israel, would suffer very seriously if it were not for the voluntary work of thousands of women. But this tradition of volunteerism, which has been so strong in this country, has meant also that women have done much less in administrative and governmental positions than, say, in Scandinavia. I was struck by this several years ago at a conference among twelve leading Russian women and twelve leading American women, and I was the only completely professional one among the American women. All the rest of them were responsible, highly educated leaders of volunteer movements, who were put vis-a-vis a great Russian heart specialist, a great Russian economist and the like. The Russians sent only professional women, and we met them with highly well informed voluntary workers.

RABBI BERKOWITZ: In some Jewish communities in Eastern Europe it was customary for a child starting Hebrew school to have a dab of honey placed on his learning slate. The child touched the honey with his fingers and tasted it, and the sweetness of the honey was intended to be a symbolic foretaste of the sweetness and pleasantness of the study of the Torah. In this discussion we have experienced the wonderful opportunity of having Dr. Margaret Mead give us a small taste, so to speak—a sweet taste—of her learning, knowledge and experience. Now, like the child first beginning to learn, we too can be better able to learn and understand what has been, what is and will be, thanks to our dialogue. It was indeed a taste of honey which will linger on and on.

IDA KAMINSKA

RABBI BERKOWITZ: We are privileged to interview a person who, through creative artistry, has in her lifetime given us a deeper understanding and appreciation of the human drama through the theater. Her career is unmatched in the annals of the Jewish stage in Russia, Poland and in the United States. Our guest has produced more that seventy plays, has played a hundred and fifty parts and received an Academy Award nomination in 1967 for her role in the film *The Shop on Main Street*. She has translated seventy plays into Yiddish, has dramatized several novels and authored two original plays. We welcome Mme. Ida Kaminska.

The history of the Yiddish theater in Poland covers a period of about a hundred years, and Madam Kaminska has been active in it for more than seventy years of that time. How is this possible?

MME. KAMINSKA: I think that in saying this we have to include the years of my mother's and father's work. Our work started with them and my work is a continuation. I cannot separate myself from the work of my mother and father, for I began with them and have not broken away to this day. Now my daughter plays in the theater with me, and I hope she will continue the tradition.

RABBI BERKOWITZ: Tell us about your parents—your mother Esther Rachel and father Abraham Isaac.

MME. KAMINSKA: My father came from a poor, proletarian and very religious family, who lived in Prage-Valya. Somehow he left and began to perform in a wandering troupe. They were amateurs. Incidentally, when he started there was not a woman in the company. As you know, it was blasphemous for a woman to act in the theater. Men played women's parts, and the greatest problem was to find men to perform.

One day he passed a shop in Warsaw and saw a young girl sitting at the window and heard her singing. He thought she was beautiful and her voice lovely, so he began to talk to her. That was the way he met my mother, Esther Rachel Halperin. She had come to live with her older sister in Warsaw after her parents had died.

My father convinced her that she should become an actress. She told her sister that she wanted to tour and act in the theater. "How come? With whom?" her sister asked. "Is the young man also going? You can travel with him only if you marry him; otherwise we cannot let you go just like that!" So they married.

For her first part she was given the leading role in *The Magician* by Goldfaden. She played Mirele. She was young and beautiful and possessed an exquisite voice. From the very beginning, without experience and without knowledge of the theater, she stood out, she made an impression. They said of her, "Why, even her shoes act."

My father was very energetic, and with a young and gifted woman at his side he became even more strongly interested in the theater. He was very progressive in his thinking and feelings, even though he sprang from a religious household, and he was a good learner who knew many languages. He was a very good actor and a Godsend to my mother, because she started acting unschooled and inexperienced. But on the stage she had something that shone forth, something unusual, unfathomable, that put him in the background. However, they complemented each other, my father guided, my mother led, and that is how they went through life. Unhappily, my father and mother both died young. Regardless of the short term of their work, they left a great inheritance for the Yiddish theater; it grew from the beginnings they had made. They were not the only ones. In the past there were others who accomplished a lot for the Yiddish theater. But the Kaminsky couple—Esther Rachel and Abraham Isaac—were the pioneers.

RABBI BERKOWITZ: You made your debut at the age of six. Can you describe your childhood in the theater? Were there many roles for children of that age?

MME. KAMINSKA: At that time parents would not permit young boys or girls to act in the theater. It was considered degrading. I do not know why, but that is the way it was then. In the plays, particularly the old plays, there were many roles for children. I had an easy road. I had an older sister, four years older than I, who played the children's parts. One day she decided that she was grown up and could not play children anymore. My mother asked me—I was hardly five years old—if I wished to play the part of her grandchild in Pinsky's *The Mother*. "What about Regina?" I asked. "Regina is too grown up for the role and it suits you better," my mother replied. "Good," I said, "I'll play." And that's how I started. Later, I took the roles of older children, primarily boys, but girls too. I traveled with my mother constantly and performed everywhere with her. Gordon's plays had many children's roles. I had very good success in these. Gordon was very clever. The children in his plays were very bright. They understood everything, and when a child utters such words of wisdom, it is no great feat to be successful.

The moment came when my mother said, "Enough, you must have an education. At the age of seven or eight one must go to school." It was very difficult for me to leave the theater. My education began, but it was not all that appealing. It was not at all like the life in the theater. One day I told her, "I don't want to go to school anymore. I want to study at home—travel with you again and act." I did again, but only for a short period. At this time my mother went to America as a guest star, and I went back to school. During vacation time I toured with mother again and played older roles of fourteen or fifteen years of age. At the age of sixteen I began to play adult roles.

RABBI BERKOWITZ: I have read that you translated plays and directed them at the age of eighteen.

MME. KAMINSKA: This is how it happened. In the Yiddish theater there were no directors. Occasionally, but only occasionally, was a director engaged. First of all, there was no money for this. Secondly, if certain people came, let us say from America, and brought a play, they put it on without a director. They presented it in Poland as they had in America. My mother also directed. One needed someone else, though, from time to time, and we had one, Mark Ornstein, who wrote *The Vilner Balebesl* (Newlywed Man), as well as other plays. For a time he toured with my mother as the director. But generally there weren't any. I was very, very young when I started to direct, not intentionally, not as a formal director, but I used to alert certain actors by saying, "I think that you didn't say *this* correctly. It's not right. I think that you have to say *this* a little differently." On stage I said, "No, you stand *here*. It's better that way." And the actors began to feel that I had a certain talent for direction. And I must say, in praise of the old Jewish actors, they called on me to assist them and pushed me into directing. They were veterans, all experienced, but they were willing to listen and learn.

The time came when I put on a play, translated from French, which my mother and father played and I directed. I didn't mind directing older and more experienced actors, but my parents? They said, "It does not matter, Idele, do it." I undertook it. I did what I could.

I was very interested in the Polish theater, I visited it day and night, and I read a lot. I read everything written by Stanislavsky, Meyerhold, and others. My parents saw that I knew what I was doing, and they permitted me to do it. Thus I was drawn in without preparation, that is, without any formal schooling, except for a lot of reading on the subject. I had people around me who were happy about it all, and this has not ceased to this day.

RABBI BERKOWITZ: What was the Warsaw Yiddish Art Theater? What was its influence and impact on Polish Jewry?

MME. KAMINSKA: My first husband, Zigmund Turkor, came to the Yiddish theater via a Polish drama school with a great deal of knowledge, which was then a rarity in the Yiddish theater. He was very young and imbued with a strong love for the theater. When my father died, Zigmund performed opposite my mother. This was during the time of the First World War, and we traveled and played a varied repertory. In Poland there was great love and moral support for the Jewish theater. There were great Jews in the Poland of yore who created an atmosphere around the theater. Nevertheless, we still had to depend on our own strength to get something done. There was no help from the others. Zigmund and I worked side by side, and apart from all the other work, I still had to deal with the entire administrative end. We created a theater called "Varshaver Yiddisher Kunst Teater"—the V.I.K.T. The theater came into existence and brought to the stage wonderful productions, marvelous and magnificent.

The V.I.K.T. played in my father's theater, the Kaminsky Theater, and we had large productions but, they were not self-sustaining. The theater was a large building and had one fault as do many American theaters: you could not hear very well. The acoustics were bad, but the stage was exceptionally large and we could spread out. And we did. There were productions that made history, but they did not remain on the boards long enough. So we just had to break it up. We toured through the provinces with smaller plays in order to earn enough money to cover the debts incurred by the new Art Theater. Some time later we reorganized the V.I.K.T. since it had established a name for itself. We had good actors, and we presented plays seen for the first time on the Yiddish stage—plays like *Wolves* by Romain Rolland and Dostoevsky's *The Brothers Karamazov*. They were really wonderful Yiddish productions. We revived a Goldfaden play called *The Tenth Commandment*. We presented a series of plays, like Ettinger's *Serkele,* the first Yiddish comedy ever written, Adreyev's play *The Seven That Were Hung,* Moliere's *The Miser.* It swa marvelous repertory, in the true sense. But even this could not exist. We had to liquidate and limit ourselves to smaller ensembles and equipment in order to support and sustain ourselves.

RABBI BERKOWITZ: What happened to your theater and your efforts at the outbreak of World War II?

MME. KAMINSKA: Prior to 1939 I had established a theater in Warsaw, in the center of the city. It was called the "Ida Kaminska Ensemble." We had accustomed our audiences—even our assimilated audiences—to come to the theater. Our performances were very well received, and just when I thought I could rest a little, that was when disaster came.

For three weeks we were in Warsaw with the Germans all around us, and then we fled. The day that we decided to flee at 5:00 A.M., not knowing whether we would succeed in our escape, a woman who worked on a Polish newspaper came to me. It was before nightfall, when people were not allowed to walk on the street, particularly Jews. She came running to me and said, "Run away! You are on the list of the Gestapo. Your name is on the list of those who must be captured first." Why? Because I was a director of a theater. They wanted to capture all the directors because at the time anti-Hitler plays as well as anti-German plays were presented.

Well, we left. Our escape was a terribly drawn-out affair. When we finally arrived in Lemberg the Russians were already there and had established a state theater. This was the first time I had played in a Jewish state theater, for at that time there were state theaters only in certain cities in Russia: in Lemberg, Moscow, Kiev, Kharkov and Odessa. In Lemberg they asked me to assume the leadership of the state theater. I directed the theater until 1941. How it all happened, how we all fled from the Germans, what the first meeting was like with the Russians, and what the theater was like and all those other experiences—for that you will have to wait and read my book. There is a lot to tell and there is not enough time to tell it.

We played in Lemberg until 1941, when war broke out between the Russians and Germans. Again we had to flee. This time our running brought us to Central Asia. Just imagine, I played Yiddish theater there. In the Caucasus, before the war, there were eighty-eight Jews, not families, just Jews. But at this time many Jews came to the Caucasus not only as fugitives from Poland but from deep inside Russia. The war kept me there in the Caucasus for two years and eight months. From there, in 1944, we went to Moscow.

I did not play in Moscow at all until the end of 1946. It was then that I was supposed to come to America. But I did not. I waited until the end of the war, but about the end of 1946 I returned to Warsaw instead.

RABBI BERKOWITZ: Why did you return to Warsaw?

MME. KAMINSKA: There are two aspects in answer to this question. The first, why did I not remain in Russia, and the second, why did I go to Poland? I did not remain in Russia because I did not experience certain emotions that could have kept me there. I guess that's clear. On the other hand, I certainly wanted to leave. Now, why Poland? I just could not go anywhere else. There is a sentiment, there is a nostalgia to the places that remind you of your youth, your parents, their work. I did not find anything but stones in Warsaw, stones and ruins. However, we recognized the places. Where I lived for nineteen years the house still stood, or at least half a house. There were other places that I remembered. I was drawn back to those places. I even found my mother's grave. It still stands to this day.

So I came to Poland and waited for my children, for my daughter, her first husband, and my grandchild, who were in Lemberg. I arrived with a five-year-old son, the same age as my grandchild. My daughter and I chose to give birth simultaneously to two children in Frunze in the Caucasus of Central Asia during the war.

However, to our great misfortune, my daughter's husband, a famous jazz trumpeter, had been arrested a day before my departure. Their child remained alone in the care of friends. I waited in Warsaw to see how this misfortune would end. It lasted a long time; my daughter was sentenced to five years in prison, my son-in-law to ten. It was a dreadful experience, but I stayed in Warsaw and did everything possible, and even impossible. Almost every day I spoke to my grandchild on the telephone. So we waited. After a year and a half, when my daughter was released and sent into exile, I was able to contact her. I could send her things; I could correspond with her. Then after nine years we saw each other. My son-in-law was released after seven-and-a-half years and again became a jazz musician. Almost everything was again as it had been. But they lost those years of their lives; they lost the most beautiful and best years of youth.

Well, during this time I could not make a move. We lived in hope. We thought perhaps that something fruitful would grow in Warsaw, a city that had been so deeply rooted in a great Jewish culture. That is what we thought. Maybe if my children had been with me after the war when the pogram in the city of Kielce broke out, we might have been driven out of Poland. But as things turned out, I could not think of leaving. I wanted to be close to my children while I waited for them, and while waiting, I worked. This will clarify why I waited, and why I waited until now to tell the story.

RABBI BERKOWITZ: In 1949 your theater became a state theater. What did this mean?

MME. KAMINSKA: There was a time in Poland when they began to think of bringing all Polish theaters under the sponsorship of the state. There were not too many positive things about Poland then, but this decision was one. For it definitely is a positive thing that the theater should be a state institution. If there is a theater, it must have money and should be subsidized by the government. An actor should not be dependent on the box office or on the taste of the audience. He should be permitted to portray what he feels and what he wishes. An actor will not get rich in a state theater. No question about that, but it is a livelihood without any worries about performing.

We were in Warsaw when they decided to subsidize all Polish theater. There were about 150,000 Jews left, out of the once three and a half million, and these were people who yearned for a Yiddish theater and were delighted to come. We were interested in what the attitude of the Polish authorities would be. We introduced a memorandum stating that we existed as a theater and that we wished to be recognized as a state theater. If they had refused us, it would have been an obvious form of discrimination. They immediately accepted us and granted us a subsidy equal to the largest of the Polish theaters, although our theater was comparatively small and had a limited audience. Our theater cost them more than the Polish theaters. Poland had very good theaters and they do to this day; ours was considered among the best. They investigated us less than the other Polish theaters; they relied on our judgment as to what was to be played and how it was to be played. They came and they were interested. We received many rewards. I especially won many state awards, more than any other actor in Poland, and more than any other Jewish actress. At that time their attitude towards our theater was one of great sympathy, and that is how it was until the end, when there were almost no Jews left in the audience.

RABBI BERKOWITZ: Would you tell us something about the film *The Shop on Main Street,* which was made in Prague. You have said that you spent a whole lifetime in the theater, but in only one film you became famous internationally.

MME. KAMINSKA: I have already mentioned something about the positive aspect of the Polish authorities toward our theater. However, we clearly saw that there were negative aspects. For instance, during this twenty year period in Poland I was never offered a role in films. I was asked once to be a guest star in a Polish theater and thought that it was very successful. I made a short film for television that had an outstanding success, but I did not play in Polish films. Then, two Czechoslovakian directors, Kadar and Klaus, came to

Poland. They had revived a short novel by a man called Grossman and were adapting it for film. They had already engaged almost all of the actors but were missing just one—the character called Mme. Lautmanova, the proprietress of a poor button shop. They came to Poland and were also planning to go to Russia to seek someone for the part. They came to the theater where I happened to be doing the same play I did in New York, *The Trees Die Standing*. The following day they arranged a meeting at which they told me the content of their forthcoming film. I was impressed. Prior to the war I had played in a few films and felt that it was right that my first film after the war should relate something of the great Holocaust. I could express my feelings by showing this period again to the public. I could not skip over that time and go on to something else. That is why I was very touched and why it was very appealing.

The directors did leave for Russia as they had intended, but at a later time they confessed that after having seen my performance in *The Trees Die Standing* they had called Prague and said, "We have found Lautmanova." Then they sent me the script. I read it and called their attention to certain changes which they made to suit me. We had a few initial rehearsals. We were very happy with each other. I also met the cast, my Slovakian co-star and the whole production staff. It was good and worthwhile working with them, and I have great feelings about it all.

The film was made. The fact is that we wanted to make an artistic film. But none of us ever imagined that it would be such a hit over the entire world. You quoted me when you implied that one film can sometimes overshadow fifty years of work. For instance, I would never have had the opportunity to play Addis Ababa if the *Shop on Main Street* had not been shown there. It played all over the world, and it had its greatest success in America. We could not have imagined it. We were flabbergasted. It received an Oscar and I was nominated for an award. It was hailed the world over as a great film. We were particularly surprised about its impact in America. We had been told that people here did not like to hear about the war. They did not want to think about it too much, they did not wish to cry. Everyone says they have enough troubles and they don't want any part of it, especially the young people. But the film was seen by Jews as well as non-Jews, old and young, and this made a great impression on us. We who did not really know America, except from what we had heard, read or seen through other eyes, had to revise our opinions, especially after we came here. We realized that there are those who are interested in something truly artistic, even though it is without music and song, or without happiness, or sensationalism. The *Shop on Main Street* had such an impact on everyone that to this day I meet people who say to me,"I saw *"The Shop on Main Street* four times"; "I saw it three times"; "Once I stood on line for three hours to see it." In America there is an audience for serious art, theater and film.

RABBI BERKOWITZ: Let us return again to Poland. How do you feel about the Polish people and its government?

MME. KAMINSKA: I really cannot talk about a whole people. I cannot talk about a nation. There are good and bad everywhere. I do not exclude Jews. Naturally, I have more of a heart for the Jews. I observe their errors with different eyes. But that does not mean that I think we are perfect. Every nation has good and bad people. There are more of the bad, as well as more of the dishonest than the honest. That is the way of the world. I came to this conclusion after many years.

I cannot say that the Poles are the worst nation or the best. There is no question that among Poles there are good and worthwhile people. It is possible that among the Poles there are large numbers of people who permit themselves to be quickly influenced, particularly when they deal with or against Jews. Perhaps these people are weaker, perhaps they are more easily dominated. This is possible, but it is very difficult to weigh or measure it. But one cannot generalize about a nation. In Poland I have marvelous friends, friends who suffer greatly. A few, perhaps, but I have them. I wish you could have seen the tears that were shed by the Poles when I left, or read the letters I have received. When I left Poland they came to the Airport at five in the morning, and they went down on their knees and cried and kissed the hem of my dress, kissed my hands, bade me farewell and said, "What do you mean, you are leaving? Whom are we left with?" I cannot say that the whole Polish nation is terrible. They are perhaps weaker than other nations. I don't know. Maybe they cannot defend themselves. They have also lived through a great deal. They have always been crushed and persecuted. About Polish Jewry I cannot answer any questions. At this time it is difficult to say anything.

RABBI BERKOWITZ: You went to Israel and had an opportunity to settle there. Why didn't you? Why did you come to America?

MME KAMINSKA: I know this question interests many, but the question cannot even be put that way. I did not leave Israel. There is no question about that. When I left Poland, I went to America because I had to fulfill contracts, make a film, tour under the auspices of the same producers for whom I had worked two years earlier, and work with Macmillan to publish my memoirs. I had to attend to those things. At the same time I was assured that the American Jewish community would not let me leave, I would have to perform here. I would have a theater and everything possible would be done to help us continue our work.

While I was in Vienna waiting to come to America, I was

invited to come to Israel. I accepted with great enthusiasm and joy for many reasons, among them the fact that I have a one and only brother who lives there. Joseph Kaminsky is a well-known musician in the Israeli Philharmonic and a composer and concertmaster. I flew there, and the short period I stayed I now refer to as the most beautiful days in my life. To my misfortune, however, an impressario in Israel quickly latched on to me and insisted that I must perform there. I did not want to because I knew I had to go to America. Perhaps I would stay for a time and then later go to Israel. I told the Israelis that I had signed a contract to make a film in America. I was not sure which movie, but I knew that the director of the movie was to be the same director as in *The Shop on Main Street,* Jan Kadar. I knew I would have very good co-stars, although I did not exactly know the subject of the film. But I was still interested. I know what a film means. So I came to America, also with the intention of fulfilling a tour and doing the film. I immediately made the film, but unfortunately I had to curtail the tour because of illness. I felt badly about that, especially after all the experiences I had lived through and after all I had overcome. It was the first time that this had happened to me. I also had to ask Macmillan for an extension on my book because I could not write while in Warsaw and certainly not during my first period here.

In the interim there was talk about performing, about establishing a Yiddish theater in America. There are so many Jews, why not here? If I wanted to perform in Israel, I could play there *and* in America. If I could establish a theater here, I could play here *and* in Israel. Golda Meir and Shazar said to me, "If you wish to remain with us in Israel, we will receive you with joy; if you wish to leave, do so in good health; we extend our blessings to you, for your work is also a labor for us. It is a Jewish cultural work that can be brought to the whole world, for it is just as good for us as it is for all Jews the world over."

These are the words that I continue to repeat before every community. That is why I disagree with the statement that my departure meant that I left Israel. I will always return to Israel. What drove and carried me out of Poland was the thought that I could go to Israel. No matter where I am, no matter where I go, no one will succeed in parting me from Israel. When I was in Israel, I said, "You need the Jews of the world, but unfortunately you cannot accommodate them all in your country. And we, Jews of the world, need you, we *must* have you. This is the bond that cannot be torn asunder.

RABBI BERKOWITZ: And we, Jews of the world, people of the world, need Ida Kaminska. Benjamin Disraeli called the stage "a supplement of the pulpit, where virtue moves our love and affection." The Yiddish stage especially has been one of the great landmarks of the Jewish people and one of the great components of our heritage. As a leading luminary of the Yiddish stage, you helped develop that theater into a voice which spoke to Jews across the breadth of Eastern Europe; moving into the world of film, you translated a moment of our history into terms understood by all peoples.

Ida Kaminska, in telling us of your life in the theatre, you have helped us to experience a vibrant, creative period of Jewish life. In telling us of your more recent emotions with regard to Europe and Israel, you have deepened our insight into matters which touch us intimately today.

Our tradition has produced many men and women who have made great contributions to the arts. Some of these have been of interest only because they have been Jews: their work has been only peripherally touched by their Jewish background. Your whole career has been bound up with the fact of your Jewish origins, your Jewish feelings, your Jewish world. We appreciate the opportunity of having visited with you and sharing for too brief a moment your experiences.

RAMSEY CLARK

RABBI BERKOWITZ: Occasionally, a poor boy, born of humble circumstances, overcomes handicaps to rise to great heights. More rare is the son of a great father who overcomes the handicap of parental greatness to rise to his own peaks of great achievement. What might have been the case of a great man's son coasting down the path built by an illustrious father is instead in the instance of Ramsey Clark an example of a man who has built his own path in life.

Ramsey Clark has the inheritance of a great name. Tom Clark, his father, was a Justice of the Supreme Court of the United States. He is a son worthy of the name he has inherited, and his illustrious father continues to live in the works of his son, who became Attorney General of the United States under President Lyndon B. Johnson.

Basically, I have used as text for this discussion a book which I hope everyone will read: *Crime in America—Observations on its Nature, Causes, Prevention and Control,* by Mr. Clark. We are going to try to cover the overall theme of justice, crime, riots and famous trials; the issues of prison, the death penalty, gun control and the judicial system.

Let me begin with a phrase from the Bible that you are familiar with, a phrase that is often quoted by preachers: "Justice, justice shalt thou pursue." A rabbi once asked, Why the repetition? Why do we need the word "justice" twice? Is it not sufficient to say "Justice shalt thou pursue"? The sages answered with great wisdom and insight. First, we have to find justice; this accounts for the use of the word the first time. But in seeking out justice, the *means* should be just. Hence the second use of the word.

From this Biblical admonition I would like to turn to some areas of justice and elicit your thinking on several issues. In your book you write, "The criminal justice system has been tragically neglected in America for generations. It is a system in theory only." Would you elaborate on this observation?

MR. CLARK: It is an observation that is hard to elaborate on briefly, but I will try. We measure things in our time, unhappily, in part by expenditures. Our total expenditure for what we call our system of criminal justice—federal, state and local—in 1967, the first year we made a comprehensive effort to measure it, was a little better than five billion dollars. That year we spent 8.8 billion on tobacco and 12.5 billion on alcoholic beverages. I think that gives you some general impression of our priorities. The neglect that has characterized public attitudes toward the elements of our system of criminal justice is manifest every day. Read the Knapp Commission findings and read about Attica. Go to your criminal courts. A very close friend of mine, a lawyer who has not really practiced although he was an assistant attorney general with me, visited the courts today for the first time and could not believe them. They reminded him of my description of the courts in South Africa; masses of people huddled together waiting for their turn to go through.

We have not provided the resources, we have not provided the personnel, we have not provided the skills, we have not provided people from all walks of life to make our efforts in criminal justice effective. The police, in typical jurisdictions, are not in contact with the prosecutor to any appreciable degree. They send files over, they send witnesses over. The prosecutor has no sense of obligation, typically, to give priority to the police and to help them set goals for what they are doing. Courts are more often than not antagonists of the police; a typical characterization of their relationship is one of friction, of waste of manpower. Jails and prisons are in a class by themselves, warehouses of human degradation.

What has to be a system, an effective system, will fail unless police, prosecutuors, courts and corrections work effectively together. If any segment in that flow of human lives fails, the whole system fails. It is not a system, it is a jungle.

RABBI BERKOWITZ: You wrote that "the nation has a crazy-quilt pattern of 40,000 police jurisdictions, remnants of history." And you discuss the desirability, and the undesirability, of a national police force. You say that while many believe a national police force is desirable, you have strong reservations. Why?

MR. CLARK: I have more than reservations. I think first that a national police force cannot be effective. We are a very diverse people, and our strength is in our diversity and our differences. My experience with national bureaucracy is that it simply cannot be sensitive to the differences, the needs of the varieties of the people in this country. People desperately need, in this time of interdependence, to have some power to affect things that are important to them. If you have to deal with a far-away police force in Washington, D.C., about your safety in the streets, there is really no chance to have that power. Second, we fear for our freedom in America; I think we have lost part of our sense of its values. To the extent that we have been a vital and creative and good people, we have known freedom. We are afraid now, and there are many who tell us that we have to sacrifice freedom for safety. That is false dogma. We must have safety and freedom, or we have neither. I fear the ideologies that can creep into a national police force; I fear the power that it can exert over our freedom. It is critically important for the individual American that we have local police that are responsive to the people where they live.

RABBI BERKOWITZ: What about the use of parapolice aides. We have seen examples of this in certain parts of New York City. Do you think this idea is of any consequence?

MR. CLARK: I believe that if we are ever going to get serious about police service and ever conceive of it as something different from a paramilitary force, the essential role of the helper is clear. What are the police doing? You cannot count the variety of activities. The range of professional skills that is essential within a police department is broader than the range of professional skills in any other function. They have to have sound lawyers if we are going to have a sound system of law. They have to have effective medical aid if we are going to avoid unnecessary serious injury and loss of life. They are not able to deal with violence without using violence and causing violence; they will have to be terribly skilled in the dynamics of family breakup, which generates most of the violence in America.

They are going to have to have helpers; they are going to have to conceive of themselves as an important social service. They are going to have to be deeply integrated in the community. To do this, they will have to have people who live in the neighborhoods and who are known there. They will have to encourage the young; they are going to have to accept young people who do not have the training, the background and maturity of professional police officers to help them with the young who are involved in so many of our crimes.

RABBI BERKOWITZ: You deal with many myths and misconceptions about crime in your book. For example, we are very much concerned with crime in the streets and with violence. Yet you say that "white collar crime is the most corrosive of all crimes." What is white collar crime, and why do you consider it to be the most corrosive?

MR. CLARK: White collar crime is generally antisocial conduct by people of opportunity, advantage and power—conduct that is prohibited because it manifests a particular degree of greed or insensitivity to others. It is the embezzlement of church funds. It is failure to support the government by cheating on taxes that are essential to all the public services that we know. It is fixing prices of milk, bread, other things that poor people have to buy to stay alive. It can reach much deeper into a family's welfare and stability than the thief who takes money from bureau drawers, than the mugger who can injure you and take your purse.

It can wipe out the frugality and savings of a lifetime. It can cause you to be swindled for improvements to your home that are never made and leave your home in a greater state of disrepair. It can give you an automobile that is dangerous or a television set that does not work.

It is corrosive because it destroys the confidence of people in the integrity of our national character. These white collar thieves do not steal because they are hungry. You remember Anatole France's phrase from *The Red Lily*—that the law in its majestic equality prohibits the rich as well as the poor from stealing bread, begging in the streets and sleeping under bridges. These are people of opportunity; they are people of means, and their crimes manifest the inherent immoral capacity of our national character. It is terribly corrosive.

I daresay that price fixing sounds very benign. We ought to ask ourselves, Is it benign or is it the theft of power? It is men with power getting together and saying that this commodity—an electric light bulb, or a loaf of bread—is essential to everyone in this community, and it is controlled by us. We can have a reasonable profit of 25 cents for the bulb or 12 cents for the loaf of bread. But let's charge 40 cents for a loaf of bread and 80 cents for a light bulb. One price-fixing conspiracy by an electrical company which went on for four or five years actually diverted more money each year than all the burglaries, larcenies or thefts in the United States combined. If you think about it, then what hope is there really for us if we condone such "benign" activities?

RABBI BERKOWITZ: You made an interesting observation that surprised me and I think will surprise nine out of ten Americans, if not ten out of ten: "To the extent that it has been reported, murder occurred less frequently per capita in the U. S. in the 1960's than during the 1920's and 1930's." Can you elaborate a bit? All of us read statistics about so many murders every day or every week, yet you say there are fewer in the last decade than in the twenties and the thirties.

MR. CLARK: It is only fair to preface this answer with my judgment that ignorance characterizes our knowledge of criminal justice more than fact. We really do not know. And statistics are dangerous for a number of reasons. One, we forget that they involve one human being at a time and they tend to be dehumanized in that way; and two, they can be quite misleading and can be used in misleading ways purposely or unconsciously. We do not really know. We began with our national crime reports in the early thirties. The rate of murder per hundred thousand population in most of those years exceeded the rate of murder per hundred thousand during the sixties. My judgment is that our recording system in the sixties was far more effective and far more proficient than it was in the thirties.

You can document, as has been done, counties in the South, and not just there, where deaths of Blacks weekly or monthly were never listed as violent deaths or accidental deaths. They just simply were not recorded. The number of police departments and the proportion of the population they covered was much less in the thirties.

Karl Menninger said that he thinks our capacity for violence—and this is a highly subjective judgment—in the nineteenth century was far, far greater than our capacity for violence today. I think that he is right. I think there are differences in the quality of violence today, too; it is an irrational, frustrated type of violence, as distinguished from the cruel, calculated, purposeful violence that characterizes other countries. But we have a high capacity for this irrational, emotional frustration that leads to violence. My reading of the statistics and of history, and my experience is that murder is substantially down from yesteryear, but far, far from where it ought to be.

RABBI BERKOWITZ: The daily newspapers are filled with stories about how organized crime is infiltrating legitimate business in the United States. But you say that organized crime, its wealth and income "are exaggerated beyond reason and that there is no one massive organization that manages all or even most of the planned and continuous criminal conduct throughout the country." Most of us have a different impression. What is the state of organized crime?

MR. CLARK: We've passed Auden's "age of anxiety" and are almost in an age of incoherence; we desperately seek an explanation for the human conduct around us. This is the essential rationale for the conspiracy theory—we want desperately to believe that a mob of Sicilians have come into this country and are causing all this trouble; it absolves us of any responsibility. But it doesn't work that way. The Crime Commission which began its studies in 1966 went to seventy-six cities and could find the presence of organized crime in nineteen and an indication of its existence in seven others. Twenty-six out of seventy-six. They found in the remainder no organized crime reported publicly or detectable by investigation. Crime was as high or higher in those places as it was in places where organized crime existed.

Organized crime is different from other crime in that it deals with goods and services that people want. This is a small part of what I mean when I say that crime reflects the character of the people. Nobody wants to get robbed or assaulted or to have his car stolen, but people want to gamble, they want narcotics and prostitution, or they need money so desperately that they will pay any amount of interest. These sources represent at least 80 percent of all income of organized crime.

There are three conditions that are essential for the existence of organized crime because it is a daily retail trade. They are, first, the accumulation in a general area of thousands of powerless people. Organized crime is not providing narcotics for the kids in the suburbs because it has to do business tomorrow. It knows how dangerous such traffic would be because the parents of the kids in the suburbs have some power, and there will be a day of reckoning. But organized crime can, as it has for years, supply narcotics with impunity to the poor and powerless people of the central city. In 1900, when we were 76 million people in this country, we had far more people addicted to opium and its derivatives than we have in the 1970's when we are probably 215 million. And organized crime was supplying it then as it supplies much of our narcotics now.

Secondly, there must be an effort to control by law enforcement conduct which you know people engage in. You know that millions of people gamble. You know that among the poor there is little opportunity or hope other than the numbers that they bet on if they can scrape up the money. You know that they are playing the numbers regularly, and you know that organized crime is annually raking off millions and millions of dollars from the poorest people among us. Yet we have no more creative way of stopping this than to say they cannot do it, and if they do, they are guilty of a crime for which they will be put in the penitentiary, knowing all the time that we cannot enforce our law. Prohibition was a classic example. Prohibition was a great fountainhead for new criminal organizations in that era.

The third element is the corruption and neutralization of the elements of law enforcement. How can it be that the police officer on the beat in Hunts Point or Bedford-Stuyvesant does not know who the bookie is—everyone else knows. He does know, and the kids who live there know he knows. That doesn't give the kids any confidence in the system, or respect for the law. They see prostitutes on the corner, and they see the guy who sold them their first fix consummating a transaction right in front of an officer.

You cannot have this situation very long and hope to have a system that is believed in. And a system that is not believed in is not going to work. That is elementary in human nature. We *can* end organized crime. It does not have to exist—there are whole nations in the world today that do not have it. There are whole states in this country that do not have it. When you neglect law enforcement while you keep millions of powerless people cramped in the central cities, when you call acts crimes but you know that millions of people are doing them and you cannot effectively merely enforce them away, you have organized crime. Organization is a symptom of social disease rather than the cause of crime.

RABBI BERKOWITZ: You just touched on my next category:

crime, the cause and the cure. I am going to suggest that two of your statements in your book may be contradictory. You write, "We have witnessed more fundamental change in the way people live and the nature of their society during this century than in all previous history. We shall witness more change in the remainder of the century than throughout history to date. It is change that causes revolution, not revolution that causes change." Then you say, "In so complex a mass society, it becomes increasingly difficult for an individual to find human dignity, a sense of purpose, a meaning in life. His impotence to affect in the slightest way things of utmost importance overwhelms him." Yet, you also say, "We can prevent nearly all of the crime in America if we care." Mr. Clark, is there an inconsistency here? If technology seems to be increasing crime, of what consequence is my caring against the forces of mass society?

MR. CLARK: My reading of Deuteronomy teaches me that one has to care. If we do not have a passion for justice we limit the extent that man can affect his destiny. I do not believe that there has ever been a people in history that so manifestly and abundantly has had the capacity that we have to solve all our problems. I think that we are going to have to *want* to solve them. Two of our chief problems today are violence and segregation.

What is the connection between the fire bombing of Dresden and our involvement in Indo-China? What is the connection between Kent State and Attica? The answer is that people who resort to violence as a problem solver will shoot their children. That is the lesson of ₁Kent State. Typically, the subject of violence is going to be the Black or the foreigner, the one we fear or despise, but when the chips are down and we have conditioned ourselves to violence as a problem solver, that is what is going to happen.

Then there is segregation. We use segregation all the time. And not only by skin but even by age, as when we segregate the elderly. Look at what this means to us. How does a little child get some sense of what life's purpose is, where we go and why we are here, without the elderly? What does he miss by not knowing that wisdom and that gentleness and that love of the old? He is segregated because the modern urban family is so fragile it cannot quite hold together. Then we segregate races and what happens? All their disabilities are compounded, and we have frustrations and fears and riots. Prisons are the classical example of segregation. There is no more complete failure in our efforts than prisons. Even in prisons we try to segregate in solitary confinement. And what happens? Suicide and rage.

We must begin to change that. We are going to have to care. We are going to have to see that we really know what the problems are. We know what the causes of crime are. We don't want to admit it, but we know. Did you ever think of the relationship between hunger and crime? It is enormous. What might you do if you were hungry? What might happen to you if your grandmother and your mother were hungry and you were retarded? Eighty percent of mental retardation in this country occurs in the 10 percent of the poorest people among us. Malnutrition is a major factor. How many billions did we spend last year to keep rich farmers from growing more food? Can we not bring those two factors together? Of course we can, and then we will begin to solve the problem.

Until we care, until we are concerned about the welfare of others, until we can see in ourselves racism and fear and greed and violence, and overcome it, and know that in our interdependence when any one person suffers, we suffer too, we are going to be in for turbulent times. Perhaps we should be.

RABBI BERKOWITZ: I couldn't agree with you more. I think

that this is the great issue in any learning process or in human dynamics—I see this in my work. I frankly don't admire people who don't care. And I have the greatest admiration for people who care; care about many things, care about people, care about conditions, care about life, care about all the issues that are uppermost in our minds.

You have been involved in a famous trial, and I would like you to comment on it. As the late President Johnson's chief law officer, you authorized the prosecution of Dr. Benjamin Spock and the Reverend William Sloan Coffin for conspiring to counsel evasion of the draft. At the time you said that they so disagreed with their government that they would sacrifice freedom itself to show their concern. Why did you feel that this prosecution was justified?

MR. CLARK: That case was my responsibility directly. I made that decision, and it is often hard to know all the things that lead one to make a decision. The time was the fall of 1967. The protest against the war in Indo-China—with which I sympathized fully—was at fever pitch. The activities of many individuals who directed efforts in the United States to conduct the war were growing, and in this system there were laws to uphold it. In my judgement if the system is to have integrity, it has to enforce its laws. If change is to be effected, where the laws are wrong and where they are not deeply rooted in moral pinciple, then the law has to be enforced so that the people can see that it is wrong. I felt that Thoreau was probably right for not paying his taxes in protest of the war, but I thought had he not been prosecuted for it, there would have been a failure of the system and an inability for him to make his point.

I had other concerns. I was concerned about the thousands of young people who were putting their futures and their lives on the line in the cruelest and hardest way—there are few things more difficult to withstand than ostracism from those whom you respect and love and the anger and heartbreak of a mother or father. I had experience in World War II with conscientious objectors. I thought that among them were the strongest and the best men that we had, and at that time I saw many of them crushed. I wanted to avoid that with as many young people as I could, so I picked on some people who could take care of themselves, with a test case of five defendants. The difficulties with the case were enormous. I think if I had been sitting on the court, I would have voted with the judge of the First Circuit Court who dissented with the majority and dismissed all the cases on First Amendment grounds.

But the main difficulties in the case were the conspiracy counts and the proximity of the conduct to the question of expression of speech, which is almost inherent in the situation.

RABBI BERKOWITZ: Why were the Chicago Seven accused of crossing state lines to incite riot at the Democractic Convention in August of 1968? What did this trial tell us about ourselves and our times?

MR. CLARK: To me, the trial of the Chicago Seven showed a total failure of the system. The Congress enacted a statute, called the Rap Brown Statute, which gives you some impression of its motivation, in fear and in anger. In my judgment, we have had many riots over the years in this country, and they have been deemed the responsibility of local law enforcement. As a practical matter, the federal government has no capacity to deal with a riot. And there was not a riot in the 1960's in which military presence was achieved before the riot was over. It just takes that long to move soldiers. Moreover, a society which wants to be free and have dignity will not use military power in a domestic disturbance.

So the statute was in many ways a fraud. It was not necessary; local government could have handled the problem.

It was not effective; the Federal government could not have added significantly to the police capacity needed to deal with it. How many times has it been used in all the turbulent situations that we have had, and what does it really say? Any bar room brawl involving five people could theoretically come under the statute if one of the participants had driven over from Newark, New Jersey, or down from Greenwich, Connecticut, with the idea that he might get involved.

The problem arose from the failure of the City of Chicago to recognize the meaning of the First Amendment. The Department of Justice had pleaded with city officials to give the protesters the opportunity to assemble, to petition their government. Soldiers Field was available. It can hold a hundred thousand people, is solid concrete and would take a lot of work to damage. The protesters had asked for permission to use it; they literally could not have filled two percent of the seats. It was safe out there, there was plenty of land around it: parking lots, freeways, Lake Michigan on one side, the Illinois Central railroad tracks on the other. There was no way in which they could hurt themselves on the concrete benches. But that was denied. If the city had lived up to the spirit of the First Amendment at the time, the demonstrators could have spoken and perhaps some steam would have been let off and frustrations eased.

The police, in my judgment, used excessive force. They struck out in anger at people. If you want to live under a government of laws, if you want to have some condfidence that the police will not strike out at you with the same emotion someday, you do what you can to see that government itself never violates the law and that the police do not act emotionally but rationally and consistent with lawful purpose. There was a riot in the courtroom which was emotionalized in large measure by the court. And the man who prosecuted the case was full of animus—I don't know whether you read the press reports of the speech he made after the trial in which he referred to the defendants as "faggots" and despicable people, none of whom he could have any respect for, except Bobby Seale. Apparently that shows that he had no racial prejudice.

The prosecutor was a witness to the events. Now, we know it is an elemental rule of justice that witnesses do not participate as judges, jurors or lawyers. At the time I was Attorney General he had been a United States Attorney, and we had removed him from the case. He was a protege of Mayor Daley and very close to the mayor, and that is just not the way the law is supposed to work. I will never understand how Bobby Seale got into this case. I had reviewed the evidence and refused to indict him. The evidence that I saw said that Bobby Seale had participated in no way in the peace movement, that he had no plans to come to Chicago. Eldridge Cleaver had accepted a fee to come and speak in Chicago. They wanted Cleaver because he could pull an audience, and they wanted to tell people from out of the state to come and hear Cleaver, but Cleaver could not come. Seale came at the last moment, and he made a speech in Lincoln Park on Tuesday night and in Grant Park Wednesday night; it was the same speech he had made a hundred times in a hundred different places in probably fifteen or twenty states, and then he left.

What do you do in a case like that? There were hundreds of people who had worked for weeks to get people to come there; what about them? I think there is some idea that you can keep the action and passion of our times out of the courtroom and that when people walk through that door their character is going to change; that there will be serenity and pure reason. However, life is not like that, neither is human nature. The trial was an abuse of the system of law and an injustice, compounded in the contempt citations and convictions which came out of it.

RABBI BERKOWITZ: As a former Attorney General of the United States you have had an intimate, day-by-day acquaintance with the office. You comment in your book on the office of Attorney General and John Mitchell and you say that during the 1960's we witnessed much information divulged wrongfully. Among those whose reputations were damaged are: Justice Abe Fortas, Senator Edward Long of Missouri, Governor James Rhodes of Ohio, Frank Sinatra, Roy Cohn, James R. Hoffa.

MR. CLARK: This manifests a failure of integrity in government. If we are to know justice, then the government can never put itself above the law. The question is not whether the Berrigans are good people or whether Roy Cohn is a nice guy. Those things will tend to take care of themselves. If they have injured society in any way society can protect itself and deal with them. But if the government can decide who are good people and who are bad people, whom it likes and whom it does not like, and if it can use the enormous power it gets from its store of information on individuals to damage them, then I see little hope of its ability to deal with the problems of the future.

The classic example is probably Dr. Martin Luther King. I do not think we begin to perceive the importance of the message that this man had for our world. Social change is what he sought and nonviolence was his method. He caused people to believe. Now we understand that the FBI had electronic surveillance on him—wiretaps—and unsavory personal qualities were said to be revealed in these. The FBI played these tapes for senators, editors, opinion makers.

If the government can do that, what is going to happen to us? Perhaps that action changed the history of the civil rights movement, a movement which struggled against racism, a problem which can be solved in our generation or which will involve us in unthinkable violence.

The government simply cannot permit such violations of personal privacy.

RABBI BERKOWITZ: You say that under Attorney General John Mitchell, the U. S. Department of Justice regularly placed investigative information from official sources in the press. You add that if the Attorney General has evidence of a crime, he should indict in court, not in the press. You state that "the Department of Justice announced that it was investigating leaders of the Vietnam Moratorium march of November 15, 1969, even citing one by name," and that "this may be good politics but it slowly destroys justice."

MR. CLARK: I think that the legal function of the prosecutor is clear: to enforce laws. And the procedure is clear: first, to cause information and facts to be gathered or to gather facts that are evidence of a violation of the law; then, in the light of our Fourth Amendment, to present them to a grand jury; and then, if the grand jury believes that there is probable cause to believe that a crime has been committed, to prosecute.

I think that this is a rational system which, when the people care, can be just. It can preserve freedom and provide safety. I think that when the prosecutor, who is also human, takes it upon himself to gather information, or not to gather information but say that he has, and characterize people to the public, he will destroy or impair the potential of those individuals. If you look back in history you will see that this tactic has almost always been used against people who seek change, against people who protest injustice.

Through the social contract the people have said that certain acts should be unlawful. The prosecutor has the responsibility of vigorously, but fairly, presenting evidence of these acts to grand juries and petit juries, but not to destroy reputations or poison minds and act as a big brother to all of us to say these are the bad people and these are the good people.

RABBI BERKOWITZ: There has been a great deal of discussion about the FBI, and at the same time about the late

Mr. Hoover. Would you want to comment on the role of the FBI? What about the man who had been the head of it for so many years?

MR. CLARK: The FBI is one of the more than twenty federal civilian investigative agencies. It is an important investigative agency, with responsibility in the areas of what we would call general federal crime. New York City has and needs at least five times the number of police officers that the FBI has for the entire country. The FBI has important responsibilities and opportunities; it deals in part with crimes that are of a dimension that can affect many people, and therefore it is imperative that it be an example of excellence.

The FBI provides one of the better chances for state and local law enforcement to learn of the general national experience and raise their own professional standards. The FBI is a critically important agency.

I think we are fortunate indeed that Mr. Hoover consistently resisted an expansion of its activities, even when there was some urging that he do so. He refused to take on many areas of federal investigation. Narcotics is one example, as is protection of the President, which is a Secret Service function. He consistently spoke against a national police force, and resisted within the limits of his own rights—and we all have that limit—the characterization of the FBI as a national police force. He brought excellence and vitality to a major bureaucracy, and that is a valuable lesson when many begin to wonder whether that is possible.

RABBI BERKOWITZ: What do you think of the present Supreme Court and those who in recent years have been appointed?

MR. CLARK: In the principal contests of our time, which are between the forces that seek change and those that resist change, the United States Supreme Court with this quality of personnel will be aligned with the forces that resist change. I believe that this is too bad, because I think that change is inescapable and desirable.

The history of the Supreme Court under the leadership of the late Chief Justice Earl Warren is epochal in the quality of its justice. The Supreme Court of the United States is inherently the most conservative institution in American government, and I defy anyone to reach a different analysis. It provides life tenure and is composed of elderly men with long training in a conservative discipline and common backgrounds of advantage and wealth, power and prestige. There are no elections to the Court. But somehow the Warren Court saw the three greatest needs of this country, and it tried within the spirit of our Constitution to create the opportunity for change.

It detected racism as something that would destroy our country, and that is what its civil rights decisions were all about.

It detected the incapacity of institutions of government themselves to change, institutions that were frozen and paralyzed in the mode of the 19th century, and that is what reapportionment cases were all about. . . . that government must represent people, not trees or acreage, in Warren's phrase.

It detected the central question of our time, human dignity, and said that the most despised and feared among us shall, to the extent that we can achieve it, know equal justice. So if you are miserable and poor, or retarded like a Mexican-American from Arizona named Miranda, and charged with rape, you have the same right as a rich advantaged man not to be taken advantage of in interrogation. If you are a drifter who never had a job or stayed in one place long like Clarence Earl Gideon, and are charged with burglary and cannot afford a lawyer, you have a right to a lawyer just like the rich and mighty.

Some Justices represent a desire to return to the past, but we cannot return to the past. I respect their legal ability, respect their integrity, but I say that they are behind the times and the demands of that Court. The needs of the people of this country are not to be fulfilled by that kind of philosophy.

With others I see more difficult problems. I am concerned about commitment to freedom. I do not believe that some of them really support or understand the Bill of Rights. The Bill of Rights to me is not just a string of old words, it stands for the spirit of man, the right to think and be yourself, speak and print and publish and pray. For example, I can hear a Justice saying that he believes that the Executive can wiretap without a court order, and I can hear him saying that he does not know what the presumption of innocence is, because the government is going to detain peole who are charged with crime until they are tried. And, for that matter, I can see him drawing up a plan for arresting thousands and thousands of youngsters who went to the nation's capital in Washington because they were concerned about our violence in Indo-China, nearly all of whom were dismissed by the courts because there weren't those stubborn little things called facts to support charges against them. Many could not even be identified by the arresting officer as having been anywhere at any time or done anything.

I just don't want that philosophy on the Supreme Court when we need freedom so desperately.

RABBI BERKOWITZ: I have from time to time asked one basic question of participants in these dialgoes. It is not an easy one. If you could go back in history, and if you could meet three people, who would these three people be and why would you select them?

MR. CLARK: You know, I am not really oriented that way. Hypotheses contrary to fact are difficult for me. I am deeply concerned about the present and future. I have my prejudices;

as Will Rogers used to say, we are all prejudiced but on different subjects. Of course, ignorance is the mother of prejudice.

I would have wanted to meet Abraham Lincoln. He left us just about a million words, his own words, and I have lived with them. You know, I worry abut our failure to speak for ourselves. It is so important to know people, particularly people in whom we have to place confidence, yet now they all have speech writers and ghost writers. How do we really know them? Lincoln wrote his own stuff. You can read it. I find in it the most tenacious truths, and I find a person who is disenthralled from prejudice, seeking truth. I find a native wisdom there and a beauty.

I would have liked to have known Beethoven and Anatole France, and all kinds of people like that. Jefferson fascinates me, with all the layers of culture and aristocracy that he must have had. But there is something raw and pure and beautiful about Lincoln.

I would like to have met Moses. This is perhaps the responsibility not of the authors of the Bible, but of Thomas Mann. It also means, you see, that I am very skeptical about history. I studied history and love it, but I think it is written largely by the force of the imagination. The more I see things written about things I know, the more I know how very hard it is.

I am interested in the movers of people. I don't really see, in our time—that is, in these last hundred years, leaders moving people. I see them for the most part safely behind where the people are. Moses was a force and he could move people, and he had what I consider to be a fierce outrage for justice. He had—and this is apart from the Tablets of the Law—a sense of pity that is an important quality to me because it is so humanly based. The pity that Moses could manifest when morality broke loose balanced his fierce strength and determination. He was a very, very interesting person.

RABBI BERKOWITZ: And why Beethoven?

MR. CLARK: Shaw called Beethoven the most turbulent spirit that ever found expression in pure sound, and I find him thrilling. I just do. The enormous passion of the man. I am still inspired every time I hear his human power. He was not afraid of turbulence or passion. He was a very interesting man who felt a need beyond his music that Mozart never felt. If Beethoven saw an arbitrary power, he would face it and even pursue it; he could be characterized as a disobliging steamroller.

His torment was his deafness. It is ironical that a man to whom sound meant so much and who could convey such beauty in human spirit through sound, should lose his sense of hearing. His pettiness in all his personal relations really, I think, spoke of his strength. But the thing I see most in Beethoven is the unbelievable richness of his human spirit.

RABBI BERKOWITZ: In your position as Attorney General is there one incident, one moment, one experience, that somehow is paramount and continues to remain uppermost in your mind?

MR. CLARK: Not really, you know. I just do not personalize things. I have had no crises in my life. My only regret is that I could not go further and do more.

RABBI BERKOWITZ: That sort of dissatisfaction with one's life is a sentiment which should motivate us all. Speaking from the other side, in a sense, I might say that you have gone a long way and done a great deal for America and for the American people whom you evidently love so greatly. In an age when concern is often replaced by indifference, when honor is often subordinated to convenience, when courage often gives way to compromise, you have given us, through your public service and your private endeavors, a glimpse of what man can achieve. Our country is the better because you have had the opportunity to hold high office. We have been privileged to hear from a truly thoughtful, concerned and effective individual, for which we extend our thanks to Ramsey Clark.

MARIE SYRKIN

RABBI BERKOWITZ: Within our lifetime, a great and unforgettable personality appeared on the Jewish scene. His name was Dr. Nachman Syrkin, a socialist and Zionist theoretician, whose contributions are still acclaimed today. We have heard it said that renowed parents do not often have famous offspring. However, a notable exception to the general rule is the very distinguished lady, Dr. Marie Syrkin. She has earned in her own name an international reputation as an author, as an editor—in particular, of the *Jewish Frontier*—as a lecturer and teacher. For many years she was professor of humanities at Brandeis University. At present she serves with great distinction and devotion as a member of the Executive Board of the Jewish Agency for Israel.

The pages of Jewish history are filled with tales and incidents of resistance, of people or groups of people determined not only to live their lives but to carry on a way of life and a mission which across centuries of history was a mandate given to them at Mt. Sinai. Too often, we associate Jewish resistance movements and Jewish bravery with something in the far distant past, in a history book. Yet in our time we have seen Jewish resistance, in Palestine. There, a handful of people were determined to survive. They said, "We shall live, we shall create a new Jewish state." And create it they did, with great glory and valor.

Also, we were witnesses, some of us even participants, in a resistance against the most diabolical force of evil that the world has ever beheld—Nazi Germany. This was a struggle that often ended in death, but was fought with bravery, honor and courage.

While Dr. Syrkin has written several books, I want to concentrate only on one because of its historical value and its insights as to what went on in the lives of our people during one of the most tragic periods of Jewish history.

In 1947, Dr. Syrkin wrote *Blessed is the Match*, unquestionably one of the most stirring and meaningful documents of the Jewish resistance movement against Nazi Germany. Dr. Syrkin, why and under what circumstances did you write this book?

DR. SYRKIN: It is always very interesting for someone who has written a book to be asked to tell what prompted the writing of it. Like most Jews in America, during those terrible years in the forties, I was concerned by a question which began to trouble us subsequently even more. The more we heard in the early forties of the destruction, the more anxious I became to find out whether there had been any attempts to act against that destruction.

In 1945 the war with Germany had already been concluded and the war with Japan was practically over. About that time I heard from many Palestinians about a remarkable girl parachutist, Hannah Senesh, who had perished in Hungary after she had parachuted in from Palestine. She had written a poem which was the theme song of Palestine in 1945, "Blessed Is the Match That Is Consumed in Kindling Flame."

RABBI BERKOWITZ: I would like to read some of the other lines: "Blessed is the match that is consumed in kindling flame,/Blessed is the flame that burns in the secret fastness of the heart./Blessed is the heart with strength to stop its beating for honor's sake./Blessed is the match that is consumed in kindling flame."

DR. SYRKIN: The poem seemed to me so wonderful. The sense of something slight, a match, that cannot be very much, but that can be consumed in kindling flame, seemed the absolute essence of sacrificial heroism. I remember asking a Palestinian to visit me and tell me about Hannah Senesh. He was an important man involved in the underground. As he talked more and more about Hannah Senesh I was very thrilled. Then he suddenly said to me, "I have to make an important telephone call." He went to make the call and came back into the living room saying, "I have to go now. Besides, why should I tell you about it; go to Palestine and find the people who were engaged in the resistance." At the moment it seemed completely logical and reasonable. The thing to do was to go there to speak to the members of the resistance and to those who had emerged from the ghettos and had escaped and made their way to Palestine. It was a little hard to get there. One could not get a plane, and it took three weeks by boat, but that was not important. I got there. And that book was the result of interviewing these people who had been in the Resistance and who had lived through it. I wrote the story immediately, as I remembered it.

RABBI BERKOWITZ: Did you limit your research and

documentation to Palestine alone, or did you go elsewhere before writing the book? Did you visit the DP camps at any time?

DR. SYRKIN: Remember this was the summer of 1945. Movement was limited. The only place to get material—directly from the people who had experienced it, the people who had been active in the Resistance—was in Palestine. There was no exception to this. Subsequently, a year and a half later, I went to the DP camps and got much more material, but by then the book had already been written.

RABBI BERKOWITZ: Let's turn to the book and the chapter called "The Underground Network." In speaking about the rescue of Jews from Europe, you stated: "At the outset the entire rescue operation was a Jewish one. The great powers displayed no active concern in the drama being enacted behind the Nazi curtain, the deliberate scientific massacre of six million men, women and children." You wrote: "It is important to stress this point, not for the purpose of leveling an accusation against the world's incomprehensible indifference with regard to history's great crime, for no accusation can be bitter or grave enough, but so that one can appreciate with what limited strength and by what few hands the work was done."

You have a fascinating chapter "The Office in Istambul"—could you tell us about this office, and, in particular, how the code using Hebrew names fooled the Germans?

DR. SYRKIN: The office in Istambul consisted of Palestinian Jews who had made their way to outposts. We must remember what the situation was. Europe was a Nazi fortress, with all of it in Hitler's hands. At certain points there were attempts to bore from the outside in. This was not the situation that existed after the war, when some frontiers were down and there were attempts to go illegally over other frontiers. During the war the continent was hermetically sealed under the control of Hitler's armies. The Jews in Istambul were individuals, small in number but great human beings with so little at their command, attempting to establish contact within. I have sometimes thought of the parallel of miners who have been entombed, where the people above are knocking and listening and trying to contact them, and when they are lucky, hearing some kind of an answering sound. It was the same process. This was an awesome attempt to get to the heart of Europe, particularly Poland, where the great misfortune was raging at its utmost in order to establish contact or even to get them out. To get someone out did not necessarily mean to get them out of Europe, but to get them perhaps from one depot to another depot, or from Poland to Czechoslovakia. From Czechoslovakia one could get to another country, farther away from the Hitler terror.

Now, they had their *shlichim,* who at times managed to penetrate. A Palestinian could not suddenly just appear in the heart of Europe. How was it done? At times they engaged German businessmen who cooperated with them. These businessmen had the right to travel, and they usually got as far as Poland, for instance, with messages. They did it for pay, rarely for idealistic reasons. Sometimes this was successful. In the office in Palestine, where I was looking for material on this, they had somehow received code communications from the heart of the Warsaw Ghetto. An example of the code they used was to write the Hebrew words for "Uncle Gus is with us," or "Auntie Sarah is in our midst this moment." Or, by using the Hebrew words for Simon, "Simon so-and-so is with Auntie so-and-so." It was a simple code, and it is hard to understand how the Germans were fooled by it.

But they were able to communicate by using just a few words allotted to them, so that somehow a pretty clear understanding of conditions within the ghettos reached Istambul and Palestine. Even when it came to the Warsaw Ghetto uprising, somehow they got the message to Palestine.

RABBI BERKOWITZ: This reminds me of a friend who tells the story of someone in his family who received a letter from relatives in the Soviet Union. It was a very enthusiastic and glowing report of life in Russia. It said that Jewish life was flourishing—that not only were they able to study Yiddish, but Hebrew, and all the things that go with it. And at the very end, the letter was signed *Moishe Kapoire*. Perhaps by this time the Politburo has learned what this means.

Dr. Syrkin, of the period of the Jewish resistance movement you wrote, "They too were zealots and visionaries, consumed with the passion to reach the Jews of Europe." You were speaking of the Palestinians. Then you said very movingly, "As I sat there with them [referring to the Palestinians] I could not help asking myself for the hundredth time, 'Why was there no such inner compulsion among the Jews in America?'"

Dr. Syrkin, why was this so, and what evidence do you have for this? What comment would you like to make today with respect to this statement of some years ago?

DR. SYRKIN: The evidence is that the Jews of America did not act, they just did not. And I do not think that this is a matter that I must in any way prove. Of course, there is the question "Why?" I think it would be presumptuous of me to answer. It is more significant to give the answer that the Palestinians gave us. We have had many discussions on it. There were 600,000 Jews in Palestine who were consumed by the feeling that it was their business to do something about the Jews in Europe. They saw to it that the British government sent the parachutists. It was not much, but it was as much as they could do. Subsequently they organized the illegal immigration; they did all these things. Here, with five million Jews in America—we had protest meetings. Now, the Jews of Palestine explained this to us: we have five million Jews, many of them rich and powerful, while there were 600,000 Jews under the British mandate, not even in a free democracy, yet they infiltrated the Axis. Why the difference? The difference, as they themselves said, was that they were 600,000 who had to fight as a people. They were accustomed to think as a people, and when a group thinks of itself as a people, they act as a people. They did not say, "We are only 600,000 individuals, what can we do?" They said, "I am a member of a people and my people is being tortured and destroyed. I cannot be indifferent to what is happening to my people because I am that people." And they did not ask, "Is it possible, is it reasonable, will it be successful?" They did what they had to do out of their passionate concern.

I do not think we can exempt any of us, we American Jews. What was our situation? In the first place, it took a long time to believe that what was happening was actually true. The Jews in Palestine, because of an entirely different psychology, because of the historic reasons that led them to Palestine, were much more psychologically prepared to believe what was happening. In addition, the first witnesses were among them. By the time it began to percolate into our minds, we also felt that we were good American citizens and we had to do what the American government wanted us to do, and the last thing the American government wanted was disturbance, uproar, change in immigration quotas, anything they thought would impede the war effort. We did nothing to rock the boat, with America in the war, with inconvenient demands and questions. The people in Palestine began by rocking the boat, and they never worried about it. They had been rocking the British boat for a long time. They were doing it for themselves and out of their enormous sense of national responsibility.

Very simply, if you are a Zionist in Palestine, you obviously have a more consuming sense of national responsibility. If you are an American, you have to face the fact that this is what happened historically, and I am not at all certain that it would not happen again. In a similar crisis, in a great crisis, what would be the reaction of American Jewry and what would be the reaction of Israel? We can just take it right down the line. Who catches Eichmann and tries him? Not the respectable American Jew, he would not do anything unlawful. It is Israel. And I think that this feeling of national responsibility is the basis of the nation.

RABBI BERKOWITZ: In your book you have a chapter called "Eichmann Makes an Offer." What is this about?

DR. SYRKIN: When you try to piece a story together, as I did in this book, you go to all sources. I went to the mother of Hannah Senesh, and she told me about how she had seen her daughter in a Hungarian prison. I went to a Palestinian, a friend of Hanah Senesh, and heard another part of her story. One day, someone came to me in Tel-Aviv, a very interesting chap. He did not seem to be doing much then, but he had a very interesting history. His name was Joel Brand, and he claimed to have negotiated with Eichmann. This was in 1945. I have a special reason for mentioning this now. He died several years ago, but this all happened about thirty years ago. I met him, he told me his story, and I put it down as he told it to me. You are familiar with the story. It was late in the war, and he was told by various intermediaries that Eichmann had made an offer that for ten thousand trucks for the Russian front, plus a certain amount of medicine and other things, the Germans would release a million Jews.

Negotiations began with Eichmann, who said—and I remember the words this man told me—*"Blut fur Waren—Waren fur Blut,"* "Blood for goods—goods for blood." They notified the Jewish Agency, the people in Palestine, and brought it to the attention of the British authorities, who in turn told Roosevelt. It was dismissed as an attempt to divide the Allies. Russia was our ally and the trucks would have been used on the Russian front by the Germans. The British and the Americans argued that this was an obvious attempt to create division among the Allies and not a serious offer. Even if it had been possible to raise the money, no Jewish organization could have followed through. It was a question of delivering trucks to Germany to be used on the Russian front. Obviously, no one could have gone to the Joint Distribution Committee and said, "Here, we have ten thousand trucks." They were in no position to hand over trucks to Germany. It could only have been done if Great Britain and America were willing.

When I met Joel Brand I asked him, "What do you think, could anything have been done?" The question thus came down to: Would the strengthening of the German war machine by this amount have been so dangerous that it was not worth the sacrifice of hundreds of thousands of Jewish lives? Joel Brand said, "The cost to the Allies would have been infinitesimal if measured by the extent to which the German war machine might have been strengthened. If, however, political division had ensued between Russia and America, that might have been a more serious matter. In any event, the tragedy was that nothing happened."

The reason I mentioned this—remember, this is what he told me in 1945—is that within the past few years, those of us who have followed the literature have seen book after book appear which made the following accusation: "The Jewish Agency—in other words, Ben Gurion and the leaders of Palestine—had a chance to save the Jews, a million or hundreds of thousands, and they did not take it." You see, the tragedy was made into a constant political argument against Moshe Sharett, and against Ben Gurion by groups who claim today that more could have been done to save the Jews of Europe. Joel Brand himself, as time passed, came under the influence of political groups who used him to make capital against the parties in power, and he lent his name to some of those accusations. For that reason, my interview with him, given in 1945, before any political issues came up some ten or fifteen years later, is, to me, tremendously valuable. At that time it was so clear in his mind, as he said, that whatever the Jewish community could have done, they did. It was wholly in the hands of Great Britain and America, and neither was prepared to act. That a tragic incident is turned into the vicious political capital of a decade or fifteen years later is one of the minor tragedies but, nevertheless, is a tragedy of Jewish contemporary history.

RABBI BERKOWITZ: In Slovakia in 1942, another person tried to negotiate with the Nazis—Gisi Fleischman. Who was she, what did she do, and what were her negotiations with the Nazi leaders?

DR. SYRKIN: Gisi Fleischman's story is a smaller version of the Joel Brand attempt. She was very valuable, very devoted, and she perished, of course. Her negotiations were with a German named Willy von Wislitzeni, who said that for a certain price he would let Jewish children escape from Czechoslovakia. The tragedy of these attempts is that on a large scale they failed. But there was a constant attempt, as you read the documents, to save, perhaps, ten children, to get them from one spot to another until that one became dangerous, then to another until that was threatened. What is significant was the constant pitting of the human spirit and intelligence, under the most incredible circumstances, in attempting to do something.

So when one reads that the Jews in Europe were passive, that they let themselves be slaughtered, it is written not in malice, I am sure, as much as in total ignorance of these undying efforts. What could they achieve? A person here and an individual there; this one or that one would perhaps be captured in the next place to which he could go, but the attempts by ransom, by hiding, by every possible means were utilized, not only by a few but by a whole network of individuals attempting to do what they could.

RABBI BERKOWITZ: This is what you meant, then, when you wrote, "The breathtaking schemes of mass salvation prodded by such optimists as Gisi Fleischman and Joel Brand never materialized, but the loss was not total." You say that between 1939 and 1940 the chief obstacle to rescue was lack of ports of entry. The Germans permitted their victims to escape if they could, but there was nowhere for them to go. Then you write, "By the end of 1941, however, the Nazi temper changed." Do you think that if Jews had been able to be rescued and ports of entry could have been found, that the Jews could have left Germany, and if so, how many?

DR. SYRKIN: It appears true that in the initial stages the Germans were not so committed to an extermination program. They wanted to get rid of the Jews. The Jews could have left, and they were prepared to let them go. An issue of the now defunct *Look* magazine tells how a ship had gotten out with hundreds of people on it, but in North or South America, no country would let them in. It was a question of quotas. That was the horror and the shame. It is undoubtedly true that there was a stage when Germany would have let them out. Maybe with money, but it was possible to get them out. But no country would give shelter to them; there was no place to go.

Later, undoubtedly, as situations hardened, the pathology of Hilter increased. When the Jews had been on the shores of salvation, there were no saviors to take them in. So apparently the world was not outraged. Consequently, there appeared to be almost consent. It is a terrible thing to say, but certainly the Germans felt that if the outrage of the world was not great enough to save the Jews when they could be saved, then the next step was not so enormous. They had a kind of tacit permission from the world, almost, psychologically.

And then, of course, as things got worse, undoubtedly Hilter and his entourage felt, first, that if they could achieve nothing else, they could at least achieve this, the extermination of the Jews, and second, they were already so drenched in blood, so deep, it would be better to go on than retreat.

This changed for a few at the very end of the war when there was an attempt to show, by some, that they were "good" Germans, but not for Hitler and his entourage, who were concerned with completing the business and, if possible, with wiping out all signs of what they had done.

RABBI BERKOWITZ: In writing about the Warsaw Ghetto, in the chapter "The Struggle of the Spirit," you have two poems by children. One little boy, Motele, wrote: "From tomorrow on I shall be sad—From tomorrow on! Today I will be gay./What is the use of sadness/tell me that?/Because these evil winds begin to blow?/Why should I grieve for tomorrow—today?/ Tomorrow may be so good, so sunny, tomorrow the sun may shine for us again;/We shall no longer need to be sad./From tomorrow on I shall be sad—from tomorrow on!/Not today; No! today I will be glad./And every day, no matter how bitter it be, I will say:/From tomorrow on, I shall be sad, not today!"

Here is a poem by Martha, a little girl, which reads: "I must be saving these days (I have no money to save),/I must save health and strength, Enough to last me for a long while, I must save my nerves,/And my thoughts, and my mind and the fire of my spirit;/I must be saving of tears that flow—/I shall need them for a long, long while. I must save endurance these stormy days. There is so much I need in life: warmth of feeling and a kind heart—/These things I lack; of these I must be saving!/All these, the gifts of God, I wish to keep./How sad I should be if I lost them quickly."

These were written by children in the Warsaw Ghetto.

DR. SYRKIN: I found these poems in the *Gazeta Żydowska*, a ghetto paper. They were written in Yiddish and I translated them. The first poem was by an eight-year-old child. The second, which is much more mature, is by a little girl, Martha, aged eleven, I believe. Of course, they both perished. Look at what that child asks for. She asks for thoughts. She asks for saving of thoughts and to have a kind heart. You see in that poem the whole desire of the ghetto not to be brutalized, not to become what the Germans tried to make them. This is a tremendous, conscious struggle to remain human, which is expressed so marvelously in the lines of this child, which does not ask for bread, does not ask for warmth, but for human qualities. That a child of eleven, under conditions of such terror, which I do not have to describe to you, could create this dream to remain human, is the greatest triumph of the spirit. This is heroism and nobility. This is one answer to the question, "How did they resist?" This is resistance, deep and profound in nature. The child perished, but she is alive due to this desire.

RABBI BERKOWITZ: I am equally moved by the other poem. Dr. Syrkin, I would like you to describe, even briefly, the community that inspired these poems. What was the Warsaw Ghetto Council?

DR. SYRKIN: The Council played a very equivocal role in the life of the ghetto. The German authorities set up the ghetto, and then they designated a certain number of people to be the

Jewish representatives vis-a-vis the German authorities. These Jews were the Council. I believe that in the beginning the Council acted in completely good faith. They acted as a buffer between the Ghetto and the German authorities. Whatever miserable rations were available, whatever work could be doled out, whatever sanitation took place, there had to be some kind of authority—an authority that dealt with the Germans. Of course, the great horror began when the Council was asked to furnish Jews, and the Council members at some point became aware that the Jews they were delivering to the Germans were not for labor, but destined for death. And the selection started.

If you read the diaries of the ghetto that exist—there are famous diaries, like the Lieberman diary, the Kaplan diary—you will notice that in the beginning they saw the Council as very ordinary people. The bitterness against the Council, of course, increased with time, as their functions became clearer and clearer. In the case of the Warsaw Ghetto, when the head of the Council discovered what was really going on, he committed suicide. There were different kinds of councils in the Ghetto, and some, when certain demands were made of them, refused to collaborate. There were probably others, under the threat of guns themselves, that did perform the bidding of the Germans, probably with the rationalization that in any case there would be a selection in the Ghetto. I think it is impossible for us to judge them. We here cannot judge what the Council was doing then. But I think there is something that we must understand. Selection for death was implicit in the Ghetto from the first day. For instance, there was something in the diaries of Dr. Emanuel Ringelblum that I cannot forget. Ringelblum was the archivist of the Warsaw Ghetto, a historian, and a marvelous human being. Certainly he was the last person to be a collaborator. He had a page in his diaries which goes something like this: "All night I heard the crying of children outside, freezing to death in the snow. In the morning, people came and took away the corpses."

You say to yourself when you read this—"All night he heard the crying of children, dying"—Why didn't he get up and bring them into his house? You say this, now and here, in America. The whole point is that there was limited warmth, limited food, and one existed at the expense of the other. Ringelblum had nothing to give the child that was dying in the snow, probably not even a bit of space to spare. There were too many dying in the snow, and this was going on throughout the Ghetto.

He describes situations and discussions which show that those still alive in the Ghetto were thinking and saying: "We have just so much left of food, should we say that we will save perhaps ten while the others perish, or shall we all perish in doling it out? And whom shall we save? Shall we try to find ten children? But the children may be too weak to live. Shall we try to find ten young people who perhaps will be able to survive, to achieve something?"

This selection, which you see in its ultimate form when the Council selects, is already an essential part of the existence of the Ghetto. The most delicate soul, the most marvelous spirit, the most dedicated beings are engaging in selecting. Even when you think of illegal immigration, it is a selection of those who will get on the boat and those who will not get on the boat. Part of the tragedy of the existence of European Jewry is that selection is, from the start, implicit in the conditions.

RABBI BERKOWITZ: Here Dr. Ringelblum in his diary writes the following: "Know then that the last surviving educational workers remain true to the ideas of our culture. Until their death they hold aloft the banner of culture in the struggle against barbarism." He concludes: "We doubt whether we shall ever see you again. Give our warm greetings to all our leaders of Jewish culture, writers, journalists, musicians, artists, all builders of modern Jewish culture and fighters for the salvation of Jews and all humanity." This was written when people knew they were going to die, the next day, the next week, the next month.

What are some of the activities that went on in spite of and against the barbarism?

DR. SYRKIN: Dr. Ringelblum organized a group called *Oneg Shabbat*—Celebrants of the Sabbath. They were determined to keep a record of what was happening. It is interesting how they maintained their historic sense, a people that was doomed. We learned so much about the Ghetto because of the people who kept the records. They buried their papers, they smuggled them out, and the record remained as written by Ringelblum, Kaplan and others.

They also kept trying to organize activities. They had lecture series on Sholom Aleichem, on Mendelssohn. This is interesting. These were Jews from all over Europe who were in the ghetto in Warsaw. Many of them were assimilated Jews. Now they were beginning to learn and talk Yiddish for the first time.

And there is a moment when Ringelblum must pause in his diary because they are giving lectures in Yiddish on Sholom Aleichem, or when they are discussing Socialist Zionism, Marxism. "Who knows," he says, "this may mean the revival of Yiddish." Can you imagine, at such a moment, to have this notion that the language is going to be revived?

They gave courses which they thought would be practical. For example, in the early stages, a lot of them were studying English for the day when they would be able to get out and use it. There was a course in cosmetology; these were practical things, you know, the desire to train for something.

There was a diary that appeared recently. It was written by a young boy and it was found and translated. The boy was named Moshe Flinker. He was killed in Belgium at the age of seventeen. This is a very different one from the Anne Frank diary. This boy's family decided that they would save themselves not by hiding but by living openly. They were well-to-do, and lived openly in Belgium, thinking that perhaps they would get away with it there. They were captured. Young Moshe left a diary in Hebrew. I think it is one of the most remarkable ever written. The boy—remember, he was keeping his diary in the forties—was a great Hebrew student, but he decided that he must learn Arabic because he sensed—in 1944, mind you—that there would be a Jewish state, and he wanted to be a diplomat for the Jewish state. So he had to know Arabic as well as Hebrew. You can picture this young boy, with the doom of death on him, sneaking into libraries in a Belgian city to get Arabic grammar books.

One more thing, which has nothing to do with this book, but to illustrate again the Jewish spirit in its intensity. I went to the DP camps for a very interesting reason in the beginning of 1947—you have to keep the date in mind to understand. There was no State of Israel yet, and things looked very black. The Hillel Foundation here had persuaded American universities to allot a certain number of scholarships to young Jews in the DP camps. The American government had agreed to let about three hundred above the quota go to American colleges. I was involved in choosing the applicants for this project.

I would like to tell you about the most remarkable examination that I ever proctored while picking the lucky three hundred. I went to the DP camps and the question, naturally, arose—here were young Jews gathered from every part of Europe—How could we choose from all the thousands? They had no documents; they had been destroyed long ago. In the past few years they had not been going to college, they had been in ghettos and concentration camps. So we had to go back a few years to where their education had been interrupted, and we decided that the only way to choose was to give an examination. We could not tell all of them that they could go to America. We announced that an examination would be held in Munich and those who passed would go to America—to Columbia, Vassar, or wherever they chose. The next question was, In what language should we test? These were people from Hungary, Poland and other countries. The examiner, of course, had to be able to read the answers. A general question on literature or history had to be answered, in depth, in French, German, Yiddish or Russian, because those were the languages that I knew. I could not read any others. A question in physics or mathematics, of a general kind, could be answered in those languages as well as in Hungarian and Rumanian, because the examiner who marked those knew these two languages also.

Then there was another question. If these boys and girls were to go to an American university, they had to know some English. They had to be able to write a paragraph in English on why they wanted to go to America. I will never forget that day as long as I live. Young people came from all the DP camps in Germany, and they sat there—hundreds of them—and the questions were given to them. Many of them looked at the test and stood up and left. They had forgotten—years and years had passed. Others began to weep. Most of them remained. Then I saw something that I had never seen in my life before—they broke out in the most horrible sweat. A beautiful blond girl, I recall, burst into tears and left. She was supposed to be very good in mathematics, but she said that she could not remember anything. Finally, they got through with the examinations. It took much longer than we expected. We had expected that it would take about two hours, but it took all day. Then came the question of grading. We could not give grades of 98, 97 or 96. We had classifications: Class 1, 2, and 3.

Eight years ago at Brandeis University I met a young professor of physics who had been in Class 1. The blond girl, who jumped up and ran away, I saw as a graduate student at Harvard—these were among the successes. But there were many more failures. I tell you this story for the courage and the zeal it shows. This examination, written in three or four languages, was taken by people who had not even looked at a book for four years. This tells much about a people and their spirit.

RABBI BERKOWITZ: One question on the Warsaw Ghetto that has been asked should again be answered. Why did the Jews of Europe begin to resist so late? Why did the Warsaw Ghetto fight back only when a mere 30,000 were left and over half a million had been massacred?

DR. SYRKIN: Because many of them still hoped. They hoped for the victory of the Allies, they hoped that there would be some kind of deliverance. They knew that resistance meant the finale. As long as there was an element of hope in their minds that something would intervene, they waited. They were mistaken, but who are we to say that they should have acted otherwise? Early resistance would have doomed them. It is the greatest delusion to assume that if they had started six months earlier, they would have succeeded. They would have been liquidated that much more rapidly. With the Nazi war machine against them, they had no chance. And they waited, hoping perhaps the Allies would do something, that the Germans would be defeated, that some change would take place.

RABBI BERKOWITZ: In addition to the Warsaw Ghetto, there were Jewish partisans throughout Eastern Europe. What about them?

DR. SYRKIN: In Vilna, particularly, there was an active group of partisans, people who had fled to the woods and who attempted to fight. That was one type. There was also an attempt to establish a community in the woods, not to fight, but simply to live. You might ask why did they not all go to the woods? I spoke to one of the heads of the Vilna partisans. If the young men, for instance, had left the ghetto and gone into the woods, they would have had to completely abandon the old, the women and the children. Only the young men and the strong could go into the woods in winter and operate from there. Those who went did so knowing that they were free to leave the ghetto and their people. Many felt that they could not leave the ghetto and all it meant: women, children, family.

The Vilna group was very active as partisans. But there was another tragedy. They could not tie up with the Polish partisans, for instance, or the White Russian partisans, because these hunted the Jewish partisans. They were as alone in the woods as they were alone in the ghettos. Anti-Semitism was so entrenched that Polish partisans attacked the Jewish partisans. There were many instances of that.

RABBI BERKOWITZ: You have a phrase in one of your chapters, "Rescue is Resistance." I think it is an unusually telling phase. Who were the rescuers in some of the countries of Europe who were also part of the resistance movement?

DR. SYRKIN: In Holland and in Denmark the situation was much brighter than in Easter Europe. There were Gentiles who assisted the Jews. There were really heroic figures who attempted to smuggle Jews out, hide them, and it is really a question why the people in the small countries showed so much more valor than those of Eastern Europe. Even in France there were not as many rescues as there were in

Holland and Denmark. The smaller the country, the more valor there apparently was in the attempts to actively assist in the rescue of Jews.

RABBI BERKWOITZ: Dr. Syrkin used the phrase "a woman of valor" as part of the title of her book on the life of Golda Meir. I should like to use the same words to describe and characterize her noble life and work. But I believe we would have to have one more element, one more word, one more phrase, and that is the word *Ahavah*—the concept of love, for this is a concept that is fundamental to all that Dr. Syrkin has done. She has through a lifetime of service indicated her love for her people and for the land of Israel and for its culture.

SAUL ALINSKY

RABBI BERKOWITZ: I begin this dialogue with a story, one of my favorites, which is probably familiar to you. It was written by Sholem Asch, who concludes one of his great books, *Salvation,* telling about a young man, Shlomo, who goes from town to town in search of his family, following the terrible massacre of the Jews in Poland in 1648. As he roamed through the Fair of Lublin among the refugees, listening to the cries and moans of his people, he yielded to despair and asked himself, Can there be a future for our people?

Then he walked a narrow street where the merchants' stores were located, and he saw an empty stall in which an old man was calling to buyers. He marveled at this, because the stall was empty and there was nothing in it to sell, so he went over to the booth and he asked the old man, "Your stall is empty, and yet you are asking buyers to come in; what can you sell?"

The old man told the troubled young man, "My son, I sell faith." I quote this story because I think it is an appropriate one to introduce our distinguished guest. The future is in desperate need of proclaimers of faith, men who believe in the worth and the importance of the human being, to work, to plan and to sacrifice in order to reach their goals. Such an unusual human being is our guest, Saul Alinsky.

Two books will be of interest to us. One is *The Professional Radical; Conversations with Saul Alinsky,* by Marion K. Sanders, and the other is by Mr. Alinsky, *Rules for Radicals, A Pragmatic Primer for Realistic Radicals.* We live in a time in which everyone seems to be frightened by the word "radical" and all that it connotes. Yet, in meeting our guest we are going to hear definitions, biography, tactics and philosophy from someone who truly understands the real meaning of the word "radical."

I would like Mr. Alinsky to begin by telling us a story, which he told my son, about the way he handled his rabbi when he was a little boy.

MR. ALINSKY: I was brought up in a very Orthodox home. We were so Orthodox that on Saturday I had to go to synagogue three times. And right after school every day I had to go to cheder. My parents were utterly committed to the importance of education; nothing else mattered. When I was about nine or ten, I had the flu. When I was convalescing they had the rabbi come to tutor me. I had read a couple of pages of the Bible and translated it, and apparently I had done it without a mistake. Suddenly a penny dropped over my head on the Bible, and I looked at my rabbi and asked, "What is this?" He said, "God has rewarded you." I thought about this and next day I was mute when I sat down. The rabbi asked, "What's the matter, are you sick, can't you read?" I said, "No, I have been thinking about it, and it's a nickel or nothing."

So my first strike was against God. The rabbi banged me across the face in the permissive manner the rabbi had in those days, and this sent me sailing across the room. When my mother came in she was horrified because he was cursing me, not unto the third generation, but unto the fifteenth generation, and screaming about my heresy. My mother was also shocked by my heresy, but at the same time she was horrified that the rabbi would strike me, her only child.

RABBI BERKOWITZ: I am sure that if this story took place today, what with inflation, you would probably ask for a quarter or a half dollar.

MR. ALINSKY: Oh, much more than that.

RABBI BERKOWITZ: In *The Professional Radical; Conversations with Saul Alinsky,* you said that "Sociologists use the term 'Primary Relationship' and they spend lecture after lecture and give all kinds of assigned reading to explain it. Professor Frank Nitti taught me the whole thing in five minutes." For those of you who do not recall your Chicago history, Frank Nitti was the right-hand man of Al Capone. How did Mr. Nitti teach you, and how did an upstanding citizen, a sociologist, a criminologist, get tied up with Al Capone and his gang?

MR. ALINSKY: They are among the most honest people I have met before or since. And the most unneurotic, I might add. The first day that I went to the University of Chicago as a freshman, I learned one of the most important lessons in my life. I was sitting with my Dean, who was registering me, and he asked me, "What would you like to take?" I wanted to reply that I would like to take a look at the curriculum, but before I had a chance to open my mouth, he said, "English 101 will be just right. What else would you like to take?" And again, he said, "Political Science 101 will be just right."

While I was no genius, I was not dumb, and I figured this guy was not going to give me what I wanted. So I started looking round at my fellow students, and he kept tugging at my sleeve saying, "You have one half-major left now, what would you want to take?" I realized he was serious. In those days I had thought of going into engineering; I was fresh out of high school, with a limited high school vocabulary, and I saw something that looked like engineering; it was called "Equestration 101" and I said: "I'll take that." The next morning at eight o'clock I showed up for Equestration 101, and before I knew what hit me, I was sworn into the U.S. Army Reserve Officers Training Corps; I was put on top of a horse and I stayed with the course for four years. Now, I have never liked horses, unless I have a ticket on one that is coming down the stretch in the lead, and I do not especially like sitting on one, and so I learned a lesson—if I did not know what something meant, to ask.

After graduation I was awarded a fellowship. It was in criminology, and I was told that I was going to get insight into crime, so I went to the dictionary to look up "insight." The definition said, "getting on the inside" and nothing else. So I went to Capone headquarters, without any tactics or anything else; I just said that I was a student and I would like to know what they were all about, and they said, "Get lost, punk."

It was nothing romantic; if you have seen things like *The Untouchables*, that is sheer fiction. The gang did not have to worry about anybody squealing or anything like that, because everyone was in on the act. The only way you could understand the syndicate was to realize that it was a quasi-public utility. Everybody owned stock—the police department, the judges, everybody. It was there to service the people of Chicago with liquor and women and other aspects of the American way of life, or the universal way of life.

This was very different from what I was learning in my classes in social pathology. I kept hanging around there, and one day I was at a table in the restaurant at the Lexington Hotel, which was the Capone headquarters, and at the next table was a very notorious character named Big Ed Stash, who was an efficiency expert, otherwise known as a killer, sitting with four guys, and he started out with something like, "Did I ever tell you about that blonde?" Someone cut in and said, "Do we have to listen to that again?" But I said, "I never heard about it, Mr. Stash; I would like to hear it." He said, "Would you, kid? Come over here."

I was apparently a good audience and from that point on he introduced me to the others, and nobody asked any questions because I was being sponsored by this man. Nitti got a tremendous charge out of being called a professor and having a student body of one.

I learned a lot about this primary-relationship question. I noticed that they had these different experts, and occasionally they would import one from New York or Detroit, time-and-a-half for overtime and Saturday, and I thought that it was all pretty efficient. I am not dwelling on the morality of it. How could you question the morality? The good people of Chicago, they were buying, they were the customers. So who or what is moral?

Nitti told me, "You see, kid, sometimes our own guys might know the guy, so we have to get somebody from out of town. You understand?" And I still had a lot of hang-up about admitting that I did not know, as though it were a stigma or something, so I said, "Yeah, I guess so." The next day I asked one of his associates to explain it, telling him that I had to explain it to those stupid college professors back at the university. "How would you put it?" I asked. He explained it to me very simply. "If you have a job to do, you go find somebody. You have a complete description of him. You put your gun to his gut and you pull three or four times. But it's another thing when you put that gun against him and look up and recognize him. You know his wife, you know his kids, you've taken him to the ball game. You know there will be a funeral, there will be tears and there will be orphans and this isn't going to be just a job, this is going to be murder. You would hesitate, and because of that they would always get an out-of-town man." This is the same basis on which all armies since the beginning of time have had an irrevocable rule— our organization has it when we engage in confrontation with different parts of the establishment: Never fraternize with the enemy. Once you start fraternizing, and once you start exchanging baby pictures, it is hard to do the things you have to do.

RABBI BERKOWITZ: You have made the following observation: "I have never encountered such a bunch of morons as in the field of criminology." Would you care to elaborate, especially in the light of the things that have been going on in the last few years.

MR. ALINSKY: I think the statement speaks for itself. I never have seen such morons. They are pretty stupid people. Criminologists know that a lot of things are wrong and none of them does anything about it. They invent a lot of professional jargon and gobbledegook and programs that are really meaningless; nobody is willing to face up to the basic issues that are involved—issues of discrimination, of rotten housing, unemployment.

RABBI BERKOWITZ: Let me interrupt to ask you your opinion of Attica. Do you think it was handled right?

MR. ALINSKY: I think it was handled very badly. First of all, you must understand what a prison situation is, and I am not just talking about the American one. I am talking about this on a world wide basis. I was state criminologist of Illinois for three years. I suppose I am still a criminologist. I think that some of our major corporations are more criminal than some of the people I was working with.

In prison none of the personnel can carry guns because they are always working in the yard or in the cell blocks and can get jumped at any point, and their gun can be taken away from them. Similarly, in institutions there is an irrevocable rule that hostages can never be honored because if the institution backs down to protect a hostage, it ends any kind of discipline or any kind of security, or what makes a prisoner a prisoner.

On this basis, once a man accepts a position in any prison he agrees to forfeit his life in the event he is taken hostage. This is the reason, for instance, why in the Marin County shoot-out in San Francisco the San Quentin guards would not accept the principle of hostages when the judge had a shotgun against him, while the sheriff and the other police did accept it.

Once the hostages were seized at Attica Prison—I am not discussing the merits of the uprising, I am only answering the question about handling it—once the hostages were seized, when New York State permitted the media to come in, permitted negotiating teams to come in, this was highly unprecedented.

This does not mean that it should not have been done. If anyone on the negotiating team had had any kind of sophistication as an organizer, he would have told the inmates that the thing to do at that point, with television and the cameras running, would have been to release the hostages right in front of the cameras and say to the networks and the American people: "We only took these hostages in order that we might have a chance to speak, so you could hear us and we could communicate with you. These are the horrible things that are happening to us." And then turn to each hostage and say, "Were you treated all right? Please carry our message outside."

This would have created a public opinion in the country which would have been a very significant force. It also would have created the kind of situation in which your governor could then have come himself to see what it was about. No leading official, no top political official can meet with the threat of danger to hostages hanging over him.

This is what should have been done on that side. On the other side, the governor took the position that he did not have the authority to quash any possible indictments—criminal indictments. You may remember one keeper was killed, or at least he died. At that point someone should have told him: "It is true you do not have that authority, but you have the authority to issue a statement that if the proceedings are instituted and if any of the inmates are convicted, then as governor you do have the authority to pardon, and you will take into consideration that all the hostages were released." That would have created a different kind of situation on both sides.

Lastly, I thought the actual use of guns was utterly inexcusable. I think what happened was that your state authorities were out of their depth with intermediaries and negotiators. With the media on the scene in force, they panicked, and there was no need for it. Instead of a shoot out, enough gas could have been dumped over there so that everybody—hostages, inmates and all—would have ended up in the hospital for two or three weeks, but nobody would have died.

RABBI BERKOWITZ: Let me ask you about one idea that you

hold which is somewhat out of step with the way some people feel today. You say in one of your books, "I don't know why this is, but I'll steal before I'll take charity." Why do you feel so strongly about the concept of charity that you would steal before you would take it?

MR. ALINSKY: I cannot answer why to that, but I would. I just cannot accept the idea of charity any more than I would take to living under a paternalistic, feudalistic system—you know, "Here, peasants, I will be a good father to all of you." That is the way I am.

RABBI BERKOWITZ: Another fascinating statement—You say, "My one regret about the atomic bomb to this day is that it wasn't dropped on Berlin instead of Hiroshima and Nagasaki."

MR. ALINSKY: I would like to add to that statement—that it was not dropped over Berlin, Hamburg, Munich, Stuttgart, over all of Germany. I hated the Nazis with a passion. I did not consider them human beings, I still do not. I was one of those who, after the war, wanted to see as part of the settlement that every storm trooper from block captain up be executed. I had too many friends in the resistance, I know what went on. We have too short a memory about what the Nazis did when they put people to the torch. I was too heavily involved in the International Brigade that fought against the Nazi Panzer divisions. I know what the Nazis did to them. Frankly, I would not have regarded the bomb dropped on Germany as a bomb, I would have regarded it as insect extermination. I know that there are many who would take issue with me on that.

RABBI BERKOWITZ: Mr. Alinsky, what is the purpose, the

philosophy, to which you have dedicated your work these past forty years? What is it concerned with?

MR. ALINSKY: This is a rough question to answer. It is so easy to toss off some cliches, like, "I want to make this a better world." Motivations shift with time. If you had asked me that question in 1940, I would not have hesitated for an instant. I would simply have said to you, "I am a professional anti-Fascist." The enemy was clear and that was the fight.

Let us say it is a combination of two things. The first is what happens if you have an imagination that is a little above normal. I majored in archeology in my undergraduate years, and I recall when looking at an Aztec sacrificial altar that while the other kids, I am sure, were seeing just a stone artifact with dark stains of blood on them, I could close my eyes and could hear these virgin maidens who had been sacrificed, almost hear them scream when they realized what was happening.

Now, when you are cursed with that kind of imagination, you see people suffering, you identify. This makes you very angry, and you want to do something about it to relieve your own self-pain, because their pain becomes part of you.

Another part is that, about twenty-five years ago, I went through a sequence in my personal life when people I loved very dearly were dying, one after the other. Before then death had been no stranger to me; my best friends are buried over in Spain. An early experience: I would have dinner with a guy whom I liked very much on Thursday, and on Friday I would see him in the morgue, undergoing an autopsy. Maybe it all accumulated, or maybe it was just those who were very close to me. But I learned a very basic lesson, which very few people have ever learned, that I was mortal. Someday, in actual fact, I was going to die.

You know it is an interesting thing, people talk about it, but death is always something—like an automobile accident—that happens to somebody else. You save for your old age and you talk about when you are going to die, but you never really believe that it will occur. You will be interested to know that in a few months a very academic and a very profound magazine is publishing a very long interview with me, a magazine called *Playboy*, and the last question to me was, "What do you want on your tombstone?" I replied, "I just want my name." They also asked me, "Suppose there is an afterworld?" and I said, "Well, in that case, after my name just put down, "Out, now organizing Hell."

That is where I would like to go. All my life I have spent with the have-nots. Here you are a have-not if you are short of money; there you are a have-not if you are short on virtue. Anyway, if I were organizing Hell, I would be in my own Heaven; this is what I would want to do.

But once you know definitely that you are going to die, a very basic question comes up, What is the meaning of being alive? What is it? Is it just a straight hedonistic experience of pleasures, or is it something more? I don't know the answer. But I am sure that I do not know anything more worthwhile to do with my life than what I am doing. If I did know, I would do it.

I will give you an example. Jacques Maritain, the great Catholic philosopher, who for some strange reason is a very close friend and great admirer of mine, while he was professor of advanced studies at Princeton had Einstein to visit one night. After dinner we were sitting in front of the fireplace and the question was propounded: If you could ask for one single thing, one thing, and get it, what would you ask for? And carrying the burden of a name beginning with "A," a burden which I have borne since the time of kindergarten, I discovered that even in this high academic society they started alphabetically. I thought for almost an hour, and years since I have often reflected as to whether I would have given a different answer. I have never been able to come up with anything else. My answer was that I would ask to know the question of what to ask for. If I knew the question, I would pretty much have the answer.

I do not have any answers. I do not think there are answers. There are so many things that relate to why you are doing what you are doing, and you are not even conscious of some of them. Many reasons that I could give are sheer rationalizations.

RABBI BERKOWITZ: Apropos to the one wish, let me ask the question: If there were three people in history whom you could meet and be with, who would they be and why?

MR. ALINSKY: First, Moses, because he was a great organizer. He kept organizing God all over the place. Then, since I am human, Helen of Troy. Third would be a combination—I would spend some time with Tom Paine, some time with Lenin, some time with Jefferson.

RABBI BERKOWITZ: Would all of these people have a common denominator?

MR. ALINSKY: They would, except for Helen of Troy. The common denominator for the others would be their efforts to create a society struggling toward the kind of world where man could really begin to create things, to live and not to exist, not to huddle in fear. Once you say that one of your major values is security, it means that you are scared, you are trying to get security in a world where there is no security.

As Montaigne remarked: "The moment we are born, we begin to die." The people I mention wanted to achieve a kind of world of peace, of equality, of worth, of education, of health, of all the goals that mankind has always striven for.

RABBI BERKOWITZ: Let me read an excerpt from the book *Rules for Radicals.* You mentioned that Moses was a great organizer, and I would like to read what you have said about him: "The episode between Moses and God, when the Jews had begun to worship the Golden Calf, is revealing. Moses did not try to communicate with God in terms of mercy or justice when God was angry and wanted to destroy the Jews; he moved in on a top value and outmaneuvered God. It is only when the other party is concerned or feels threatened that he will listen—in the arena of action a threat or a crisis becomes almost a precondition to communication.

"Now, a great organizer like Moses never loses his cool as a lesser man might have done when God said, 'Go get thee down; *thy* people whom *thou* hast brought out of the land of Egypt hath sinned.' At that point if Moses had dropped his cool in any way one would have expected him to reply, 'Where do you get off with all that stuff about *my* people whom *I* brought out of the land of Egypt. I was just taking a walk through the desert and who started that bush burning, and who told me to get over to Egypt, and who told me to get these people out of slavery, and who pulled all those power plays, and all the plagues, and who split the Red Sea, and who put a pillar of cloud in the sky and now all of a sudden they are *my* people?' But Moses kept his cool, and he knew that the most important center of his attack would have to be on what he judged to be God's prime value. As Moses read it, it was that God wanted to be Number One. All through the Old Testament one bumps into 'There shall be no other gods before me'; 'Thou shalt not worship false gods'; 'I am a jealous and vindictive God'; 'Thou shalt not use the Lord's name in vain.' And it goes on and on, including the first part of the Ten Commandments.

Knowing this, Moses took off on his attack. He began arguing and telling God to cool it. (At this point trying to figure out Moses' motivation, one would wonder whether it was because he was loyal to his own people, because after all he was pushing a hundred and twenty, and that's asking a lot.) At any rate, he began to negotiate, saying, 'Look, God, you're God. You are holding all the cards. Whatever you want to do you can do, and nobody can stop you. But you know, God, you can't just scratch that deal you've got with these people—you remember, the Covenant—in which you promised not only to take them out of slavery but that they would practically inherit the earth. I know you are going to tell me that they broke their end of it all, so all bets are off. But it isn't that easy. You are in a spot. The news of this deal has leaked out all over the joint. The Egyptians, the Philistines, the Canaanites, *everybody* knows about it. But as I said before, You are God. Go ahead and knock them off. What do you care if people are going to say, 'There goes God, you can't believe anything He tells you. You can't make a deal with Him. His word isn't even worth the stone it's written on. But after all, You are God and I suppose you can handle it.' And the Lord was appeased from doing the evil which he had spoken against his people. Another maxim in effective communication is that people have to make their own decisions. It isn't just that Moses could not tell God what God should do; no organizer can tell a community, either, what to do. Much of the time, the organizer has a pretty good idea of what the community should be doing, and he will want to suggest, maneuver and persuade the community toward that action."

I was captivated because I would say that in the spirit of the modern Midrash, in the spirit of modern interpretation of Biblical incidents, this really approaches the matter in a very interesting, very understandable manner to people.

MR. ALINSKY: I am doing the whole Bible that way. You see, we use it as compulsory reading for our trainers, not as religion. Moses and Paul were two of the greatest organizers that came down the pike. If Paul had not come to organize the Church, I think Jesus would have been just another guy hanging up there because they killed about three hundred and sixty that year. You read it over and over again in the Epistles and the Corinthians. The organizers are called missionaries now—you can see Paul getting an epistle from one of his Corinthians: "I have a whole batch who are ready to sign up but they do not want to be circumcised, they say it hurts too much." Scrub circumcision—from now on, nobody has to be circumcised. A good organizer always counts off a secondary thing for the primary thing. "I have a group over here and they love to eat seafood." Sign them up; from now on anyone can eat anything he wants.

You see the development on an organizational basis and the pragmatics of it. One of the things that really intrigued me was the first time the race issue came up—when Moses married a black woman, remember that? There are a lot of rabbis that do not, you know. And the Jews really hated it—Aaron and Miriam organized against him, and they got Moses in a corner where Moses had to go back to God and say, "Do something." So God then turned Miriam into a leper, the whitest leper of all. That was the first time it dawned on me that God might have a sense of humor. You want to be white, I will make you so white. It is an interesting treatment.

RABBI BERKOWITZ: What is the Industrial Areas Foundation of which you are the head?

MR. ALINSKY: Basically, what we are trying to do is very simple. There are different kinds of societies that man can live in, and these societies are not ends unto themselves but are regarded as mechanisms trying to achieve certain ends. For example, a free and open society—and remember that all definitions are relative. "Free," or any other word, is dependent on many factors. For example, there can be no such thing as a successful traitor, because if he succeeds he automatically becomes a founding father. If we had lost the American Revolution, the name that would be glorified by us would be Benedict Arnold, whom we now call a traitor. Jefferson, Adams, Madison, Paine, Franklin and all the rest of them would be regarded as traitors today. You have to keep this in mind in terms of definitions; they are relative and dependent upon where you stand.

This is a pragmatic world. If you are living in the world as it is you have to recognize this, or you become a political astronaut out in some kind of mystical space. You make all your decisions in terms of the kind of society you want. Your value judgments, judgments in tactics are never made on the basis of what is best, because life never affords you that luxury. It is always on the basis of alternatives.

On this basis, consider Hamilton in the Federalist papers, arguing against giving the vote to the people who were poor and illiterate. Most of the colonists at the time of the American Revolution were illiterate. They did not have a public school system. When Hamilton was confronted by Madison and Jay, with whom he was arguing, they said, "All right, if you do not give them the vote, that is the end of our kind of democratic society. What is the alternative to it?" The alternative would be a system of elitism, a system of dictatorship or monarchy, or something else. On that basis of alternatives, Hamilton, as a realist, relinquished his position.

On the same basis, to me, a free and open society has been the most promising mechanism for achieving some of the high goals, a platform, a jumping-off place for things I mentioned before—freedom, equality, peace. The only way a free and open society can develop is through citizen participation. To put it into the cliche that has been used too much in recent days, "power to the people." When I use the word "power"—all words are loaded words—I am using it strictly as defined in Webster's Unabridged: the ability to act. No morals are involved—the power of this microphone carries my voice. The power of my heartbeat keeps me alive, the power of government keeps a society.

The one way that a free and open society dies is the development of a situation where people do not have the power to limit, the power to participate. The only way that people can have the power to operate in this kind of society is through organization. The times of the town hall, of participation on an individual basis, went out as far back as 1825. So organization and power become synonymous, and it is on this basis that a commitment to a free and open society requires that organization be done. The difference between organizations and movements comes and goes, but organizations carry with them the basic core of a power operation.

If you are talking to Mayor Daley in Chicago, you can have twenty-five thousand people in a mass demonstration outside of City Hall, but Daley is a sophisticated politician, and he is looking at you. He does not care if you have fifty thousand demonstrators—he is smart enough to know that in a couple of hours they are all going to go home, and tomorrow everything is going to be just as it was. But when he is looking at you he is thinking: How much of an organization does he have? How is it going to grow? How many votes will he have come Election Day? How much power can he deliver? It is on that basis that a deal is made. There was a time when I assumed that by setting up demonstrations, the fallout would start other organizations elsewhere. People came from all over the world in those days—and they still do now, but for a different reason—just to watch what we were doing and see how we were doing it. Well, that didn't work. True, there were upsurges all over the country, but they all subsided. One thing that came through loud and clear was that a mass organization is not the consequence of an immaculate conception; it needs the sperm of the organizer. The organizer is always working out different action programs, helping to develop the kind of tactics which provide a real adventure for people, winning victories, constantly keeping in action. Otherwise, nothing useful will happen.

I can get up here and give you a talk and turn you on with reference to two or three or four different issues, and you will all sign things, and most of you will, on the way out, join together for this, and two weeks from now you will forget about the whole thing—you will be tied up with something else. It just does not work unless you have that politically sophisticated organizer.

We therefore decided that the big job ahead was to train organizers, and this is the purpose of the training institute, from which organizers have gone out almost every three or four months. We have trained people from all over the world except Asia. I go to Asia and hold seminars and training sessions there. I stay there until the government kicks me out, which is usually at the end of five days.

Going back to an earlier question—why I am doing what I am doing. Just a few weeks before the Democratic Convention in 1968, I was on CBS television with George Wallace, and at one point, Wallace completely blew his cool—which is very unusual—and turned on the moderator. The program was live, and Wallace literally screamed, "You promised me when I got on this show with Alinsky that you would keep him under control." What had happened, among other things, was that Wallace had taken the position that if the people of Alabama had voted for school segregation, that would be a democratic decision and therefore segregation would be a democratic policy. What Wallace could not understand was that there are certain high values for which democracy is simply the means to the end. Freedom and equality are basic to democracy; you cannot vote on these, you cannot discuss them, you cannot debate them, they are the basic articles of faith. And if any so-called democratic society or mechanism should violate any of those, then democracy has just become a prostitute.

RABBI BERKOWITZ: In these books, *Rules for Radicals,* and *The Professional Radical,* there were a number of interesting stories and each story tells a lesson. I am going to read just one, and I am going to ask you to tell the others. It says: "Even Alinsky's everyday habits and gestures are intended to demonstrate the uses of power. Once while addressing students at an Eastern college in the campus chapel, he lit up a cigarette. The college president rose to tell him that smoking was not allowed. Whereupon Alinsky started to leave. No smoking, no speech. The embarrassed president at once relented, and having made his point, Alinsky refrained from smoking. He upheld the public's right to good service in restaurants; to get attention, he will throw a glass on the floor or level insults at the waiters." Speaking of waiters, can you tell us about the mixing up of the orders and what happened to the waiter?

MR. ALINSKY: First, let me comment. I do not go around restaurants throwing glasses and doing things like that. You know, legends get built up around these things. Once when I was sitting with a half-dozen top educators in a hotel in Boston and I asked for coffee twice and had not gotten it, I said, "Well, I am going to get my coffee." I reached over just to get a drink of water, and six men moved to take the glass from my hand. They thought I was going to throw it; they had read that story. Nothing was further from my mind. I'll tell you the basis of that story. I was with some friends at Toots Shor's, and they had theater tickets. In New York, you know, when you have theater tickets you have an early dinner—at least you used to. And there it was already quarter to eight and we still had not gotten our entree, and I asked, "Do you want me to get your entrees for you?" They asked, "What can you do? Do you know Shor?" I said, "No, but I am an organizer, I know how to get things done." So I took the water pitcher, and I just held it up and while the rest of the people and the waiters stared at me, I dropped it. It went off like a bomb. Instantly we got our steaks; we got everything we wanted. This is what started the whole story.

I had a more interesting experience. I went to the University of Kyoto, which is about 150 miles south of Tokyo, to lecture just a couple of months ago, and apparently the word had gotten around that I was coming. Just about every American and British student for miles around came to the lecture. So, instead of the lecture audience being what it would ordinarily have been—about a thousand Japanese students—there were about a thousand Japanese students and about 300 American and British students.

The whole point of this is that when you go outside of experience, you don't communicate. I was talking about communication and making a point that you can only communicate within someone's experience. For example, I am communicating with you when suddenly your eyes light up and you say, "Hey, I know just what you are talking about. I had something just like that happen to me, let me tell you about it." Then you start telling me about your experience. Otherwise, there is no communication.

I was explaining this at the lecture. Incidentally, English is not a second language to the Japanese; it is rare that you run into Japanese who speak English, so I always had an interpreter who would interpret sentence by sentence. While I was talking I was getting back this intelligent plastic look that college students have in a classroom when they don't know what the professor is talking about, but they nod when he nods and shake their heads when he does. This is not too tragic, because usually the college professor does not know too much about what he is talking about either. But I wanted to break through this, and I said: "Now look, you really don't understand what I am talking about. So I am going to explain it to you." I turned to the interpreter and said: "Don't interpret what I am talking about, and tell the Japanese students to keep their eyes on the American and British students." Then I told the following story.

Tactics is doing what you can with what you've got. In Rochester, New York, we were organizing in a Black community. All we had was bodies—thirty-five thousand people. Rochester prides itself on its culture; you have heard about their symphony. We bought about a hundred tickets for the Rochester Symphony and planned for one hundred people to go from the Black ghetto. They were going to get dressed in their good suit or good dress, and it would be unusual in Rochester to have a hundred Blacks at something like that. They were subjected to a pre-concert dinner back in the neighborhood, where for three hours they were stuffed and stuffed with nothing but baked beans, and then they were sent to the concert. Obviously this was going to blow the concert very quickly. There is no law against this, you see, nothing that anybody could do about it.

The Junior League is one of the big sponsors for the symphony season, and we could see these Junior League gals with their husbands the next morning at breakfast, when a man's defenses are really down. "John, you are not going to sit still and have our whole symphony season ruined by those people. We don't know what they want, but you'd better do something." Once you get that kind of pressure going it is very helpful.

When the tactic was described the American and British students laughed, and the Japanese students were just sort of smiling, looking at the Americans and British who were cracking up. So I repeated the story again for the interpreter to tell, and he came all the way down to the punch line and the Japanese students were all sitting there with an expression saying, "So, what else is new?" Because, you see, the Japanese don't eat baked beans, they eat rice, and they have no way of knowing what baked beans means in any way. This was completely outside of their experience.

For the first time, therefore, the kids realized what is meant by going in and out of experience.

Let me give you a little organizational test, a very simple and elementary one. In Hyannisport three weeks ago, I opened a Massachusetts teachers association meeting. I was in a Holiday Inn, and I was supposed to talk at 10 A.M. and it was eight o'clock. I called downstairs for room service and said that I wanted half a grapefruit, two poached eggs, coffee and toast. A voice on the other end said, "Sorry, we do not have any elevators in this Holiday Inn, the kitchen is all the way over at one end and we have a constant series of complaints about any hot food, like eggs. So we can send you grapefruit and coffee, but that's it."

I said, "Just a minute, I'll call you back." It was a simple organizational problem; I wanted my eggs. Then I picked up the phone and said, "This is Room 502 calling again," and I got my eggs. How did I get them? I'll tell you what I did. I said, "This is Room 502; I want my half grapefruit, two cold poached eggs, coffee and toast." There was nothing he could say. My eggs came up nice and warm.

RABBI BERKOWITZ: There is another incident I would like to ask about. You lectured at a college,—I think it was a fundamentalist college—and you mentioned that college students came to you saying, "Mr. Alinsky, we can't have any fun." You advised them about effecting some kind of change on the administration. It is a beautiful story, and I would like to hear you share it with us.

MR. ALINSKY: This was a college in western Washington, a fundamentalist college. The kids came up to me after a lecture and said, "What do we do, they don't let us dance on campus, they won't let us have any beer, they won't let us smoke or do anything." I asked, "What will they let you do?" "Well, they let us chew gum." I said, "Fine, tactics is doing what you can with what you've got." I told them to use their imagination. I said, "Look, you stick about five or ten sticks of gum in your mouth and chew it. You drop it down on the walks. Have you ever stepped on a wad of chewing gum? You could tie up the city of Chicago with five hundred wads of chewing gum on State and Madison streets. Even the traffic cop would be trying to scrape it off his feet. And that's it."

I left, and about two or three weeks later when I got back to my office there was a letter signed by about twenty or twenty-five students stating, "It worked, it worked. We can do anything now, we can dance, drink beer on campus, we can do everything except chew gum."

RABBI BERKOWITZ: You have said, "I have run into more senility among the nineteen- and twenty-year-olds in America than among the aged." What did you mean by this?

MR. ALINSKY: Senility occurs when life becomes too much for you, life right here and right now. When life in the here and now becomes so threatening and so beyond understanding, then what happens with people, particularly in the aging group, is that they then turn back to the past with its familiarities and begin to reminisce. They are always talking about the good old days; they start living in the past.

Now, with a lot of kids, particularly within the last ten years, life in the here and now has been just too much, just too incomprehensible, too maddening. But not having lived long enough to have had a past security to run back to, they jumped off into a mystical future. And when you would say, "Well, all right, what kind of a world do you want, what kind of a world is it going to be?" their answer would be, "We don't know, but it will rise like a phoenix out of the ashes of the old one."

In either case, whether going back or ahead, it is an escape from the immediate present and life here.

RABBI BERKOWITZ: You have been asked about the danger of a demagogue or a dictator taking over one of our organizations, and you have proved that this is not very likely, but you do say that you worry about the radical right these days, specifically the John Birch Society.

MR. ALINSKY: Well, I mean more than the John Birch Society—there is a whole complex of them. I personally am much more concerned about the Minute Men, particularly if their aim gets any better than it has been the last two times with me. When the extreme right talks about "law and order" it brings back that campaign statement, "Our country is torn with violence, disorder, there is crime rampant on the street, what we need in our country is law and order. Elect me and I shall bring law and order." Speech given in 1932 in Hamburg, Germany, by Adolf Hitler. Sounds familiar, doesn't it?

RABBI BERKOWITZ: How about the Black Panthers?

MR. ALINSKY: I think it is all over, and I think by the time the internecine warfare between Eldridge Cleaver and Huey Newton is resolved, it will be a lost cause, so to speak. My own sympathies, in terms of people, are with the West Coast group, some of whom are very good friends of mine. I watched the Panthers from the beginning; I knew a number of them personally, and they were very sincere. They were not choosing the race issue for their own personal aggrandizement, or using it to fatten their own pockets, but they went off the track on a number of things. It is just one of those episodes of the boiling of the times. I would say, to me, as a human being, apart from being an organizer, I have infinitely more respect for someone like Newton, who stays in the arena, instead of copping out over to Algeria and sounding forth with all sorts of pontifical statements like Cleaver. And I would go even a step further than that, as far as my feelings are concerned; his next book is going to be called "Brain on Ice." I don't like him; I feel very negative about him.

RABBI BERKOWITZ: Your views on this specific subject are especially cogent because you know the people intimately, rather than through the medium of newspaper headlines.

And this is, I think, one of the important aspects of our conversation. We have heard a great deal about Saul Alinsky, his organizing methods and his organization, but it was always through a secondary source—some medium other than the personality himself. We have, at long last, had the opportunity to talk directly with you about events and techniques which bear directly on the communities in which we live.

I began with a story out of our tradition, and both you and I have had occasion to call on references to our Jewish heritage in the course of our discussion. Jews have always been thinkers, but in the final analysis we have always been doers as well—doing on the basis of our thinking. We have been privileged to get behind the action phase of social action—in the Alinsky pattern—and see some of the thinking which moves it. It has been a revealing discussion, one which deepens our understanding of some of today's problems as well as some of the means being taken to alleviate them.

ERICH SEGAL

RABBI BERKOWITZ: The achievement of fame or popularity in any area of endeavor is a difficult task, acquired by few. Yet occasionally there are some who are able to succeed in many fields. Such a person is Erich Segal. He is a screen writer, an author of scholarly books on classical antiquity, a professor of literature at Yale University and a marathon runner. He is the author of the best-selling novel *Love Story* and has seen his novel brought to the screen as an outstanding motion picture.

Dr. Segal, I begin with that part of you that is an author. What special sensitivity is it that the writer must have to be a good author?

DR. SEGAL: In a way you answered part of the question. Not every author has to have a special sensitivity, I think. There are brilliant observers, people who can see things in minute detail and rather unsympathetically relate this detail in brilliant fashion. The result is a mosaic that glitters. There are some artists who can see, who have sensitivity and who can convey it. And then there are people who perceive, who are sensitive, but who in no way can express what they see.

RABBI BERKOWITZ: You are, of course, a teacher and an author. Are writers set apart from other people? Are they more lonely? Are they, for want of a better word, different?

DR. SEGAL: They are different in a way. Some of them are not at all lonely. There are real loners among writers—writers such as Truman Capote, who says that he will never write for the theater, that he detests team sports. He is a very gifted man and he can go his own way. I, on the other hand, write for give-and-take. For me, writing is not a lonely enterprise. I do the first draft, and it is always lousy; I show it to someone who gives his reaction and shares with me the criticism that will help make it not lousy. The loneliest job I did was the novel *Love Story*, because all I had the editor do at the end was to help edit it. But usually—and my main experience in writing is with the theater and movies—it is not lonely. Sometimes I wish it were, and that people would go away, but the modern writer, especially for the modern media, is anything but lonely. He is involved with directors and producers of all sorts. It is not a lonely profession unless, of course, one is a poet or a novelist who cannot stand being involved with people.

To the other part of your question, how are we different. Each writer is different in his own special way. I could not really, except by being incredibly pompous, tell you how writers are different. They just are. If I might change your question to: "How am I different?," I might say that I sometimes prefer to live my experiences on the typewriter than to live them in the world.

RABBI BERKOWITZ: When you write, do you plan the story

in advance, or let the characters take you where they want to go, in a sense.

DR. SEGAL: In *Love Story* I knew where I was going to go. I knew I was going to write about a girl who was going to die. I knew I had the first sentence: "What can you say about a twenty-five-year-old girl who died?" When I sat down at the typewriter I did not know whom I would write about, or who the girl would be or who the boy would be. I sat down at the typewriter and they started to talk and they took me along. I must say the one moment in *Love Story* that people—critics and laymen alike—single out as the most moving was the moment that I myself did not know was going to occur until, in fact, it did occur. The boy walked out of the hospital and embraced his father. I said, What, come again? And then I said, Yes, that's what he does. Then I said, Yes, I guess that must be the end of the book. And that was the end of the book.

I know, to cite a classical example, that Virgil, author of the *Aeneid* and other works, would have not only a diagram of what he was going to do, but would have a prose outline and turn it into verse. That is just the opposite extreme. Flaubert, for example, had maps and charts when he was writing *Madame Bovary*, and she would do this and do that, according to his organization of the story. There are probably living authors who are that careful. I suppose that I have done this sort of thing before. In fact, I know I have.

I have read about some strange things with respect to myself. One of the rumors is that I sprang full-grown from the head of Zeus or whatever; that I never had any writing experience prior to *Love Story*. The truth is that I have had an incredible career of non-successes, writing a script for a movie that was not a success. I am not ashamed of what I did. I am ashamed of what the director did to what I did. There was a movie called *The Games*. It was all about Olympic games.

When writing that, I boiled things down onto index cards because that kind of structure was the answer to the writing problem. Here was the story of four people intertwined, all of whom would ultimately meet as antagonists in an Olympic climax. There were four separate stories, and I had index cards—not to the extent that Flaubert had his maps—but my index cards were of different colors for the different parts. I put them all together, shuffled them up, and put them in the right order, and that really was the hardest structural part.

RABBI BERKOWITZ: What is the difference between writing for the movies and writing a novel?

DR. SEGAL: First, what is prized in a movie writer is his attention to visual detail. There is a paradox here, because you will note that in *Love Story* there is no detail, so that those who say that it was only cinematic could not be more wrong. It may be wrong in a lot of other things, but it is not cinematic because it omits the very details that make the screen writer valued. Writing for the screen is a new art, in the sense that the writer is the junior partner to the director. It is a collaborative kind of thing. The writer's vision is not always realized, and the director with a flip of the lens can change it, whereas the novel is totally the author's. Unfortunately, that privilege, that dictatorship, is often not a benevolent dictatorship over the reader, in my opinion. Writers have these despotic powers of literature, and they make you read whatever they want to write.

There are certain novelists that I would tax for non-brevity. They write a sentence five times. They feel sure that one of these five ways must be the right one, and since they do not know which, they include all five. This is what you are subject to in a novel, unless it is written by a conscientious novelist or there is a good editor. In any case, if the novelist has any strength of ego he can get all that he writes printed, and he can get his vision presented completely. If a person aspires to divinity, I suggest that the nearest he can come to it is to be a novelist. Everything will happen just the way he wants it and writes it, and the type will be set just the way he wants it.

The difference in writing for a screenplay is that actors are involved—actors who somehow can never read what one has written as perfectly as that actor in your head. If you are honest with yourself and admit that the real actor can read it better than the imagined actor in your mind, it's wonderful. In a conversation with Hollis Alpert, the movie critic, I said that in a movie script there is a greater downside risk than in a book. He said, "That's a great word; I have never heard of it, what does it mean?" I said that it comes from the stock market. It is the only market phrase I know, and I am not taking any downside risks. But there is a greater artistic downside risk when you commit your writing to the hands of someone else.

RABBI BERKOWITZ: Isaac Bashevis Singer once said the following (in fact he said it on this platform): "A Jewish writer is not such merely because he is a Jew, but because he writes about Jews. You must have a very big background in Jewish tradition to be a Jewish writer. From my point of view this excludes a man who does not know Yiddish, who does not know Hebrew, who does not know our history, does not know our customs and our laws. I would not call this man a Jewish writer, even if he happens to write about a Jewish storekeeper, or a Jewish worker, or a Jewish doctor. From this point of view I would say that there are very few fiction writers in English whom I would call Jewish writers."

Then, someone whose life was cut off at a very early age, a most gifted man, David Boroff, when asked on this platform for a definition of Jewish literature, said somewhat the opposite. "In our own culture, the American culture, the common sense answer is the best, which is to say that anything about Jews, whether written by Jews or non-Jews, represents some aspect of American Jewish literature. That means that a novel by Ernest Hemingway, like *The Sun Also Rises*, is in a sense American Jewish literature."

"If we are going to accept Singer's definition," concludes Mr. Boroff, "there is very little American Jewish literature except by Singer himself and possibly by Saul Bellow; of the other Jewish American writers there are very few that meet this requirement. Philip Roth is out, Bernard Malamud, even though he writes with a kind of Yiddish flavor, is out; he is not well schooled. Norman Mailer and others are out. I am afraid that Mr. Singer's definition will not work for us." Against this background what is your definition of the American Jewish writer?

DR. SEGAL: I think Mr. Singer's definition is highly idiosyncratic, highly so. And it is selfish in a way, because he does not want to share the mantle with many people. I am really trying not to do what is so easy in making literary comment of any sort—to disparage, or to see anything other than the thing as it is. A Jewish writer is a Jew who writes.

RABBI BERKOWITZ: Who in your estimation are the outstanding Jewish writers of today?

DR. SEGAL: Saul Bellow, for one. The trouble is, I always feel that I am going to miss a few people that I do not know are Jewish. When I think of writers, I think of all kinds of writers. To me a man is not just a writer who writes novels. We are not living in the age of the novel only. There are movies too, which may be proven in the perspective of eternity. For all we know, when the twentieth century is evaluated, critics will consider movies to be a higher art form. So we have to consider the great contribution of the cinema. I cannot begin to judge the great Jewish contribution to the cinema. There are the movies, and there is the musical stage, with all of the Jewish writers who work in these media. The literature of the American musical stage is created by very great American Jewish writers.

RABBI BERKOWITZ: What is your position, if any, on negative and positive writing about Jews and Judaism? Many people are very critical of books which in their estimation are unfair to the Jewish theme, the Jewish family, the Jewish home.

DR. SEGAL: I am against unfair books, of course, but I would not dare generalize even about the work of a single author, the work being his collective lifetime achievement. I do not like to read books which disparage any ethnic or religious group, even under the guise of satire. There are limits to satire.

RABBI BERKOWITZ: What makes a book great? Is it literary style, universal appeal? What books in your judgment stand the test of time?

DR. SEGAL: I do not know what "great" is, or what one means by using the term "great." Is it a euphemism for success? Take, for example, *Mood Indigo,* a recently translated French book by Boris Vian. This *is* an incredible book about what it is like to be young in a mechanized age. It is about love and death and life and hope and war and peace, and all the things that sound resounding and need volumes to say—it says it in 187 pages. This is a great book, but it is not a successful book.

RABBI BERKOWITZ: Then let me express it for you in these terms. What is it that the average reader in America wants from a book?

DR. SEGAL: Obviously some entertainment value, preferably coupled with edification, hence the appeal of a book like *Zelda*. It is biography in which you get some interesting insights about Mrs. Fitzgerald, F. Scott Fitzgerald and Hemingway. You put down the book with some satisfaction, feeling you have learned something. I think that is a normal kind of thing. But you have asked a question to which any publisher would like to have the answer. And indeed, if I had it, I would not be here, I would be having dinner with the publisher, and he would be trying to get the answer from me.

RABBI BERKOWITZ: Then let me hit directly home and specifically ask about *Love Story*. To begin with, how did this book come about? You must have been asked this question many times, but I would be interested in the process of its genesis and development.

DR. SEGAL: It was a screenplay before it was a novel, because when I got the idea for writing the story, I had never written a novel before. I know I was grabbed by something. It really happens to you, that poetic frenzy you hear about. I was in a frenzied state. It was a Thanksgiving holiday, when some Yale students of mine came to visit me—graduates who kept in touch. They told me the story of a young classmate whose wife had put him through graduate school, not law school as in the book. It is a common story and they liked it. Even when parents can afford to send a child through school, the students like to do it themselves, they get a certain satisfaction out of it. At any rate, the girl did not live to have this satisfaction, because she died of a disease which was, of course, also not the same as in *Love Story*.

I was struck by what this young man would feel, at the age of twenty-five, having completed his studies, ready for life in every respect. He had, in fact, paid his wife back for her sacrifices. These were not really sacrifices, but he would never believe that.

Now, one always has regrets, one always has Kaddish said, when someone close dies. I did not know the boy and, obviously, I would not invade anyone's privacy. The story of *Love Story* was based on a melodramatic occurrence, and I built around it. But this is not an uncommon occurrence, as I later found out from a multitude of letters. It occurs more often than one thinks.

I sat down to write, and from somewhere in my imagination, not really my imagination but somewhere from the happiest of my experiences, came this girl Jenny. She was a girl I knew, who is alive and well, blushing a bit, at least among her friends, who realize that it is obviously a portrait of her. Her husband is very proud of her. This was a very wonderful and unique character, and so I put her down on paper. This is an answer to an unasked question—where writers get their characters. More or less they are refractions, not reflections, because it is cruel to put a mirror up to what your friends are doing. Perhaps they are a reflection of the better or at least the salient qualities of people one knows.

So, actually, there are three truths involved, blended together by the writer's affection. These three truths were woven into what is absolutely fiction, but what you might call true fiction. A boy who actually existed; in fact, I saw him walking to his law office the other day in New York, but I did not say "hello" because I was embarrassed. A girl whom I knew, admired and loved—still know, admire and love. And an incident which triggered it all off, which happened to neither one of these two parties. The story happened to a Yale boy, but I wrote about it using the setting of Harvard because Harvard was what I knew best. I could never pretend to know what it is like to be a Yale undergraduate. I have no idea what it is like to be in one of my classes. I am on the other side.

RABBI BERKOWITZ: And what about the conflict in the book between father and son?

DR. SEGAL: That was an afterthought, as far as I was concerned. I wanted to convey a subtle conflict to depict the deepest of all possible grief, the greatest of all possible isolation. I wanted that to be so sad. I wanted to somehow, without saying it, show that this boy had nothing, absolutely nothing, and so, not very subtly, I divested him of his rich parents. I added a cliched melodramatic factor because I wanted him to be alone for the effect, for the artistic purpose. Added to that, there is a more subtle, but nonetheless present, alienation, a slight feeling of guilt that the boy has to face. With ostensible good humor his father has had to suffer through his child marrying in a way he and his wife had not wanted. You know, parents care about that sort of thing. The father was big-hearted and said "I don't care," but deep down Oliver caused him hurt. Now, had Jenny lived and presented him with a half-dozen grandchildren, he would have really felt fine about it.

RABBI BERKOWITZ: I was moved by the story. I felt that it had a kind of low-keyed style that leaves the reader to delve further into his own imagination. Not everything is said explicitly or brought to its logical conclusion.

DR. SEGAL: I appreciate your noticing that. I really mean it, because the initial impact of *Love Story* in this country made it an item of conversation and people were so enthusiastic that they did not read as carefully as they might have had they been less enthusiastic. The key to the style, which is exactly as you describe it, is in the attitude of the French poet Verlaine, who said, "I took out all the colors, all that is left are the nuances."

Perhaps the most astute of the letters I received were the ones that said: "Dear Mr. Segal, thank you for the hundred pages you did not write." I did not write what color hair Jenny had, or what Oliver looked like—deliberately so, and for two reasons. I believe MacLuhan—although the man has gone overboard and is drowning in the swimming pool of his own theory—says, essentially, that environment is drastically changed by media. I do not have time to read the description of a Balzac, the kind of minute detail which you get in a single second on TV. If you read a book it has to be something other than what you can get through the electronic media. It should be evocative rather than descriptive.

You may have realized that in the story there are only three colors mentioned—three places where I describe something by color. One, her eyes are brown, then her kitchen is yellow. That was deliberate, yellow kitchens are chic, and I wanted to show that they had moved up into a world where they had the superfluities of life, not just a stove that worked, but one that was also yellow and a bit fancy. And then the most deliberate—and you may see the effect of it—is the third and only other color that is used. After three years the boy visits his father and says, "I noticed that my father's hair had grown grayer in the three years I had not seen him." Now, you notice that and you get a little upset, at least if the novel is working for you. You are affected and you really feel that he had not seen his father for three years because we never knew what his father's hair looked like in the first place. But the boy notices that his father's hair had grown grayer—ergo, it is important. It has the effect of, "Oh, my God, three years have gone by."

So, by my deliberately leaving out the colors of the trees in Cambridge, the red Georgian brick, the lovely pastel gray of the library, when color finally appears, you pay attention. This was absolutely deliberate.

RABBI BERKOWITZ: In the transition from the book to the film, was any of this quality lost?

DR. SEGAL: It was thrown away, absolutely, because a book is a book and a movie is a movie. Anyone who tries to make a book into a movie book is going to have a lousy movie. They made it into a movie, and I must say it is good, but obviously one cannot make a movie in which one does not know the color of the heroine's hair. They would be in bad trouble, if they played it all in shadow.

You will excuse me if I sound pompous about my own thoughts, but you must understand two things. First, this is the year that I am popular, and second I am a professor, so I am entitled. You do understand that in real life I do not regard this as the world's greatest literature. There is no copy of *Love Story* next to Sophocles on my shelf. It is in the closet with the manuscript, the typed stuff, and my term papers from Harvard.

A movie is a movie. Indeed, one of the valid techniques of translating a novel with nondescription to a movie, is to give the movie maker some help. You are in bad shape if you hand in a script in which you make no specifications at all as to what the characters look like. One of the joys of a movie is indeed its visual quality.

Now, obviously, I win or lose, but what makes the movie win is really something I have nothing to do with. It walks the line between *Peyton Place* and something that is a little special for one occasion. The slightest bit of miscasting, the slightest bit of misdirection, the slightest bit of an over-anything can bring it into the *Peyton Place* area.

Certainly I had three lucky breaks. One is that Ali MacGraw is a person—I mean a *person*—she photographs like a person. This is a girl who can convey a soul onto Eastman Kodak film stock. Other people cannot ordinarily be so photographed. This girl is not the world's most trained would probably make the film "R" automatically, but for all the others, the dialogue is as it is. The four-letter words are mostly not in the dialogue of the book, they are in the descriptions. These are inner thoughts that are really emotional and call up four-letter words. Listen to yourself the next time you drop something on your foot—and then write to me. It is truth, and it is the writer's job to tell the truth.

When the script was finished, the producer, a neophyte who had never produced before, brought the script to be rated. Dr. Stern of the rating commission said, "Well. . . PG." Our producer was very upset—worried in fact—that the picture would be banned in Boston or something. At the last minute he had a crisis of faith, and he said, "But tell me, Dr. Stern, why did you give this picture with that word and this word, which admittedly I and my wife never use, why did you give it a PG?" Dr. Stern said, "I want to tell you something. I want young people to see this picture because it is *moral*. It is moral, it talks about love and fidelity and a physical commitment. You know, kids are making physical commitments, or whatever euphemisms are used, at the age of thirteen. I would like in some way, in their language, to show them that there are some spiritual values that can and should be attached to this physical involvement. What better way than to clothe it in the credibility of the language in which they speak?"

RABBI BERKOWITZ: I want to read a passage from the book. When the young man proposed marriage, he said, "What about our marriage?" It was I who spoke those words, although for a split second I wasn't sure I really had. "Who said anything about marriage?" "Me, I am saying it now. Do you want to marry me?" "Yes." She tilted her head, did not smile, but merely inquired, "But why?" The young man looked her straight in the eye. "Because," I said. "Oh," she said, "that's a very good reason."

Now, is this typical of a lack of sentimentality in the expression of emotion? Would you say that this is characteristic of young people?

DR. SEGAL: That "because" is very, very fraught with emotion. There is enormous sentiment behind that "because," there is a whole world behind that "because." That "because" is to say that I will be here for forty years to tell you all the reasons why I want to marry you. Your question is really a good one and a very valid observation about the life style of young people today. When Jenny says, "You want to marry me?" she knows darn well that he does, and that she wants to marry him, but it is a way of reacting. It is a kind of language they speak. It is part of the reason for the four-letter words; it is a kind of fake toughness, a toughness that hides an enormous tenderness. Why are the Beatles such heroes? Because they get away with the incredible tenderness that the average young person is afraid to express. They are part of an enormously sensitive generation. They hide it—at least from the people who do not understand that kind of talking. Underneath it they cherish and nourish a real tenderness. How did I learn all about this? How did I become such a *maven*? I learned something about this by reading French reviews, because in France they delve into this sort of sociological literary analysis. The only other persons who put it into such terms were the college-age reviewers in student newspapers. The sociological beat was missed by all except the French critics and the young kids.

RABBI BERKOWITZ: This summer, I believe you took a trip to Europe. Was your book translated into many languages while you were there?

DR. SEGAL: Oh, yes, I had a lot of fun, because *Love Story* was translated into all kinds of languages. The hardest of all was English—and I will get to that. I took a voyage to Europe where *Love Story* was published in many languages, and I worked on many translations. You know, it is a very tough thing; an example of this was in the Italian version. The line referring to the lady lawyer, Bella Landau, referred to her as "a cool chick"—in the Italian translation it came out as "a frigid woman."

There are a lot of innocent mistakes. In the Spanish version, for example, they are at the wedding, and the father is looking "slack-jawed" in wonderment at his daughter. The Spaniard actually wrote there that he was looking with slacks in his jaw. Well, maybe he thought it was some surrealistic thing that happened. When one sees something like that one thinks in horror, "What am I getting when I read Tolstoy?" We really do not know, we just have faith in the translation.

Thank God, it was a short book. I worked with the translators every chance I had. I even compiled a glossary of Americanisms, which is good for a few guffaws. But it was nice to go to Europe, and it was nice to be received on the Continent. It was almost more than I could bear to be received as I was in England. There I did not change a word. I did not have to do anything, just get published and go over there.

In the *Times* in London, regarding the publication, Navla O'Faolin, Sean O'Faolin's daughter, and herself a professor of literature at the University of Dublin, said that *Love Story* represents the death of the novel. I thought that this was the worst it could get, until the *New Statesman* said I was "sexually anemic." How do you write a letter to an editor and say "Test that."? Or do you? And it really got worse—they all jumped on the bandwagon and tried to outdo each other. One writer in England, who was quoted in the Sunday papers here, had enormous guts. He came out at the same time everyone else did but praised the book. He said, "It is a book about human goodness, and I was profoundly moved." I wrote him a letter.

I did not have many thank-you notes to write to England, however, so I had time to write him a long one.

There was an enormous reaction on the part of the younger people. They wrote letters to me apologizing for this establishment kind of reaction, saying that it was not representative of what English people really feel. Fortunately, after that I went to France where I read about the tradition of the American novel and saw myself in a line that culminated with J. D. Salinger, and I said, "Well, they are more astute, these French," and I became a Francophile. The French reviews were enormously observant about the sociological aspect, as I mentioned.

I also had the experience of talking on some of the talk shows. They have them in France too, but they cover the whole country. You are not just talking to your friends in Queens or in Boston—you are talking to Marseilles and Strasbourg, and even across the border into Belgium; you are talking to everyone. You are talking to a nation and a half, and people call on the phone and they ask you questions. So little is our society understood that the first question asked me on Radio Luxembourg was, "Etes-vous raciste?" (Are you racist?) It took me a while to get my balance. It was not television and the host said to the caller: 'Sir, I wish you could see the face of our distinguished guest because it is on the floor." I said, "Do you think, sir, that there is apartheid in America as in the Union of South Africa?" He said, "Well, yes, there is apartheid and you either are or you aren't." I responded, "You asked a question that reveals how little you understand us."

If you think they misjudge us because of our foreign policy, imagine what they think of us as people. And this was a responsible young man—I could tell by his tone of voice. He was shocked that I was shocked. Anyway, it was very edifying, being on that program, it was hands-across-the-sea kind of thing, and I really felt that we as a people came off a bit more human as a result of this contact.

RABBI BERKOWITZ: Now, I would like to turn to more personal aspects. We have spoken about the book market, Jewish writers, the contemporary scene, young people, about *Love Story*. Let us talk about you. Where were you born and educated? What was the extent of your Jewish education and background?

DR. SEGAL: They are synonymous, because I was born the son of a rabbi, in Brooklyn, on June 16, 1937. I was not consulted in the matter, but it was decided that I should learn Hebrew, which my late father taught me. I guess I was three or four when I started. Early he said, "Get with it! *Bereshis*; the next word is *bara* and the next word is up to you." I can still quote the whole of *Bereshis* by heart. I think I read Hebrew before I read English; I don't remember anything as well. From there it was very quickly to the Crown Heights Yeshiva where it was Hebrew in the morning until we had a quick luncheon break and then English was crowded in. But it was good, it was a good education. It was rigorous, it was fine, and I must tell you an astonishing fact—as I look over my educational career from the first year on it became easier and easier because nothing could be harder than a Yeshiva.

I later went to Midwood High School, and it was much easier, not because I did not have to go to Hebrew in the morning—my parents saw to that—although I traveled up to the Jewish Theological Seminary at night. That was okay too; you see, there was no pressure. I don't think we had report cards. Midwood High School was easier than the Yeshiva.

I don't remember anything about the Crown Heights Yeshiva except the hard work and being there at an assembly and hearing the most emotional speech I ever heard a rabbi give, excluding my father, when the State of Israel was established. We were in school, and he made a speech. I do not recall what he said, but I was never so moved as I was at that moment.

RABBI BERKOWITZ: Without being sentimental, Erich Segal's appearance here evokes within me and the memories of other people a great feeling of warmth and nostalgia. His late father, of blessed memory, was Rabbi Samuel Segal. I had the privilege of knowing your father, and I want to say that I loved him dearly and respected him for his gifts and many talents. He was a warm-hearted individual, a writer of plays, a great artist and sculptor, and an unusual human being.

Have you continued your Jewish studies in recent years? What of your Jewish identification, knowledge of language, history?

DR. SEGAL: I interpret that question as: "What kind of a Jew are you?" And that is a very good question, and I have asked myself that question. I do not find myself in Temple on very many Friday nights. On the High Holy days and Passover, yes. For some reason, I have always enjoyed sharing religious services with kids who were there not because their parents told them to be there. The kids whose parents had to call them up at school to remind them to go to *Shul* on Saturday usually went to football games. The parents were none the wiser, but the ones who really wanted to go were there. It was a pleasure to be there; there was no constraint.

This is a very eccentric way of describing it. I felt it, whether in a converted gym or Phillips Brooks house, or even when on some occasions a Unitarian church was taken over for the day, and was a Temple by virtue of the fact that people were there who wanted to be there to give testimony to their Judaism. I read every year in the Yom Kippur service. It has become a tradition for me, at least for the six years or so that I have been at Yale. As far as attendance is concerned, I think I have become one of those three-day-a-year Jews against whom my father used to sermonize on the holidays.

I don't know whether or what young people are rethinking

today. I do not consider myself one of them. I am an observer of the young, and I learn what I can. But I imagine that they are rethinking about all kinds of institutions, such as churches. What is a church? Is it a place where a cross hangs or a place where people gather? Can any place become a church, or by analogy, a synagogue if a couple of Jews get together and in some way share something spiritual? In that sense, if I talk about Jewish matters with my friends—I had one such conversation yesterday with the associate provost at Yale who happens to be a Jewish boy from Carolina—is that a Jewish experience? Is it a kind of new, outside-of-synagogue kind of Judaism? My background is there. I appreciate the Bible as literature, and I do not deny it as truth. Sometimes I study the Psalms and I think about why this is this way or that way. There is sometimes more song than feeling in the Psalms, and I say, "Was the Psalmist sincere, or was he trying to be clever? This is the kind of literary analysis I would make, fairly or unfairly, with any kind of thought. Maybe that is a secularization of me; maybe I am finished as a Jew.

RABBI BERKOWITZ: You are, in accordance with all reports, an intensely disciplined individual. I think it is important that we discuss the need of discipline in life.

DR. SEGAL: Absolutely! We are in a particular period of undiscipline. We oscillate from one extreme to another. This business of the laxity and permissiveness of a whole generation is serious. Obviously even the most dedicated rebel against the establishment who gets on an Eastern Airlines plane for Washington to bomb Mr. Agnew's front lawn is not going to want one of his own cohorts to be pilot of the plane just because he has enthusiasm or has soul. He wants him to be trained. There is a discipline to becoming a pilot, and he wants the guy piloting the plane to go through pilot school and do his homework. Right? Likewise, when you get on the operating table and are about to be opened up, you would like the surgeon to be a nice fellow who gives you good vibrations and is a beautiful person, but you would also like him to have some training, to have gone through the discipline of medical school so that he knows how to cut very well.

I am using extreme examples, but this is really true. I mean we accept discipline in the surgeon and in the doctor. Everybody gets sick, even radical thinkers get sick, and they want to get cured, which comes only by "reactionary" training. It is a paradox, no?

So, I think that people will come to realize that discipline is needed even though there are exceptions, like gifts from God—people who can run fast, for example. I know about that; I trained like a maniac and still people who never trained beat me on the track. There are some areas in which one can excel without discipline, but on the other hand, the majority of areas, especially intellectual ones, require discipline.

Any person, any young person with a goal in life, will realize that his goal requires discipline. To use an absurd reflection, which has some truth in it, even the revolutionaries who are now bombing are training themselves to be better bombers, unless they want to blow themselves up. Of course, this is a terrible way to learn discipline, but it is, in a way, an example of the fact that expertise is needed in everything.

RABBI BERKOWITZ: According to your biography you run ten miles a day. I would like to know how you do it and why you do it?

DR. SEGAL: I have done it with my two feet and wearing a pair of track shoes ever since my days in high school. I was a member of the track team there and had an undistinguished track career which I went on to perpetuate at Harvard and thereafter. It is not hard to run ten miles. The first time, yes, believe me, but after that you get accustomed to it, it is the most refreshing thing in the world. It makes you healthy, it makes you happy, it can do what two martinis could never do.

RABBI BERKOWITZ: How has all this affected your life—a best seller, these many personal appearances, commuting to California for weekends? How would you say this has affected your teaching, your thoughts and values? Has it made any kind of change in your outlook and life style?

DR. SEGAL: In toto, the result of having done these various things and being able to do some of them is a feeling of fulfillment, and I am very, very grateful. I know how rarely it comes to a person at any stage of life. It is a feeling of total fulfillment, of happiness, of not grinding, of not being jealous of anybody in the world. This may be an evanescent kind of feeling. You know, I have not always lived this kind of life. As my mother will testify, we had a standing joke in our house when I was a kid. The phone would ring and I would say, "Is it from Hollywood for me?" I really used to say that. And now, the phone rings, and it is for me and it *is* from Hollywood. And it is great.

RABBI BERKOWITZ: The word "fulfillment" was used a moment ago. It is refreshing to find a public figure who is willing to admit that he has experienced fulfillment in his work. In these days of "cool cats" (to use another of your terms), it is more fashionable to be dissatisfied, or, at the least, detached about what one does and the way one does it. I detect an undercurrent of enthusiasm in you about everything that you do, and the scope of your activities is, as I said in the introduction, not inconsiderable.

Perhaps this is one of the keys to the success which you have enjoyed—the freshness which you bring to your task. It most certainly provides an example for those of us who are prone to take a dim view of the world and our place in it.

I surely do not want to advocate that everyone become an incurable optimist. . . We all recognize the serious need for change in our world, just as we understand—deep down—the values inherent in turning in a good performance in whatever we undertake. Blind optimism is not the way in which we can accomplish this. However, a zest for challenge and a clear comprehension that life is not all negative are, I think, imperative if one is to survive and make a contribution to life.

This spirit, at least as much as the content of what you have to say, is a gift that you have brought us, Dr. Segal, and we thank you for it.

JACQUES LIPCHITZ

RABBI BERKOWITZ: Jacques Lipchitz spent his youth in Paris, where he was a close friend of Soutine, Modigliani and Chagall. A story about him tells of another painter who maintained that he was dissatisfied with the light that he painted on his canvas and went off to Morocco, seeking a change of light. But he found that the light on his Moroccan canvases was no different. This artist discussed it with Mr. Lipchitz, who said to him, "An artist's light comes from within, not from without." His life story shows that the artist needs and follows an inner force, but also needs an inner spiritual fire. Mr. Lipchitz demonstrates that the greatest art is the art of living, and the true creative spark is that which burns within the heart and soul of all of us. Our guest has succeeded, as have few others, in interpreting both life and work, so that a lifetime of creative communication has been combined with a lifetime of deep commitment to the humanistic doctrines of eternal Judaism.

Every person looks at life through his own experiences and his own interests. It is normal for me to view life through the eyes of a rabbi; others view life through the eyes of doctors, dentists, businessmen, lawyers. We are going to try to view a fascinating and interesting life through the perceptive eyes and creative and idealistic soul of an artist.

Mr. Lipchitz was born in 1891 in Lithuania. His father was a banking contractor and came from a rich banking family. His biographer tells us that he began at a very early age to draw and to model in clay and bread. His father wanted him to be an engineer and his mother sent him to Paris illegally and without his father's knowledge. Sounds a bit like the Scriptures—Jacob and Esau, Isaac and Rebecca. What effect, if any, did these early years have on your later work?

MR. LIPCHITZ: They are with me in every step I take.

RABBI BERKOWITZ: Your biographer says that you are grateful to your mother, who had faith in you, who showed you the way and gave you the inspiration for later sculpture.

MR. LIPCHITZ: She was a marvelous woman. She was very simple, without any education. She could darn and cook, and that was about all. She learned everything from us—her six children. By the time all of us received our education, my mother was more knowledgeable than we were. She was also, I would say, a bit superstitious. You know, the *shtetl* where I was born was a summer resort, and many people came there to cure their ills because of the sulphur waters. When I was born—I was told about this—my father invited a rabbi to bless me. He took me by the hand and said, "My boy, the first thing that I wish for you is *not* to be a rabbi." He said, "You will nevertheless be a *godol b'yisroel*, a great man in Israel." My mother always took it for granted. After all, I was the first-born and for a long time the only boy.

RABBI BERKOWITZ: Your mother had great faith and interest in your work, but your father was opposed. Why was he opposed at first, although I know that as your career developed he gave up his opposition. Why did he change his mind?

MR. LIPCHITZ: My mother, as I said, was always protecting me, and I knew that I wanted to become a sculptor. My father was opposed because as he did more business and became more prosperous and started to buy factories, he wanted me to be an engineer who would take care of all these factories. However, when I finished high school, I told my mother that I wanted to go to Paris. I had an uncle who was living on the German frontier, and she communicated with him. One day she said, "I give you my permission. Go to your uncle, he will arrange for you to go. But when you are in Paris, take care, be careful of women."

I went to my uncle's home, which was in Lithuania, in a town called Stanislav. I went back and forth across the border a few times with my uncle. Then, one day, he brought my luggage along, and I went on to Paris. My mother had told me, "It would be wise to write your father a letter asking him to forgive you. I will arrange things." And she did.

RABBI BERKOWITZ: She must have had a profound influence on your father.

MR. LIPCHITZ: She was a very intelligent woman, a very beautiful, marvelous person. A real *Yiddishe* mama, really a *Yiddishe* mama.

RABBI BERKOWITZ: Mr. Lipchitz, you opened your first studio in Paris in 1911. In 1912-1913 you began exhibiting. Your biography records that you were called to Russia for military service, and after serving you returned to Paris.

There, you began to meet and make friends. Among those were such personalities as Modigliani, Soutine and Picasso.

MR. LIPCHITZ: That biography is touched up a little bit and occasionally mixed up. For instance, I received a letter from my mother one day asking me to come back. I was afraid that perhaps somebody was sick, so I sent a telegram and told her a letter would follow, asking what was happening. She replied that my father had lost all of his fortune and they could not support me any more. I was a spoiled brat, as you can imagine. I had never worked, everything was taken for granted. I wrote back that if they could not support me, I would try to support myself. You see, something had happened to me. I had an itch and had to satisfy it. You have an itch, you scratch.

RABBI BERKOWITZ: You had an artistic itch.

MR. LIPCHITZ: Yes, when I was a child, I had this desire to work with my fingers. I started to make sculpture without seeing sculpture. In my own *shtetl* there was none, and I did not know I was doing sculpture. I thought I was making toys. I remember that one day I made a lot of animals out of bread. The only animals that I saw were pigs, so I made pigs. My mother looked at me and she said: *"Chaimki,* you make animals. All right, but why not make *kosher* animals?" She was marvelous. Years later, I made a head, and it was without the eyes. She saw it and she scratched out the eyes. She said, "I couldn't bear it that my son makes such a blind thing." She was very simple at the start. Later, she became more sophisticated.

RABBI BERKOWITZ: Tell us about Picasso and Soutine.

MR. LIPCHITZ: I was an old Parisian by the time I met

Picasso. Diego Rivera, the Mexican artist, who was my good friend, took me one day to meet Picasso. When we arrived at the studio, Picasso was not there. A little pompous man who was there showed me around the studio. You would have thought that he had made everything himself. There was a little sculpture that Picasso had made, and the man said, *"That's* the sculpture of Picasso," as though saying, "That's sculpture—what you are doing is nothing."

Later, when Picasso came, he showed us many things. Then I asked him about one particular work. "Mr. Picasso, tell me, please, do you consider this a sculpture or a painting?" because it was painted. He said, "And you, young man, could you tell me what is sculpture and what is painting?" I said to him, "No, certainly I cannot tell you what is painting and what is sculpture, but I can tell you one thing—that's not sculpture."

RABBI BERKOWITZ: What was his reaction?

MR. LIPCHITZ: He said, "Why, because it is painted? Look at this mask, it is painted also." I said, "But look how it's painted." He said, "This mask is black, but there are parts that are white. Do you know what is the white?" They were shadows, because he could not make dark shadows on dark wood, so he made them white. "That's a transposition," I said, "but that's not sculpture." When we came down, I was with the assistant, who said, "You have now made an enemy of this man." And I said, "I couldn't do otherwise. I had to tell him what I thought." Well, a day later, Picasso was in my studio, and we became close friends.

RABBI BERKOWITZ: You were part of a school in Paris, one of the first sculptors to apply the principles of Cubism. I would like to read a statement: "One should not think of Cubism in those years as a system or a fixed discipline, but rather as an ever-changing, even unsystematic movement." What is Cubism and how was it first received?

MR. LIPCHITZ: Cubism in painting became absolutely an attitude. I would say that a man like Cezanne was more of a Cubist than the first Cubist painter. When I started to understand a little about art, I was dissatisfied with everything I saw around me. I couldn't bear Rodin, I did not like my own work. I did not appreciate, too much, the people that were around me at that time. It was out of dissatisfaction that I drifted away from the classical aspects of sculpture. I was at that time attracted by the Cubists. My first Cubism was very superficial, I would say. It led me, very shortly, to Dada. I remember that it was in 1916 that I came to an art which was nonrepresentational—almost what young sculptors are doing today.

In 1915 I had a visit from a man named Jules Romains who became a very great French writer. At that time he was a young doctor beginning his writing. He was interested in what I was doing and he questioned me. I told him, "I would like to make sculpture as pure as a crystal." He said to me a bit sarcastically, "What do you know about crystal?" I couldn't answer. When he went away I asked myself what, indeed, did I know about crystals?" Crystals are not alive, they are inanimate. I wanted to make real life, and I was going about it all wrong. A crisis, a very deep crisis! So I said to myself, "What did my father do when he was building? He would take a brick and make from it a cozy house. What am I doing? I take a cozy house and I make from that a brick. And I am wrong.

So I became, for a very short time, very realistic, more than before, in my sculpture. And then I saw that I was wrong. I was very unhappy, very sick.

RABBI BERKOWITZ: Let me read something you said, and I

would like you to comment on this. The biographer said of you, "In 1925, he now arrived at a period of growth and of positive sculptural symbols. We should be on guard against the idea that pictorial content could be translated into his sculptural symbolism. His work has nothing to do with verbal symbols." And I believe this is your statement: "Sculpture depends on the sense of sight and touch, not on the instrument, language, employed by contemplative reasons." Will you explain this?

MR. LIPCHITZ: I considered that I was a newcomer to the Cubist generation. Our generation came to some kind of a closed road. We were not satisfied with things which were done in our time and before us, and I speak about the Impressionists. We had different roads. We felt that we as artists did not use all our human potentialities. The impressionists were just painting what they saw in front of them, with a theory of color that was revolutionary at that time but which later was repudiated. We wanted to use all human potentialities and also imagination, not only what the eyes saw, but what can be imagined. So we took the road of imagination. And on that road we found many people. Old Negro art, Mexican art—we shook hands with them. It was an encounter—very aesthetic—which used imagination. The first Cubist painting by Picasso, *La Table*, is not very much. It is over-agitated, it is added, it is not very tangential, it is flat. We were trying to figure out whether we were really right.

RABBI BERKOWITZ: Mr. Lipchitz, in the thirties the threats to freedom found fertile soil. In your Jewish youth in Czarist Russia you had known the meaning of terror. When you turned to mythological figures, you chose Greek or Biblical names for some of your sculpture. Why did you use figures and names from the Bible?

MR. LIPCHITZ: Well, you see, the first ethic of Cubism is merely, I would say, grammatical—we were looking for a language, a language which would be adequate to the feelings that we had. When we learned that language, we started to tell our story. I chose the Biblical and Greek because they have meaning. When you say Prometheus, you know what is meant. The same is true for the Biblical. If you think about Abraham or Moses, immediately you have meaning, and the image has meaning.

RABBI BERKOWITZ: What kind of an image does Abraham bring to your mind?

MR. LIPCHITZ: Well, first of all, he is the father of our religion, and, something which is more important to me, he represented the first step away from human sacrifices.

RABBI BERKOWITZ: How about Moses?

MR. LIPCHITZ: He is, of course, the great-grandfather of our religion. He said that we should not have or make graven images of what we see around us. I absolutely agree with him. I am absolutely in accord with him. I would say that this is what makes my sculpture special.

RABBI BERKOWITZ: You arrived in America in June 1941. Your only possessions were two statuettes, a portfolio of drawings and a few dollars. How was it that you arrived with so little?

MR. LIPCHITZ: My wife and I were living in Paris when friends of mine, a couple, came to us and said, "Hitler is on the outskirts of Paris. We are going away but we do not want to go without you. However, do what you want to. We will rent rooms in a hotel, we'll leave our car at your disposal.

Tomorrow morning at seven o'clock we are going away." Well, we had a house, food and clothing and a dream, and, of course, my work. But money we did not have. I had a few thousand francs, but that wasn't money. Our friends came at seven o'clock in the morning, and we left with them.

So we started a new life on the road. It is a long story. There was supposed to be an English boat to take all the refugees. We went to meet it but it did not come, so we went on toward Spain in a car. One morning while traveling, we saw refugee carts covered with mattresses and other possessions going in our direction. Later we started to see cars. We asked for information and said that we wanted to go to a certain town. They told us we could not go there since it was occupied by the Germans. We asked if there was a train we could get to. They said there was, but that they could not tell us exactly where, but that if we went north, we might find it. So we went north to get to this train and as a result, we stopped in a small town. I don't remember the name of the place. When we bought a paper, we learned that we were in the free world. From there we went to Toulouse, where I had many good and powerful friends. One day I received a letter from a man who asked, "What can we do for you? We are here in Marseilles and we would like to help you." I wrote him and said, "I have some drawings; if you would, please send them to America, to the Museum of Modern Art."

You see, artists are always a bit vain. We are always sure that we will somehow die soon, and I wanted to save my last drawings. I received another letter from my friend saying that not only would he send my drawings, but if we wanted to go, he would bring us to America. I do have to say that I was very stupid. I said that I didn't speak any English and that in America there were only skyscrapers. What would I do over there? I would die anyway, so better to let me die here. But he would not let us alone.

He insisted in his letters and finally I went to Marseilles

with my wife, and he got passports for us. We went back to Lourdes and waited there with our passports. After six months I recieved a very severe letter from him. "People are dying to go to America. We get you passports and you stay. You are crazy." So I said, "Maybe I am crazy." I was stupid, completely stupid, you know. They say that there is a German Valhalla where there exists one little god who is not very powerful but can take sense away from his enemies. They said that I was under his influence, because I was stupid, absolutely. I was ashamed of myself.

RABBI BERKOWITZ: Mr. Lipchitz, while we were sitting in my study, you shared with me a facet of your life which you said was rather personal. I asked your permission to ask a question about it. I asked if you are an identified Jew. You said, *"Ich bin gemahlt.* I am a Jew and I am remaining a Jew." I then asked, "How do you identify yourself, what is your identification?" You said that you put on *tefillin* every day. I think that we would be very inspired if you could share with us the background and development of your identification.

MR. LIPCHITZ: I was born into an Orthodox family, but left Orthodoxy when I was in Paris. But in spite of myself, I am a believer and always was. About three years ago I was very sick. They operated on me and took away almost all my stomach at that time. And while I was so sick, I was a Jew. My present wife comes from a very, very Orthodox family. Her brother told her, "You should go to see the Lubavitcher Rebbe and ask him to pray for you," so she did. He listened while she told her story, and said, "I know. I know you and I know him. Go home, and don't bother. He will be all right. When he gets out of the hospital, ask him to come to see me." So I did. I went with my wife and he received me.

He knew a good deal about me, because his father-in-law had lived in a hotel which had belonged to my mother in our little Russian village. When he was a young rabbi, he would from time to time visit his father-in-law. The old rabbi told my mother that his son-in-law was living in Paris and studying at the Sorbonne. My mother told him that she had a son in Paris. The son-in-law, when he came back to Paris, inquired and found out everything about me. When I visited him he started to question me about my Jewishness. I told him, "I'm not *kosher*, I do not pray, I do not go to synagogue, I sculpted a virgin for the Catholic Church." He said to me, "I will ask you one thing, only one thing. I want you to *daven* every day. That is the only thing I ask." A few days later, he sent a man with *tefillin*. I *daven* every morning. It is of great help to me. He really did something for me by advising me to do that, because I cannot take a step during the day if I do not *daven*.

RABBI BERKOWITZ: What does it mean to you?

MR. LIPCHITZ: First of all, it puts me together with all my people. I am with them. And I am near to my Lord, to the Almighty. I speak with Him. I cannot make any individual prayers, but I speak to Him. He gives me strength for the day. I could not move otherwise.

RABBI BERKOWITZ: Of all the rituals that you might observe, such as *kashrut*, keeping the Sabbath, or going to the synagogue, why do you think that the rabbi told you to put on *tefillin*?

MR. LIPCHITZ: I can't speak for him. I know that it did something very important for me. I could not live any more without it.

RABBI BERKOWITZ: You made a very interesting observation when you said that prayer puts you at one with your people. A basic sense of identification for the Jewish people has been achieved through study. One of the fundamental reasons for the Jew to put on *tefillin* in the morning is to enable every Jew, tutored or untutored, to have an opportunity not only to commune with God, but to say something from the Torah, something from the Bible, so that he can begin his day with some element of study.

You accepted a commission in 1946 or 1947 for a baptismal font for the church of Notre-Dame-de-Taite-Grace at Assy. You accepted it on the condition that it be inscribed as follows: "Jacob Lipchitz, a Jew, true to the faith of his ancestors, made this Virgin to further good will among men so that the spirit may triumph on earth."

MR. LIPCHITZ: I will tell you how it happened. I had a large exhibition in Paris in 1946. I was here in America, but I went there for the exhibition. While there, a man approached me, complimented me on my sculpture, and said, "Would you like to make a Virgin for a Catholic church?" I said, "Look at my work, it is not exactly suitable for a Catholic church." "We know everything about your work," he said. "In fact, I have been charged to approach you and ask you about it." I said, "You know I am Jewish," and he said, "If it doesn't disturb you, it doesn't disturb us."

I liked his answer so much that I said, "Well, we'll see about it, but in principle I accept." I thought about this Virgin from time to time but went away without seeing the people. I had been thinking for a long time about this adventure, and in 1947 I accepted it on the condition that I be permitted to put that inscription in a highly visible place on the sculpture. I received a very enthusiastic letter saying that they admired my work and admired the spirit of the inscription. So I started to make the Virgin.

RABBI BERKOWITZ: Why did you want the inscription included?

MR. LIPCHITZ: First, of course, because I am a Jew and because my spirit was with it. Then, with the ecumenical spirit starting to prevail in the Catholic Church, it was a beginning. I would like to see this idea spread over the entire world. You know, I never have seen this sculpture installed. I have never gone there, but I often receive letters about it.

RABBI BERKOWITZ: Have you received letters from Jews? Have you been criticized?

MR. LIPCHITZ: Oh, yes. I always finish one work at a time and this statue took about a year, and it had time to get into all the papers. I had two kinds of reactions. Some people sent me money, but I had my secretary send it back with a note of thanks. But I also had many letters saying, "You shouldn't do a Virgin," or remarks like that.

RABBI BERKOWITZ: I understand that you are working in Italy. What are you working on now?

MR. LIPCHITZ: I have always dreamt of doing large pieces of sculpture, but for many years I did not have the opportunity. Nobody asked me. Now that it is not easy for me to get around, people give me only big things to do. I have a commission for a sculpture which may be the second in size to the Statue of Liberty. I have a big statue to make for a music center in Los Angeles and another for Philadelphia, for a plaza. I'm busy!

RABBI BERKOWITZ: How big is this very large one that you mentioned?

MR. LIPCHITZ: "It's about thirty-three feet wide. I work, you know, suspended in the air, in a little chair. When my brother saw it—he is an engineer—he told me that it was too dangerous and that I was too old to work like that. But I feel marvelous. I have been in this country for two weeks, I have not done any work, and I am tired. In Italy I work in a huge warehouse all the time, but I am happy.

RABBI BERKOWITZ: What is involved in this kind of project?

MR. LIPCHITZ: Well, the model for the Los Angeles sculpture is finished. Now they are preparing the rocks and in about two and one-half months we will be ready to retouch them. Now I have started on my Columbia sculpture.

RABBI BERKOWITZ: What does this involve?

MR. LIPCHITZ: I will explain. I have an enlarger, a man who works mathematically. In Italy I have three mechanics who are making the armature. It looks like a space rocket—it's enormous. This is only the preparation, the support, but it takes about four months to do. After that we start to work in plaster. I have been working on it for three years. It will take three more years to finish it. It's ready to be enlarged. They asked me to do a sculpture that had something to do with law. I did not want to make the blind lady with the scales. I began with Bellerophon. He was a simple man who was in love with the daughter of Zeus. Of course, Zeus gave him a number of assignments; if he succeeded in doing them, he would win his daughter. Zeus thought Bellerophon would not be able to do them. But Bellerophon first tamed Pegasus; that is to say, he tamed the natural forces of nature. With the help of these natural forces, he accomplished his goals. I said that this would be a good theme for law. They accepted it, so I am doing that.

RABBI BERKOWITZ: We'll look forward to seeing it. Weren't you invited to do a sculpture for the State of Israel?

MR. LIPCHITZ: A few years ago I had a visit from the Mayor of Jerusalem, Teddy Kollek, and he commissioned me to do a medal commemorating the unification of Jerusalem. I am working on that now.

RABBI BERKOWITZ: What kind of a medal will this be? How will it be expressed?

MR. LIPCHITZ: Before going to Italy some months ago, a gentleman asked me to do a little statue for a Jewish charity. I made one of Samson and Delilah. I found that after the Six Day War, it was somehow prophetic. So I used this subject for my medal.

RABBI BERKOWITZ: Does an idea such as this, about Samson and Delilah, have to be approved by the person giving the commission?

MR. LIPCHITZ: I don't think, in this instance, that they were too happy with the subject, but having made this Samson and Delilah before the war, I had this kind of prophetic feeling and I stuck to it.

A medal is two-sided, you know, and on the other side is the inscription—something from the Bible, which has to do with something with Samson and with the Lion of Judah. I am making a large version of it—a medal is always made large and then reduced to whatever dimensions wanted. For instance, I made a medal for President Johnson, also large, and they reduced it to whatever dimensions they wanted. It was a scholarship medal which he gave out. It was very interesting because I was in the White House for a week and he was busy most of the time. One night on a Friday evening, he said, "Well, now I can give you some time." I was very angry, but I went and made a sketch. He posed for me, but he was embarrassed. He called me afterwards. I did not call him, he called me and asked me to come the next day. I told him that this was my Sabbath and that I did not work on the Sabbath. He looked at me as if I were some kind of prehistoric animal. I finished it at home, and he sent some men to take it for approval. It was approved and it was done.

RABBI BERKOWITZ: What constitutes Jewish art to you, beyond having a Jewish theme?

MR. LIPCHITZ: There is no need to look for Jewish art. We go around the entire globe, looking for universal life. Why Jewish life? I am a Jew, I am a Jewish patriot, but art is a universal language. If you are a Jew, what comes out will be Jewish.

RABBI BERKOWITZ: For example, would you say that Michelangelo's Moses and David are Jewish art?

MR. LIPCHITZ: No, they were made by a non-Jew. I had an argument when I was in Israel some years ago. Ben-Gurion received my wife, my daughter and me, and he said to me at an odd moment, "Do you like Chagall?" I told him, "He is a marvelous jewel in our Jewish crown." Ben-Gurion did not like it. He asked, "Where did you ever see Jews flying in the air?" I replied, "Mr. Prime Minister, you must be a great scholar of the Bible, which is full of angels flying in the air. Did you ever see an angel flying in the air?" He did not like my answer. I waited very patiently for the right moment when we were discussing politics, and I said, "In politics, I don't understand anything," hoping he would say the same about art. But he was so clever, he glanced at me and said, "In politics, I don't understand anything either." And I said to myself—"Our business is in good hands."

RABBI BERKOWITZ: You say that universalism is the goal and that there cannot be specific Jewish art in painting and sculpture, just as there cannot be purely French, American or Italian painting and sculpture, since the language employed is a universal one and is understood everywhere. But you say that if the artist is a Jew it will come through. How does it come through?

MR. LIPCHITZ: Before I went to Paris, I was the president of a society of Jewish artists, and we were always discussing this question of "What is Jewish?". We argued and said that this is Jewish and that is not. We don't have to bother about the question of what is Jewish and what is not. If we are Jews, everthing that comes out of us is Jewish.

RABBI BERKOWITZ: Renoir, the great French painter, suffered from rheumatism in his hands during the later years of his life, and he painted by being placed in a chair that was moved as he directed. As he applied the paint to the canvas he suffered intensely but he continued to paint. One of his disciples pleaded, "Master, why torture yourself to do more?" Gazing at his student, he replied, "The pain passes, but the beauty remains." The artist understands that the creation of beauty helps to make life endurable and worthwhile. As we attempt to express our deepest feelings through the creation of beauty, we become more than mere mortals. We feel noble and uplifted. Beauty endures beyond any one lifetime. It is created through intense concentration, passionate devotion and honest expression. As man thinks and feels at his highest level, he hallows his life and draws closer to his Creator. Truly, then, the artist is the instrument for transmitting God's beauty to man. And what the artist brings forth is God directed and God-inspired. By understanding the intention of the human artist, man can grasp some of the beauty of the

Divine and carry out God's Commandments to worship him in the beauty of holiness. This Mr. Jacques Lipchitz has achieved through a noble and meaningful lifetime of bringing the message of the beauty of holiness.